THE RATIONAL UNIFIED PROCESS MADE EASY

The Addison-Wesley Object Technology Series

Grady Booch, Ivar Jacobson, and James Rumbaugh, Series Editors

For more information, check out the series web site at www.awprofessional.com/otseries.

The Component Software Series

Clemens Szyperski, Series Editor

For more information, check out the series web site at www.awprofessional.com/csseries.

THE RATIONAL UNIFIED PROCESS MADE EASY

A PRACTITIONER'S GUIDE TO THE RUP

Per Kroll
Philippe Kruchten

✦✦Addison-Wesley

Boston • San Francisco • New York • Toronto • Montreal
London • Munich • Paris • Madrid
Capetown • Sydney • Tokyo • Singapore • Mexico City

The publisher offers discounts on this book when ordered in quantity for bulk purchases and special sales. For more information, please contact:

> U.S. Corporate and Government Sales
> (800) 382-3419
> corpsales@pearsontechgroup.com

For sales outside of the U.S., please contact:

> International Sales
> (317) 581-3793
> international@pearsontechgroup.com

Visit Addison-Wesley on the Web: www.awprofessional.com

Library of Congress Cataloging-in-Publication Data

Kroll, Per.
   The Rational unified process made easy : a practitioner's guide to the RUP / Per Kroll, Philippe Kruchten.
      p.   cm.
   Includes bibliographical references and index.
   ISBN 0-321-16609-4 (alk. paper)
   1. Computer software—Development. 2. Software engineering. I. Kruchten, Philippe. II. Title.

QA76.76.D47K75 2003
005.1—dc21   2002043780

Text printed on recycled and acid-free paper.

ISBN 0321166094

7 8 9 10 11 12 CRS 07 06 05

7th Printing   August 2005

To Susan and Sylvie

CONTENTS

FIGURES

TABLES

FOREWORD

Every software development team follows some sort of process, whether intentionally or not. In small teams of one, two, or just a handful of developers, that process is typically lightweight. Very few if any documents are produced, analysis and design does take place but is often informal and transitory, and the project's source code serves as the center of gravity around which all other activities of the project orbit.

In large teams of dozens or even hundreds of developers, typically spread across buildings or flung around the globe, that process is much more prescribed. Many more formal and officially reviewed documents are produced; analysis and design involves the collaboration of a number of nondeveloper stakeholders and is made manifest in meetings, presentations, documents, and other artifacts; and the project's code is just one—albeit the most important—of the tangible artifacts that compose the deployed system. This is not to say that lightweight processes and heavier ones are at opposite ends of the spectrum of goodness: Every problem domain, every development culture, and every individual project requires a process that is just right for its specific context.

That said, all successful projects have some fascinating elements in common, no matter what their size. These elements are notably absent in unsuccessful projects. Observe a jelled project and you'll sense a distinct rhythm of cooperative work, with individual developers driving their own activities and artifacts, but at the same time working frictionlessly yet intentionally with other organically formed sets of developers. Such projects are typically quite agile, resilient to change, and adaptable, but also predictable, reliable, and able to craft quality code that really matters. In short, for these projects, the process followed is

so much a part of the way its developers work that it is virtually invisible, yet its spirit moves every artifact produced by team members working in concert.

The spirit of the Rational Unified Process, or RUP, is exactly this kind of invisible process. The RUP has evolved over the years to embody the experience of literally thousands of projects in every conceivable domain. Per Kroll and Philippe Kruchten are especially well suited to explain the RUP in an approachable and eminently pragmatic way because they have been the central forces inside Rational Software behind the creation of the RUP and its delivery to projects around the world.

When you talk about process to many developers, there is often an immediate push back because process is so often viewed as something that gets in the way of cutting code. This is simply not so with the RUP, for its very purpose is to reduce the friction of development teams so that they may focus on producing quality systems that are of value. Per and Philippe begin by explaining the spirit of the RUP and then proceed to show how the RUP may be applied to projects of many different shapes and sizes.

After explaining the pragmatics of the RUP, they then discuss several meta topics, including how you can introduce the RUP to an organization and what pitfalls to avoid in doing so. Making the RUP approachable to different stakeholders, they then examine the RUP from the viewpoint of the project manager, analyst, architect, developer, and tester.

The most successful project makes process look easy, but in reality, some really deep currents are at work. In this book, Per and Philippe explain those currents in an approachable and practical way, so that your projects too will follow the spirit of the RUP.

Grady Booch
Chief Scientist
Rational Software Corporation
February 2003

PREFACE

The Rational Unified Process, or RUP,[1] is a software engineering process framework developed and marketed by Rational Software. It comprises many software development best practices, harvested by many contributors, over many years of experience, in a wide variety of situations. It provides a disciplined approach to assigning and managing tasks and responsibilities in a software development organization. By applying this process, software development teams can produce high-quality software that meets the needs of its end users, and do so within a predictable schedule and budget.

The RUP guides software practitioners in effectively applying modern software best practices, such as developing iteratively, taking an architecture-centric approach, mitigating risk at every stage in the process, and continuously verifying the quality of the software. Although thousands of projects today are using the RUP effectively, many teams are intimidated by the thought of implementing a new process that they perceive as large and complex. The RUP does not have to be large, and it is not complex.

The goal of this book is to show you how simple the RUP actually is. It explains the underlying software development principles behind the RUP and guides you in the application of the process in your development organization. It will also show you the way to carve a RUP Process Configuration of the right size for your organization or project.

---

1. Rational Unified Process, RUP, and Rational Process Workbench are registered trademarks of Rational Software Corporation in the United States and in other countries.

Special permission to use and reproduce excerpts and images from the RUP product in *The Rational Unified Process Made Easy* is granted by Rational Software Corporation.

Why We Wrote This Book

During more than a decade of assisting companies in adopting the RUP and its predecessors and six years of leading the development of the RUP product, we have had the opportunity to see what works and what does not. We have seen the rewards of successful adoption of the RUP, and we have seen the challenges that projects and team members may encounter along the way. We have also been privileged to work with many leading software practitioners and have learned from them through daily interaction and practical experience in actual projects.

We felt there was a need for a book on the RUP that not only tells you what to do, but also what not to do.

Lately, we have seen a number of companies adopt *too much* of the RUP. Yes, there is such a thing as "too much of the RUP." We felt there was a need for a book on the RUP that not only tells you what to do, and what artifacts to produce, but also tells you how to streamline your process and what *not* to do. We wanted to explain *how* to adopt the RUP in practice, and *when* to apply *what* parts of the RUP in a given project. We wanted to help you understand how to apply the RUP to projects of different sizes or of different types.

Through this book, we want to share some of the insights we and our colleagues have gained over the years: Our intent is to provide Project Managers, Analysts, Architects, Developers, Testers, Process Engineers, and other team members and stakeholders with an easy-to-understand guide to the RUP. We have done this by extracting, from our practical experiences with the RUP, the essence of what each role needs to know about the RUP and explaining their role within it.

This book is not a substitute for the RUP product itself. While the book provides a couple of hundred pages of practical guidance, the RUP product provides thousands of pages of direction for a wide array of roles and activities, as well as templates for accelerating your work. It also provides tight integration with desktop tools, a search engine, graphical navigation, and other features you expect from a Web-based knowledge base. Unlike this book, the RUP is continuously evolving, bringing you up-to-date guidance to apply to your projects. Finally, this book will also guide you in customizing the RUP framework to suit your specific needs.

What You Will Learn from This Book

By reading this book, you will learn

- The RUP's underlying principles, which have been validated by hundreds of successful software projects
- How these principles are applied in practice, by walking through each phase of a RUP project
- The roles and responsibilities of Project Managers, Analysts, Architects, Developers, Testers, and Process Engineers in a RUP project
- How to incrementally adopt and configure the RUP with minimal risk
- How to identify common patterns for failure, and how to avoid them

Who Should Read This Book?

This book is targeted specifically to

- All members of a team using, or about to use, the RUP, including Managers who need an *introduction and overview* of the RUP and who would like to understand *its practical application*
- Practitioners on a software project: those Project Managers, Analysts, Architects, Developers, Testers, and Process Engineers who want a *detailed understanding* of the RUP and their *specific role* within a RUP project
- Managers, Process Engineers, and others who want to understand *how the RUP can be adopted* in their organization

Structure and Contents of This Book

This book is divided into four parts: introduction, walkthrough, adoption, and role-specific guidelines.

Part I introduces the RUP. Chapter 1 explains what the RUP is and the motivation behind its development and its application. Chapter 2,

"The Spirit of the RUP," describes the underlying principles behind the RUP—these are based on the experiences gleaned from a number of successful projects and distilled into a few simple guidelines. Understanding these principles will help you better apply the RUP to your own projects. Chapter 3 provides a method for comparing processes, and we use it to compare the RUP to other agile processes, to more conventional processes, and to process assessment frameworks such as SEI CMM and SPICE. These comparisons will help you understand which project type should use what type of RUP configuration. Chapter 4 provides an example that applies the RUP to a very small project: one person for one week. By peeling away the ceremony needed for larger projects, you can focus on the essential elements of the RUP.

Part II presents the RUP by walking through each of the four phases in a RUP project: Inception, Elaboration, Construction, and Transition. Chapter 5 addresses some common misconceptions of the four phases by explaining how the iterative approach applies to them. Chapters 6–9 describe each of the four phases in detail. We focus on what is to be achieved—that is, the *objectives* of each phase—and guide you in reaching those objectives. This will help you to stay focused on the most essential activities in an actual project. Additionally, we present the RUP activities in a time-based perspective—that is, in the order they are applied in a real project—to give you a reference to understand *when* to do the activities as you work through a project.

Adopting the RUP requires some preparation and some preliminary knowledge on the part of the adopting organization. **Part III** provides basic knowledge in key areas to support a streamlined implementation. Chapter 10 walks you through the RUP product, detailing how it can be extended and configured to meet project- and organization-specific needs. Chapter 11 briefly outlines some strategies that may be useful for implementing the process including incremental rollout, pilot projects, and training curricula. Our experience shows that moving from a waterfall approach to iterative development can be a difficult transition for Project Managers, and Chapter 12 provides guidelines for planning a RUP project. Over the years, we have seen patterns of success and patterns of failure in RUP adoptions. Chapter

13 discusses the patterns of failure and how to avoid them, guarding you from repeating the mistakes of others.

The RUP product provides comprehensive guidelines for a wide array of software development activities. **Part IV**, Chapters 14–18, presents guides for each of the five key roles in any software project: Project Manager, Analyst, Architect, Developer, and Tester. For each role, we present the RUP from that role's perspective, and we describe the mission, the desired qualifications, and the key activities, as well as recommended reading and training. Note that there is no separate chapter for the Process Engineer: Most of this role is described in Chapters 10 and 11.

How to Read This Book

Based on your role in your software organization and what you want to learn from this book, we recommend the following readings:

- If you are looking for a brief overview of the RUP, read Chapters 1, 2, and 4.
- If you are looking for a detailed overview of the RUP, read Chapters 1–9.
- If you are looking for a detailed understanding of the RUP, including specific role responsibilities:
  - For Project Managers, read Chapters 1–14.
  - For Analysts, read Chapters 1–9, 13, and 15 (optionally, browse through Chapters 8 and 9).
  - For Architects, read Chapters 1–9, 13, and 16.
  - For Developers, read Chapters 1–9, 13, and 17 (optionally, browse through Chapter 6).
  - For Testers, read Chapters 1–9, 13, and 18.
  - For Process Engineers, read Chapters 1–11 and 13.
- If you are an executive looking for a brief overview of the RUP and what it takes to adopt the RUP, read Chapters 1, 2, 4, and 11.

For More Information

Latest information related to this book, including updates, relevant articles, discussion forums, and author speaking schedules can be found on http://www.rupmadeeasy.com.

Additional information about the RUP product, including a data sheet and a product demo, can be obtained from Rational Software at http://www.rational.com/products/rup.

If you are already using the RUP product, additional resources are available from the RUP Knowledge Center on the Rational Developer Network (RDN) at http://www.rational.net.

Academic institutions can contact Rational Software for information on a special program for including the RUP in a software engineering curriculum: http://www.rational.com/corpinfo/college_relations/seed/index.jsp.

Acknowledgments

The Rational Unified Process captures the experiences of thousands of talented software practitioners, and we are honored to have been able to work with them to evolve the RUP product and to write this book.

This book would not have been possible without the RUP product and its current product team: Mike Barnard, Amanda Brijpaul, Susan Buie, Margaret Chan, Fionna Chong, Erin Curtis, Philip Denno, Carlos Goti, Debra Gray, Björn Gustafsson, Sigurd Hopen, Kelli Houston, Lars Jenzer, John Lambert, Bruce MacIssac, Bryant Macy, Glenys MacIsaac, John Ringoen, Dan Shiffman, Paul Szymkowiak, and Chinh Vo.

Over the years, the Rational field teams and technical experts have accumulated a lot of experience in implementing and using the RUP. We are grateful for the many insightful review comments and ideas from these experts, which added a lot of insights on what works and what does not out in the trenches. Especially, we would like to recognize Goran Begic, Thomas Bichler, Kurt Bittner, Anthony Crain, Sam Courtenay, Jérôme Desquilbet, Maria Ericsson, Carlos Goti, Jim Heumann, Joe Marasco, Pan-Wei Ng, Andy Phillipson, Gary Pollice, Leslee Probasco, Walker Royce, John Smith, and Ian Spence.

Our external reviewers provided invaluable feedback, forcing us to rethink the structure and content of the book, hopefully helping us to create a book that is easier to read and address the issues you find most relevant in a book about the RUP. These insights were provided by Susan Burk, Celso Gonzales, Gary Pollice, and Dan Rawsthorne.

We are also thankful to Grady Booch for reviewing the book and for writing the foreword.

When you put a French guy and Swedish guy together to write a book, needless to say huge opportunities to improve the manuscript's language are created. Rational Software editors Catherine Southwood, Mike Perrow, and Marlene Ellin dove into this task with a lot of energy and professionalism, as did our external editors Kelly Sweeney and Joseph Fatton.

We also wanted to give special thanks and love to our wives, Susan Kroll and Sylvie Kruchten, for being patient with the many weekends and nights spent writing and rewriting the book.

And finally, many thanks to our publisher, Mary O'Brien, and the production and marketing teams at Addison-Wesley, including Tyrrell Albaugh and Christopher Guzikowski, for helping us get this book out.

PART I

INTRODUCING THE RATIONAL UNIFIED PROCESS

CHAPTER 1

Introducing the Rational Unified Process

What Is the Rational Unified Process?

When you ask this question, you typically get different answers, depending on whom you ask and the context of your question. What makes matters confusing is that the Rational Unified Process, or the RUP, actually denotes three very different things:

- The RUP is a **software development approach** that is iterative, architecture-centric, and use-case-driven. It is described in a variety of whitepapers and books. The most comprehensive information can be found in the RUP product itself, which contains detailed guidelines, examples, and templates covering the full software lifecycle.

- The RUP is a **well-defined and well-structured software engineering process**. It clearly defines who is responsible for what, how things are done, and when to do them. The RUP also provides a well-defined structure for the lifecycle of a RUP project, clearly articulating essential milestones and decision points.

- The RUP is also a **process product** that provides you with a **customizable process framework** for software engineering. The RUP product supports process customization and authoring, and a wide variety of processes, or Process Configurations, can be assembled from it. These RUP configurations can be made to support small or large teams and disciplined or less-formal approaches to development. The RUP product contains several out-of-the-box Process Configurations and Process Views that guide analysts, developers, testers, project managers, configuration managers, data analysts, and other team members in how to develop software. The RUP is used by a wide variety of companies in different industry sectors.

In this chapter we will get a better understanding of what the RUP is by elaborating on each of these three perspectives of the RUP.

The RUP—The Approach

In this section we discuss the essential principles the RUP uses to facilitate successful software development, as well as the keystone iterative approach to applying those principles.

Underlying Principles of the RUP Approach

At the core of the Rational Unified Process lie several fundamental principles that support successful iterative development and that represent the essential "Spirit of the RUP" (which is discussed in Chapter 2). These principles were gleaned from a huge number of successful projects and distilled into a few simple guidelines. These principles are listed here:

- **Attack major risks early and continuously. . . or they will attack you.**[1] Rather than addressing business risks, technical risks, or other risks later in a project, identify and attack major risks as early as possible.

- **Ensure that you deliver value to your customer.** Document the requirements in a form that is easily understood by customers, but work closely to the requirements through design, implementation, and testing phases to ensure that you also deliver the requirements.

---

1. See Gilb 1988.

The Spirit of the RUP

Essential Principles

- Attack major risks early and continuously…or they will attack you.
- Ensure that you deliver value to your customer.
- Stay focused on executable software.
- Accommodate change early in the project.
- Baseline an executable architecture early on.
- Build your system with components.
- Work together as one team.
- Make quality a way of life, not an afterthought.

- **Stay focused on executable software.** Documents, designs, and plans are all good, but they are a poor indication of true progress because their evaluation is subjective and their importance is secondary compared to the code itself. Executable code that compiles and successfully passes tests is the best indication of progress.

- **Accommodate change early in the project.** Today's applications are too complex to enable us to get the requirements, design, and implementation correct the first time. This means that to develop a good enough system, we need to allow and adapt to change.

- **Baseline an executable architecture early on.** Many project risks can be mitigated by designing, implementing, and testing the architecture early in the project. Establishing a stable architecture early on also facilitates communication and localizes the impact of changes.

- **Build your system with components.** Applications built with components are more resilient to change and can have radically reduced system maintenance cost. Components facilitate reuse, allowing you to build higher quality applications faster than using functional decomposition.

- **Work together as one team.** Software development has become a team sport,[2] and an iterative approach emphasizes the importance of good team communications and a team spirit where each team member feels responsible for the completed end product.
- **Make quality a way of life, not an afterthought.** Ensuring high quality involves more than just the testing team. It involves *all* team members and *all* parts of the lifecycle. An iterative approach focuses on early testing and test automation for more effective regression testing, thus reducing the number of defects.

These principles are covered in more detail in Chapter 2.

The RUP and Iterative Development

Most software teams still use a **waterfall** process for development projects, where they complete each phase in a strict sequence of requirements, then analysis and design, then implementation/integration, and then testing. Or, more commonly, a modified waterfall approach with feedback loops added to the basic overall flow just described. Such approaches leave key team members idle for extended periods of time and defer testing until the end of the project lifecycle, when problems tend to be tough and expensive to resolve, and pose serious threats to release deadlines.

By contrast, the RUP uses an **iterative** approach (iterate = repeat), that is, a sequence of incremental steps or iterations. Each iteration includes some, or most, of the development disciplines (requirements, analysis, design, implementation, and so on), as you can see in Figure 1.1. Each iteration has a well-defined set of objectives and produces a partial working implementation of the final system. Each successive iteration builds on the work of previous iterations to evolve and refine the system until the final product is complete.

Early iterations will have a greater emphasis on requirements and analysis and design; later iterations will have a greater emphasis on implementation and testing.

The iterative approach has proven itself superior to the waterfall approach for a number of reasons:

---

2. See Booch 2001.

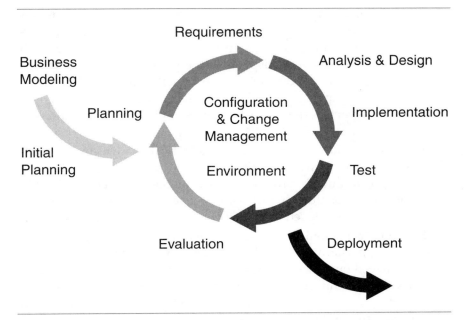

FIGURE 1.1 Iterative Development in the RUP. *The Rational Unified Process promotes an iterative approach—in each iteration you do a little requirements, analysis, design, implementation, and testing. Each iteration builds on the work of the previous iterations to produce an executable that is one step closer to the final product.*

- **It accommodates changing requirements.** Requirements change and "feature creep"—the addition of features that are technology- or customer-driven—have always been primary sources of project trouble, leading to late delivery, missed schedules, dissatisfied customers, and frustrated developers. Instead, iterative development focuses the team on producing and demonstrating executable software in the next few weeks, which forces a focus on the most essential requirements.

- **Integration is not one "big bang" at the end of a project.** Leaving integration to the end results in time-consuming rework—sometimes up to 40 percent of the total project effort. To avoid this, an iterative approach breaks a project down into smaller iterations, each ending with an integration in which building blocks are integrated progressively and continuously, minimizing later rework.

- **Risks are usually discovered or addressed during early integrations.** The RUP's integrated approach mitigates risks in early iterations, where all process components are tested. Since each iteration exercises many aspects of the project, such as tools, off-the-shelf software, and team members' skills, you can quickly discover whether perceived risks prove to be real and also uncover new, unsuspected risks at a time when they are easier and less costly to address.

- **Management has a means of making tactical changes to the product**—to compete with existing products, for example. Iterative development quickly produces an executable architecture (albeit of limited functionality), which can be used for quick release of a product with a reduced scope to counter a competitor's move.

- **Reuse is facilitated.** It is easier to identify common parts as they are being partially designed or implemented in iterations, than to recognize them during planning. Design reviews in early iterations allow architects to spot potential opportunities for reuse and then develop and mature common code for these opportunities in subsequent iterations.

- **Defects can be found and corrected over several iterations,** resulting in a robust architecture and a high-quality application. Flaws are detected even in early iterations rather than during a massive testing phase at the end. Performance bottlenecks are discovered at a time when they can still be addressed, instead of creating panic on the eve of delivery.

- **It is a better use of project personnel.** Many organizations match their use of a waterfall approach with a pipeline organization: The analysts send the completed requirements to designers, who send a completed design to programmers, who send components to integrators, who send a system to testers. These many handoffs are sources of errors and misunderstandings and make people feel less responsible for the final product. An iterative process widens the scope of expertise of the team members, allowing them to play many roles and enabling a project manager to use the available staff better, while simultaneously removing harmful handoffs.

- **Team members learn along the way.** The project members have several opportunities along a development cycle to learn from their mistakes and to improve their skills from one iteration to another. More training opportunities can be discovered as the result of assessing the earlier iterations. In contrast, in a waterfall approach, you have only one shot at design or coding or testing.

- **The development process itself is improved and refined along the way.** The assessment at the end of an iteration not only looks at the status of the project from a product or scheduling perspective, but also analyzes what, in both the organization and the process, can be improved in the next iteration.

Some project managers resist the integrated approach, seeing it as a kind of endless and uncontrolled hacking. In the Rational Unified Process, the integrated approach is very controlled: The number, duration, and objectives of iterations are carefully planned, and the tasks and responsibilities of participants are well defined. Additionally, objective measures of progress are captured. Some reworking takes place from one iteration to the next, but this, too, is carefully controlled.

The RUP—A Well-Defined Software Engineering Process

The Rational Unified Process itself was designed with techniques similar to those used in software design. In particular, it is modeled using the Software Process Engineering Metamodel (SPEM)[3]—a standard for process modeling based on the Unified Modeling Language (UML).[4] Figure 1.2 shows the overall architecture of the Rational Unified Process. The process has two structures or, if you prefer, two dimensions:

Modeling of the RUP is based on the Software Process Engineering Metamodel (SPEM).

- **Dynamic structure.** The horizontal dimension represents the **dynamic structure** or time dimension of the process. It shows how the process, expressed in terms of cycles, phases, iterations, and milestones, unfolds over the lifecycle of a project

---

3. See OMG 2001.
4. A standard for specifying, visualizing, and documenting models of software systems, including their structure and design. The standard is managed by the Object Management Group (www.omg.org).

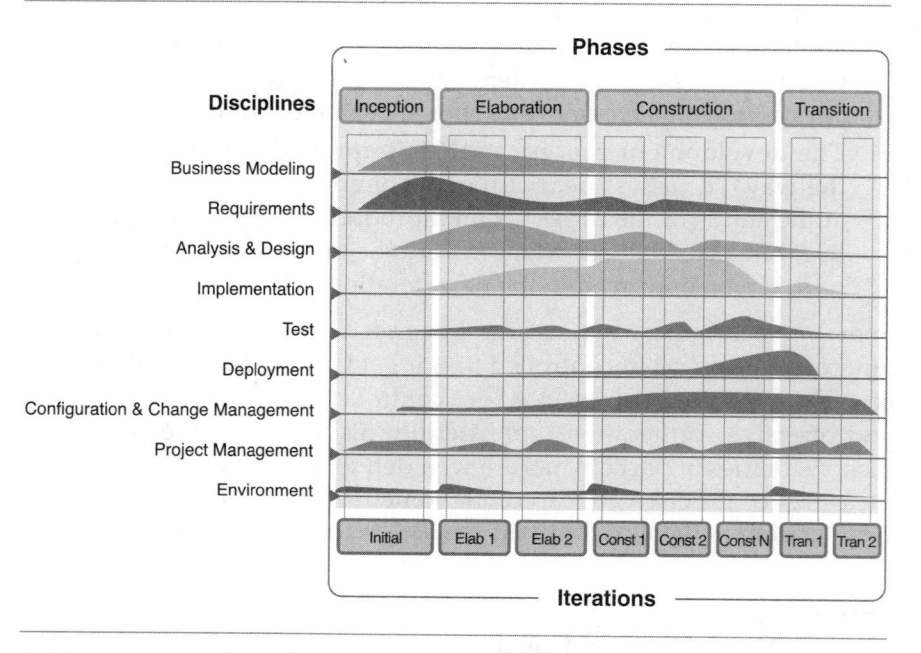

FIGURE 1.2 Two Dimensions of the RUP. *The Rational Unified Process is organized along two dimensions: The dynamic aspect (horizontal) expresses cycles, phases, iterations, and milestones; the static aspect (vertical) expresses activities, disciplines, artifacts, and roles.*

- **Static structure.** The vertical dimension represents the **static structure** of the process. It describes how process elements—activities, disciplines, artifacts, and roles—are logically grouped into core process disciplines (or workflows).

These dimensions are discussed in the following sections.

The Dynamic Structure of the Rational Unified Process

The dynamic structure deals with the lifecycle or time dimension of a project. The RUP provides a structured approach to iterative development, dividing a project into four **phases:** Inception, Elaboration, Construction, and Transition (see Figure 1.3).[5] Chapters 6 through 9 discuss

---

5. See Kruchten 2000a.

these phases in detail. The objectives and milestones of the phases are listed in the sidebar RUP Lifecycle Phases, Objectives, and Milestones.

RUP Lifecycle Phases, Objectives, and Milestones

Inception Phase

Objectives:

- Understand the scope of the project
- Build the business case
- Get stakeholder buy-in to move ahead

Milestone: Lifecycle Objective Milestone (LCO)

Elaboration Phase

Objectives:

- Mitigate major technical risks
- Create a baselined architecture
- Understand what it takes to build the system

Milestone: Lifecycle Architecture Milestone (LCA)

Construction Phase

Objective:

- Build the first operational version of the product

Milestone: Initial Operational Capability Milestone (IOC)

Transition Phase

Objective:

- Build the final version of the product and deliver it to the customer

Milestone: Product Release Milestone (PR)

Each phase contains one or more **iterations**, which focus on producing the technical deliverables necessary to achieve the business objectives of that phase. There are as many iterations as it takes to address the objectives of that phase sufficiently, but *no more*. If objectives can't be addressed within the planned phase, another iteration should be added to the phase—which will delay the project. To avoid this, make

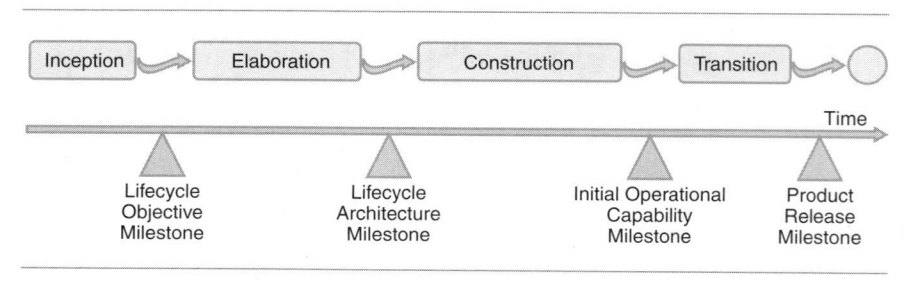

FIGURE 1.3 Milestones for the RUP Lifecycle Phases. *Each of the RUP's four phases has a milestone and a well-defined set of objectives. Use these objectives as a guide for deciding which activities to carry out and which artifacts to produce.*

Each iteration is sharply focused on just what is needed to achieve the business objectives of the phase.

sure that each iteration is sharply focused on *just* what is needed to achieve the business objectives of that phase. For example, focusing too heavily on requirements in Inception is counterproductive. Chapter 12 discusses project planning.

- **Inception.** Establish a good understanding of what system to build by getting a high-level understanding of all the requirements and establishing the scope of the system. Mitigate many of the business risks, produce the business case for building the system, and get buy-in from all stakeholders on whether to proceed with the project.

- **Elaboration.** Take care of many of the most technically difficult tasks: Design, implement, test, and baseline an executable architecture, including subsystems, their interfaces, key components, and architectural mechanisms, such as how to deal with inter-process communication or persistency. Address major technical risks, such as resource contention risks, performance risks, and data security risks, by implementing and validating actual code.

- **Construction.** Do most of the implementation as you move from an executable architecture to the first operational version of your system. Deploy several internal and alpha releases to ensure that the system is usable and addresses user needs. End the phase by deploying a fully functional beta version of the system, including installation and supporting documentation and training material (although the system will likely still require tuning of functionality, performance, and overall quality).

- **Transition.** Ensure that software addresses the needs of its users. This includes testing the product in preparation for release and making minor adjustments based on user feedback. At this point in the lifecycle, user feedback focuses mainly on fine-tuning the product, configuration, installation, and usability issues; all the major structural issues should have been worked out much earlier in the project lifecycle.

The Static Structure of the Rational Unified Process

The static structure deals with how process elements—activities, disciplines, artifacts, and roles—are logically grouped into core process disciplines. A process describes **who** is doing **what, how,** and **when.** As shown in the sidebar Four Key Modeling Elements of the RUP and Figure 1.4, the Rational Unified Process is represented using four key modeling elements.

Four Key Modeling Elements of the RUP

- **Roles.** The *who*
- **Activities.** The *how*
- **Artifacts.** The *what*
- **Workflows.** The *when*

Roles

A **role** is like a "hat" that an individual (or group) wears during a project. One individual may wear many different hats. This is an important point because it is natural to think of a role as an individual on the team, or as a fixed job title, but in the RUP the roles simply define how the individuals should do the work, and they specify the

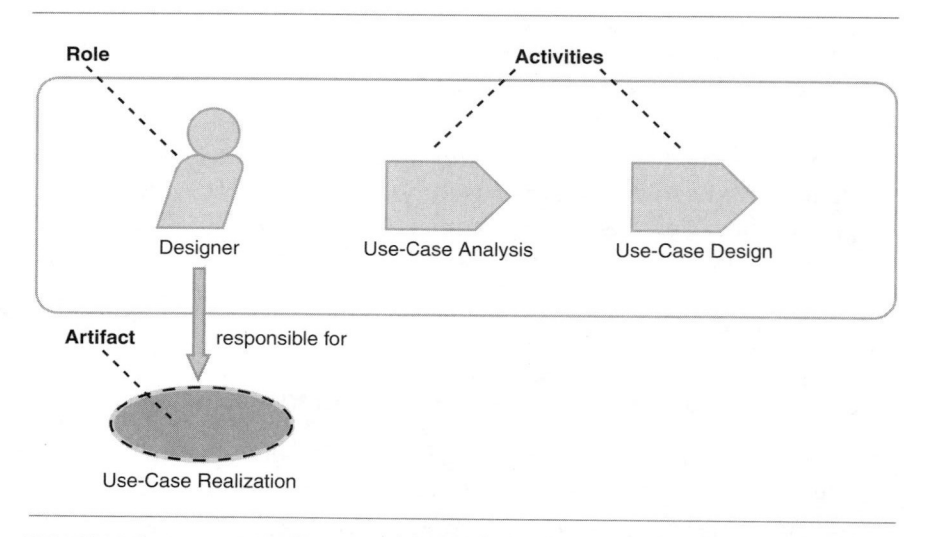

FIGURE 1.4 Roles, Activities, and Artifacts. *A* role *expresses who (an individual or a group) is doing the work; an* activity *describes how the work is done; and an* artifact *captures what is done.*

competence and responsibility that the individual(s) playing that role should have. A person usually performs one or more roles, and several people can perform the same role.

Activities

An **activity** of a specific role is a unit of work that an individual in that role may be asked to perform. The activity has a clear purpose, usually expressed in terms of creating or updating some artifacts, such as a model, a component, or a plan. Each activity is assigned to a specific role. An activity generally takes a few hours to a few days to complete, usually involves one person, and affects one or only a small number of artifacts. An activity should be usable as an element of planning and progress; if it is too small, it will be neglected, and if it is too large, progress would have to be expressed in terms of an activity's parts. Activities may be repeated several times on the same artifact—especially when going from one iteration to another, refining and expanding the system—by the same role, but not necessarily by the same individual.

Steps

Activities are broken down into **steps,** which fall into three main categories:

- **Thinking** steps, where the person playing the role understands the nature of the task, gathers and examines the input artifacts, and formulates an outcome
- **Performing** steps, where the role creates or updates some artifacts
- **Reviewing** steps, where the role inspects the results against some criteria

Not all steps are necessarily performed each time an activity is invoked, so steps can be expressed in the form of alternate flows.

Artifacts

An **artifact** is a piece of information that is produced, modified, or used by a process. Artifacts are the tangible project elements: things the project produces or uses while working toward the final product. Artifacts are used as input by roles to perform an activity and are the result or output of other activities.

Artifacts may take various shapes or forms:

- A **model,** such as the Use-Case Model or the Design Model
- A **model element,** that is, an element within a model, such as a class, a use case (UC), or a subsystem
- A **document,** such as the Vision or Business Case
- Source code
- **Executables,** such as an executable **Prototype**

An artifact can be documented formally (using a tool) or informally (captured in an e-mail message or on a whiteboard). This will be discussed in more detail in Chapter 3 and Chapters 6–9.

Workflows

A mere listing of all roles, activities, and artifacts does not quite constitute a process. You need a way to describe meaningful sequences of activities that produce some valuable result and to show interactions between roles—this is exactly what **workflows** do.

Workflows come in different shapes and forms; the two most common workflows are **Disciplines,** which are high-level workflows (see the section Disciplines that follows), and **Workflow Details,** which are workflows within a discipline.

People are not machines, and the workflow cannot be interpreted literally as a program for people to be followed exactly and mechanically.

In UML terms, a workflow can be expressed as a sequence diagram, a collaboration diagram, or an activity diagram. Figure 1.5 shows an example workflow. Note that it is not always possible or practical to represent all of the dependencies between activities. Often two activities are more tightly interwoven than shown, especially when carried out by the same individual. People are not machines, and the workflow cannot be interpreted literally as a program for people to be followed exactly and mechanically.

Additional Process Elements

Roles, activities (organized in workflows), and artifacts represent the backbone of the Rational Unified Process static structure. But there are some other elements added to activities or artifacts that make the process easier to understand and use and that provide more complete guidance to the practitioner. These additional process elements are

- **Guidelines,** to provide rules, recommendations, or heuristics that support activities, steps, and artifacts.
- **Templates,** for the various artifacts.
- **Tool mentors,** to establish a link with and provide guidance on using the development tools.
- **Concepts,** to introduce key definitions and principles.
- **Roadmaps,** to guide the user into the RUP from a given perspective.

Figure 1.6 shows how these elements enhance the primary elements.

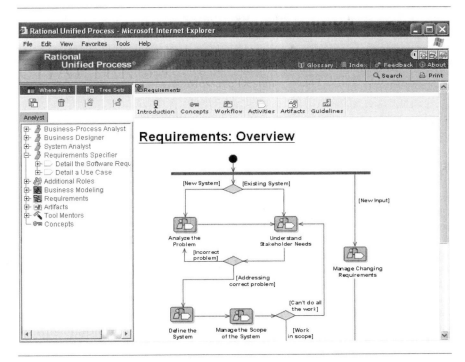

FIGURE 1.5 The Workflow of the Requirements Discipline. *A workflow shows in what order to carry out activities to accomplish something of measurable value. RUP workflows typically show only the most essential dependencies between activities to avoid cluttering the view.*

Disciplines

Finally, all process elements—roles, activities, artifacts, and the associated concepts, guidelines, and templates—are grouped into logical containers called **Disciplines**. There are nine disciplines in the standard RUP product (see the RUP Disciplines sidebar).

This list is not definitive, and any company doing extensions to the RUP product could introduce additional disciplines.

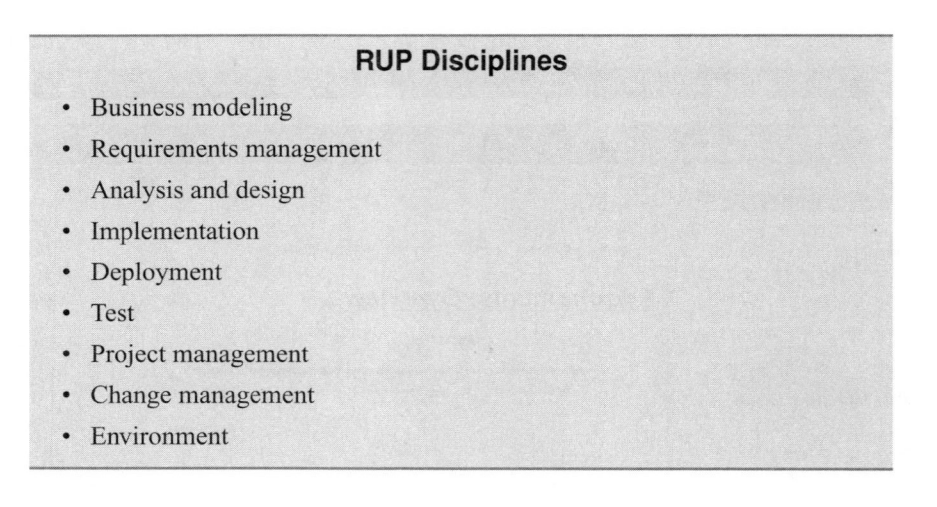

RUP Disciplines

- Business modeling
- Requirements management
- Analysis and design
- Implementation
- Deployment
- Test
- Project management
- Change management
- Environment

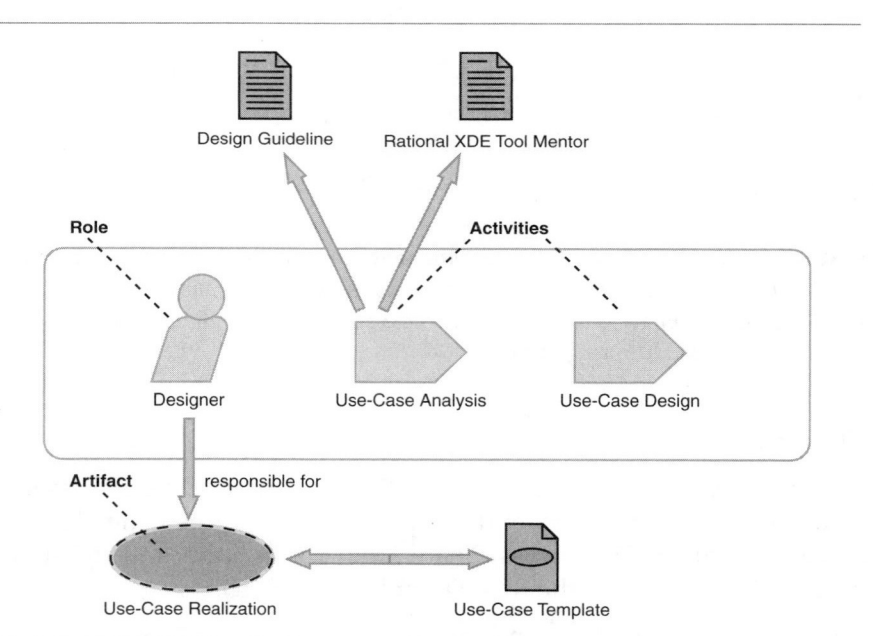

FIGURE 1.6 Adding Templates, Tool Mentors, and Guidelines. *Templates jump-start the production of an artifact; tool mentors provide detailed guidance for carrying out an activity, or step, using the tools at hand; and guidelines provide detailed guidance on activities, steps, or artifacts.*

The RUP—A Customizable Process Product

Each project and each organization have unique needs requiring a process that is adapted to their specific situation. To accommodate this requirement, the RUP product constitutes a complete process framework (see Figure 1.7) composed of several integrated parts:

The RUP product constitutes a complete process framework.

- **Best practices.** The RUP comes with a library of best practices, produced by IBM Software and its partners. These best practices are continually evolving and cover a broader scope than this book can cover. The best practices are expressed in the form of phases, roles, activities, artifacts, and workflows.

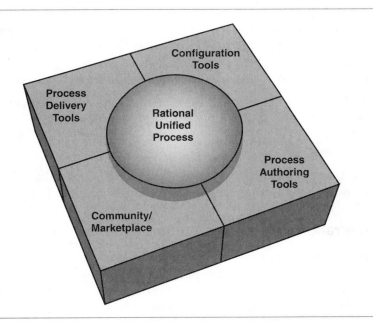

FIGURE 1.7 The RUP Process Framework. *The RUP product consists of a broad set of best practices, configuration tools for selecting appropriate best practices, process delivery tools for accessing these best practices, an online community for exchanging artifacts and experiences, and process authoring tools for adding your own best practices to the RUP.*

- **Process delivery tools.** The RUP is literally at the developers' fingertips because it is delivered online using Web technology, rather than using books or binders. This delivery allows the process to be integrated with the many software development tools in the Rational Suite and with any other tools so developers can access process guidance within the tool they are using.
- **Configuration tools.** The RUP's modular and electronic form allows it to be tailored and configured to suit the specific needs of a development organization. This is discussed briefly in the section Configuration and Process Authoring Tools, and in more detail in Chapter 10.
- **Process authoring tools.** Rational Process Workbench (RPW) is a process authoring tool, allowing you to capture your own best practices into the RUP format (see Chapter 10 for details).
- **Community/Marketplace:** The Rational Developer Network (RDN) online community allows users to exchange experiences with peers and experts, and provides access to the latest information in terms of artifacts, articles, or additional RUP content.

The RUP product is designed, developed, delivered, and maintained like any software tool. It is upgraded approximately twice a year, so the process is never obsolete and its users benefit from the latest developments.

Let's take a closer look at two areas of the RUP's capabilities: configuration and process authoring tools and process delivery tools.

Configuration and Process Authoring Tools

A process should not be followed blindly, generating useless work and producing artifacts that are of little added value. Instead, the process must be made as lean as possible while still fulfilling its mission to help developers rapidly produce predictably high-quality software. An adopting organization's best practices, along with its specific rules and procedures, should complement the process.

Since the Rational Unified Process is a **process framework,**[6] it can be adapted and extended to suit the needs of an adopting organization. The RUP framework is made up of components, divided into a base unit and a series of RUP Plug-Ins. As shown in Figure 1.8, you can produce a Process Configuration by selecting a set of RUP Plug-Ins to add to the base. You can even make a fine granular selection of which process components to deploy within your plug-ins and base. This makes it easy to create a Process Configuration that addresses the spe-

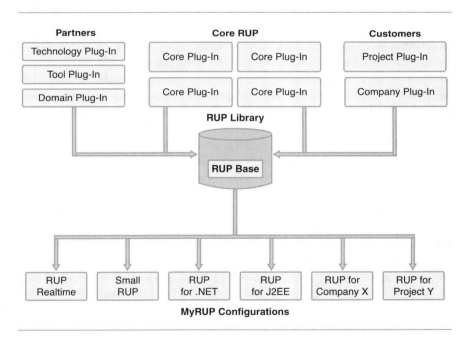

FIGURE 1.8 The RUP's Component-Based Architecture Allows the RUP to Be Configured to Project Needs. *The component-based architecture of the RUP product allows RUP users to choose from a wide variety of plug-ins and to deploy those that are appropriate for their project.*

---

6. See Kroll 2001.

cific needs, characteristics, constraints, culture, and domain of your project or organization.

You can also produce different views of the process, so-called Process Views, to allow each person in your project to view the Process Configuration from a perspective that is relevant to his or her role and responsibilities. The RUP product also comes with a number of out-of-the-box configurations and process views that you can use as a starting point. Chapter 10 details how to configure the RUP product.

Companies using the RUP process authoring tool can package their know-how of a certain technology, tool, or domain into a RUP Plug-In and make it available to other RUP users inside or outside their organization. RUP users can also produce plug-ins that are specific for a project, a division, or their entire organization, and thus make their know-how easily accessible to all their software engineers. When configuring the RUP, projects can take advantage of the best practices captured in these partner and in-house plug-ins and create configurations that fit their specific needs. Chapter 10 details how to build RUP Plug-Ins.

Process Delivery Tools

Using a process can be complicated; the RUP product helps users by providing MyRUP (a Web interface that can be personalized), tool mentors, and Extended Help. The combination of tool mentors and Extended Help provides a two-way integration between the RUP and the tools at your desktop. This integration helps practitioners make more effective use of their tools, allowing them to get more value out of their tool investment and facilitating effective implementation of the process.

MyRUP provides a role-based tree browser containing links to the parts of your project's RUP Process Configuration that are relevant for you.

MyRUP

The RUP product can be delivered through a personalized Web browser, called MyRUP. MyRUP provides Process Views, a role-based or personalized tree control containing links to the parts of your project's RUP Process Configuration that are relevant for you, as well as links to files or URLs external to your configuration (see Figure 1.9).

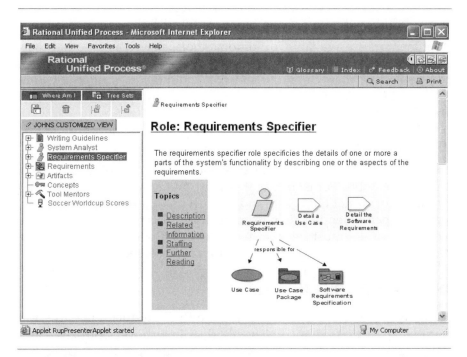

FIGURE 1.9 MyRUP Provides Personalized Views. *MyRUP is a personalized Web interface with the RUP that allows users to find information easily through a personalized view, search engine, graphical navigation, and tree control.*

Each user can customize his or her own Process View or use one of the predefined Process Views. MyRUP also provides a search engine, a glossary, and a Getting Started tutorial.

Tool Mentors

The bulk of the RUP product is tool-independent, although many of the RUP activities need to be carried out using various tools, and practitioners need to understand how to implement the process with the tools at hand. **Tool mentors** provide step-by-step guidelines for implementing the various RUP activities using the tools at hand. The tool mentors describe which menus to select, what to enter in dialog boxes, and how to draw diagrams to accomplish the specified tasks.

Tool mentors are available for Rational tools, as well as for other tools such as IBM WebSphere Application Server and BEA WebLogic. Customers and partners can write additional tool mentors, and tool mentors can be included in RUP Plug-Ins, as can any process element in the RUP product.

Extended Help

Extended Help provides context-sensitive process guidance within the various tools. For example, if you are trying to use the Class Diagram editor in Rational Rose and you do not know what to do next, you can open Extended Help from the Rose tools menu. This will give you a list of the most relevant topics within the RUP, depending on the context, in this case, a Class Diagram in Rose, see Figure 1.10.

Who Uses the RUP Product?

Roughly 10,000 companies are using the RUP product. They use it in various application domains, evenly distributed over both large and small projects. This variety shows the versatility and wide applicability of the RUP product. Here are examples of the various industry sectors around the world that use it:

- Telecommunications
- Transportation, aerospace, defense
- Manufacturing
- Financial services
- Systems integrators

The RUP has become widely adopted over the last few years, which is a sign of change in our industry. As time-to-market pressure increases, as well as the demand for high-quality applications, companies are looking to learn from others' experience and are ready to adopt proven best practices.

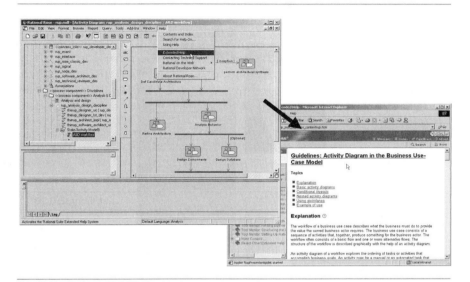

FIGURE 1.10 RUP Context-Sensitive Extended Help. *Extended Help provides context-sensitive help from the tools being used. When launched, it presents a list of the most relevant topics in the RUP product.*

The way these organizations use the Rational Unified Process varies greatly. Some use it very formally and with a high degree of discipline; they have evolved their own company process from the RUP product, which they follow with great care. Other organizations have a more informal usage, taking the RUP platform as a repository of advice, templates, and guidance that they use as they go along, as a sort of knowledge base on software engineering.

By working with these customers, observing how they use the RUP product, listening to their feedback, and looking at the additions they make to the process to address specific concerns, the RUP development team at IBM Software continues to refine the RUP product for the benefit of all.

Conclusion

We discussed that the Rational Unified Process, or the RUP, denotes three very different things:

- The RUP is an **approach for developing software,** which is iterative, architecture-centric, and use-case-driven. It is described in whitepapers and books, and the most complete set of information about the RUP approach can be found in the RUP product itself.
- The RUP is a **well-defined and well-structured software engineering process.** It clearly defines project milestones, who is responsible for what, how things are done, and when you should do them.
- The RUP is also a **process product** that provides you with a **customizable process framework** for software engineering. You can configure the RUP product to support small or large teams and disciplined or less-formal approaches to development. It also allows you to add your own best practices and to share experiences and artifacts with peers and experts.

Now that we have a better idea of what the RUP is, let us go deeper to understand its essence and its spirit, that is, the fundamental principles behind the RUP.

CHAPTER 2

The Spirit of the RUP: Guidelines for Success

We are often asked, "How do I know when I apply the RUP correctly?" There is no black-and-white answer to this question. It is not meaningful to seek the answer by counting the number of activities in the RUP that you follow or how many artifacts in the RUP that you produce. Rather, the question can best be answered by looking at how well your project adheres to the fundamental principles that represent the essential "Spirit of the RUP." These fundamental principles capture our experiences and those that thousands of Rational Software customers and colleagues have made over the last 20 years. Although these principles represent neither a complete view of the RUP nor the full complexity of those projects, understanding these principles will guide you to better apply the RUP to your own projects. These principles are

- Attack major risks early and continuously, or they will attack you.
- Ensure that you deliver value to your customer.
- Stay focused on executable software.
- Accommodate change early in the project.
- Baseline an executable architecture early on.
- Build your system with components.
- Work together as one team.
- Make quality a way of life, not an afterthought.

Iterative development can be done without applying all of these principles; however, using them will enhance project success. To optimize the implementation of an iterative approach, you should attempt to apply as many of these principles as is feasible for your project. You may find that one or several of these principles are unsuitable for your project—that's fine. Even at its essence, the RUP should be considered a smorgasbord—a Scandinavian buffet—from which you choose the dishes that fit your needs.

These principles also characterize how the Rational Unified Process differs from other iterative approaches, in particular through its strong emphasis on attacking risks and on producing an executable architecture early on.

We'll discuss each of these underlying principles in the following sections.

Attack Major Risks Early and Continuously, or They Will Attack You

The iterative approach allows you to identify and address major risks early in the project.

As Tom Gilb said, "If you don't actively attack the risks, they will actively attack you."[1] As Figure 2.1 shows, one of the prime benefits of the iterative approach is that it allows you to identify and address major risks early in the project.

Why address top risks early on? Unaddressed risks mean that you are potentially investing in a faulty architecture or a nonoptimal set of requirements. This is bad software economics. In addition, the amount of risk is directly correlated to the difference between the upper and lower estimates of how long it will take to complete a project. To come up with accurate estimations, you need to identify and address risks up front.

How do you deal with risks early on? At the beginning of each iteration, the RUP advises you to make, or revise, a list of top risks. Prioritize the risk list; then decide what you need to do to address, typically, the top three to five risks. For example, the risks may look as follows:

---

1.   See Gilb 1988.

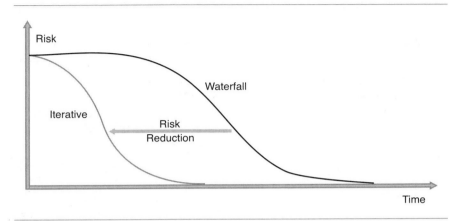

FIGURE 2.1 Risk Reduction Profiles for Waterfall and Iterative Developments. *A major goal with iterative development is to reduce risk early on. This is done by analyzing, prioritizing, and attacking top risks in each iteration.*

- **Risk 1:** You are concerned, based on past experience, that Department X will not understand what requirements you plan to deliver, and as a result will request changes *after* beta software is delivered.
- **Risk 2:** You do not understand how you can integrate with legacy system Y.
- **Risk 3:** You have no experience in developing on the Microsoft .NET platform or in using Rational Rose.
- **Risk 4:** ...And so on.

Now, how will this risk list be used? Addressing risks should be a priority for everyone throughout the project. Look at what you would "normally" do for the iteration at hand, then slightly modify the plan to make sure that you deal with your risks. Typically, risks need to be addressed from multiple perspectives, such as requirements, design, and testing. For each of these perspectives, start with a coarse solution and successively detail it to diminish the risk. You

Risks need to be addressed from multiple perspectives, such as requirements, design, and testing.

may, for example, add the following actions to address the earlier-identified risks:

- **Risk 1:** As the use cases related to Department X are developed, complement them with a user-interface (UI) prototype. Set up a meeting with Department X, and walk them through each use case, using the UI prototype as a storyboard. Get a formal sign-off on the requirements. Throughout the project, keep Department X in the loop on progress, and provide them with early prototypes and alpha releases.

- **Risk 2:** Have a "tiger team" with one or two skilled developers build an actual prototype that shows how to integrate with legacy system Y. The integration may be a throw-away, but the prototype should prove that you actually can integrate with the legacy system. Throughout the project, ensure appropriate testing of the integration with legacy system Y.

  An alternative would be to cut the scope of the project, so you do not have to integrate with legacy system Y. This strategy is called "risk avoidance" and is typically highly effective. Note that all other examples in this list are of the strategy type "risk mitigation."

- **Risk 3:** Send a couple of people for training on Microsoft .NET and Rational Rose, respectively, and find the budget to bring in a Rational Rose mentor two days per week for the first three weeks of the Elaboration phase. Recruit a team member with an understanding of the .NET platform.

- **Risk 4:** ...And so on.

The risk list continuously changes. Attacking risk is a constant battle.

Many project risks are associated with the architecture. This is why the RUP's primary objective in the Elaboration phase is getting the architecture right. To do this you not only design the architecture, but you also implement and test it. (Find out more about this in the section Baseline an Executable Architecture Early On.)

One thing to keep in mind is that the risk list continuously changes. Attacking risk is a constant battle. In each iteration you will be able to reduce or remove some risks, while others grow and new ones appear.

Summary

The RUP provides a structured approach to addressing top risks early, which decreases overall costs and allows you to make earlier, more realistic, and more accurate estimations of how much time it will take to complete the project. Remember that risk management is a dynamic and ongoing process.

Ensure That You Deliver Value to Your Customer

Delivering value to your customer is a pretty obvious goal, but how is it done? Our recommendation is closely related to iterative development, with continuous feedback loops from customers, and the "use-case-driven approach."[2] So, what are use cases? Use cases are a way of capturing functional requirements. Since they describe how a user will interact with the system, they are easy for a user to relate to. And since they describe the interaction in a time-sequential order, it is easy for both users and analysts to identify any holes in the use case. A use case can almost be considered a section in the future user manual for the system under development, but it is written with no knowledge about the specific user interface. You do not want to document the user interface in the use case; instead, you complement the use-case descriptions with a UI prototype, for example, in the form of screen shots.

Many people have learned to love use cases for their simplicity and their ability to facilitate rapid agreement with stakeholders on what the system should do. But this is not their primary benefit. We think their major advantage is that they allow each team member to work very closely to the requirements when designing, implementing, testing, and finally writing user manuals (see Figure 2.2). Use cases force you to stay externally focused on the user's perspective, and they allow you to validate the design and implementation with respect to the user requirements. They even allow you to carefully consider user needs when planning the project and managing scope.

---

2. For more information, see Jacobson 1992.

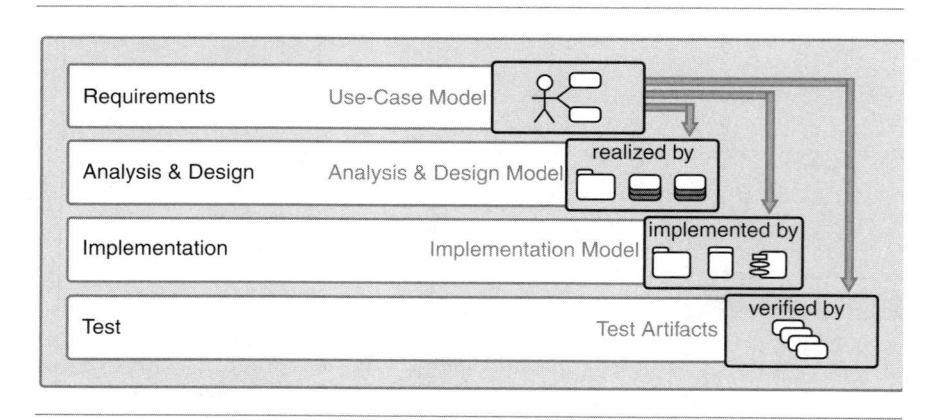

FIGURE 2.2 How Use Cases Relate to Other Software Engineering Models. *Use cases are a highly effective vehicle for capturing requirements. They also allow you to work closely to the requirements when doing design, implementation, and testing, ensuring that you deliver the requirements.*

Use cases make it easy to document functional user requirements and to help all stakeholders understand the capabilities that are to be delivered.

Since a use case describes how a user will interact with the system, you can use UML notation such as sequence diagrams or collaboration diagrams to show how this interaction will be implemented by your design elements. You can also identify test cases from a use case. This ensures that the services the users expect from the system really are provided. Since the use cases are "user manuals without knowledge of the UI," they make a solid starting point for writing user manuals. And when prioritizing which capabilities to deliver when managing scope, you choose which use cases to implement. And as we noted above, use cases allow you to work closely to the requirements throughout the development lifecycle.

Summary

Use cases make it easy to document functional user requirements and to help all stakeholders understand the capabilities that are to be delivered. More essentially, use cases allow you to work closely to the requirements when doing design, implementation, and testing, thereby ensuring that you not only document, but also deliver, the user requirements. Combined with iterative development, they help ensure that you deliver customer value.

Stay Focused on Executable Software

This third essential RUP principle has several facets. First, you should, to the extent possible, measure progress by measuring your **executable** software. It is great to know that 10 out of 20 use cases have been described, but that does not necessarily mean that 50 percent of the requirements are completed. What if you later find that half of those use cases require major rewrites because you did not properly understand the user requirements? That could mean that you were only 25 percent complete, right? So what you can really say when you have completed half of the use cases is that you are probably *not more than* 50 percent done with the requirements.

The best way of measuring progress is by measuring what software is up and running. This allows you to do testing and, based on testing and defect rates, assess the true progress that has been made. When the typical developer states, "I am 90 percent done," you should ask, "Great, but can you please demo what is up and running?" This will give you a solid idea of what has actually been accomplished. As an architect, team leader, or manager, you should always strive to have working software demonstrated and to look at test coverage and test results, rather than be fooled by the often false reality of completed documents. This does not mean that you should disregard the information in completed documents, but when considered in isolation, they provide a poor measure of true progress.

You should always strive to have working software demonstrated.

Second, a clear focus on executable software also promotes right thinking among your team; you run less risk of overanalyzing and theorizing, and instead get down to work to prove whether solution A or B is better. Forcing closure by producing executable software is often the fastest way of mitigating risk.

A third attribute of this focus on executable software is that **artifacts other than the actual software are supporting artifacts.** They are there to allow you to produce better software. By staying focused on executable software, you are better prepared to assess whether producing other artifacts—such as requirement management plans, configuration management (CM) plans, use cases, test plans, and so on—will really lead to software that works better or is easier to maintain. In many cases the answer is yes, but not always. You need to weigh the cost of producing and maintaining an artifact against the benefit of producing it. The benefit of producing many artifacts typically increases as your project grows larger, as you have more complicated stakeholder relations, as your team becomes distributed, as the cost of quality issues increases, and as the software is more critical to the business. All these factors drive toward producing more artifacts and treating them more formally. But for every project, you should strive to minimize the number of artifacts produced to reduce overhead.

If you are in doubt as to whether to produce an artifact, don't produce it.

A good guideline is that if you are in doubt as to whether to produce an artifact, don't produce it. But do not use this guideline as an excuse to skip essential activities such as setting a vision, documenting requirements, having a design, and planning the test effort. Each of these activities produces artifacts of obvious value. If the cost of producing an artifact is going to be higher than the return on investment (ROI), however, then you should skip it.

One of the most common mistakes RUP users make is to produce artifacts just because the RUP describes how to produce them. Remember, the RUP is a smorgasbord, and it is typically unwise to eat every dish at a table like the one in Figure 2.3.

Summary

Working software is the best indicator of true progress. When assessing progress, as much as possible, look at what code is up and running and which test cases have been properly executed. A strong focus on working software also enables you to minimize overhead by producing only those artifacts that add more value to your project than they cost to produce.

Photo by Dorling Kindersley

FIGURE 2.3 Consider the RUP as a Smorgasbord. *Consider the RUP as a smorgasbord of best practices. Rather than eat everything, eat your favorite dishes, the ones that make sense for your specific project.*

Accommodate Change Early in the Project

Change is good. Actually, change is great. Why? Because most modern systems are too complex to allow you to get the requirements and the design right the first time around. Change allows you to improve upon a solution. If there is no change, then you will deliver a defective solution, possibly so defective that the application has no business value. That is why you should welcome and encourage change. And the iterative approach has been optimized to do exactly that.

But change can also have severe consequences. Constant change will prevent project completion. Certain types of change late in the project

Modern systems are too complex to allow you to get the requirements and the design right the first time around.

typically mean a lot of rework, increased cost, reduced quality, and probable delays, all things you want to avoid. To optimize your Change Management strategy, you need to understand the relative cost of introducing different types of changes at different stages of the project lifecycle (see Figure 2.4). For simplicity, we group changes into four categories.

- **Cost of change to the business solution.** Change to the business solution involves major rework of requirements to address a different set of users or user needs. There is a fair amount of flexibility in making this type of modification during the Inception phase, but costs escalate as you move into the Elaboration phase. This is why you force an agreement on the vision for the system in Inception.

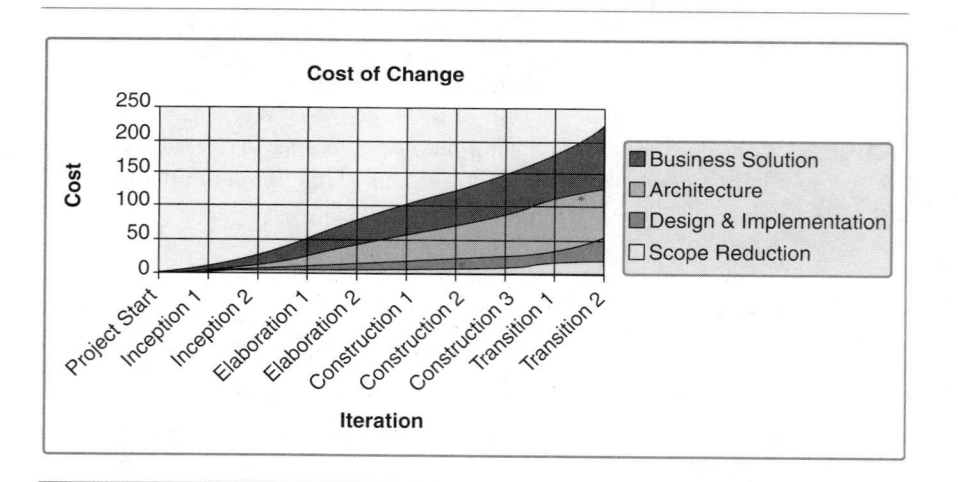

FIGURE 2.4 The Cost of Introducing Change Varies Throughout the Lifecycle.
The cost of introducing a change varies according to the lifecycle phase, and each type of change has its own cost profile. The RUP milestones at the end of each phase are optimized to minimize overall cost of change, while maximizing freedom to make changes. In general, as the project progresses, you should be more careful about introducing change, especially to the overall business solution and the architecture.

- **Cost of change to the architecture.** When following the RUP, you can make fairly significant architectural changes at low cost until the end of Elaboration. After that, significant architectural changes become increasingly costly, which is why the architecture must be baselined at the end of Elaboration.

- **Cost of change to the design and implementation.** Because of the component-based approach, these types of changes are typically localized and can hence be made at fairly low cost throughout the Construction phase. These types of changes are, however, increasingly expensive in the Transition phase, which is why you typically introduce "feature freeze" at the end of Construction.

- **Cost of change to the scope.** The cost of cutting scope—and hence postponing features to the next release—is relatively inexpensive throughout the project, if done within limits. Scope cutting is greatly facilitated by iterative development; project managers should use it as a key tool to ensure on-time project delivery.

These cost considerations mean that you need to manage change. You need to

- Have procedures in place for approving whether to introduce a change.
- Be able to assess the impact of change.
- Minimize the cost of change.

Change approvals are done through a combination of manual procedures, such as Change Control Boards (CCBs), and tools, such as Configuration and Change Management (CCM) software. Assessing the impact of change is primarily done through traceability between tools for requirements, design, code, and test. When changing a class or a requirement, you should be able to understand what other things are potentially affected; this is where traceability saves a lot of grief.

The cost of change is minimized by having procedures in place for managing changes and also by assessing their impact. Again, the right tool support can have a tremendous effect. Automatic synchronization between design and code is an example of automation reducing the cost of change, since it allows you to do some code changes by working on a higher level of abstraction—the design.

Summary

The RUP forces agreement on the overall vision at the end of the Inception phase, a baselined architecture at the end of the Elaboration phase, and feature freeze at the end of the Construction phase.

The cost of change increases the further you are into a project, and different types of changes have different cost profiles. The RUP's phases have been set up to minimize overall cost of change, while maximizing the ability to allow for change. This is why the RUP forces agreement on the overall vision at the end of the Inception phase, a baselined architecture at the end of the Elaboration phase, and feature freeze at the end of the Construction phase. Using the right tools can play a powerful role in managing change and minimizing its cost.

Baseline an Executable Architecture Early On

A lot of project risks are associated with the architecture, especially when developing the first generation of an application. That is why you want to get the architecture right. In fact, the ability to baseline a functioning architecture—that is, to design, implement, and test the architecture—early in the project is considered so essential to a successful project that the RUP treats this as the primary objective of the Elaboration phase, which is phase two of this four-phase process.

First, what do we mean by architecture?[3] The architecture comprises the software system's most important building blocks and their interfaces, that is, the subsystem, the interfaces of the subsystems, and the most important components and their interfaces (see Figure 2.5). The architecture provides a skeleton structure of the system, comprising perhaps 10 to 20 percent of the final amount of code. The architecture also consists of so-called "architectural mechanisms." These are common solutions to common problems, such as how to deal with persistency or garbage collection. Getting the architecture right is difficult, which is why you typically use your most experienced people for this task. We will discuss architecture in more detail in Chapters 7 and 16.

Having the skeleton structure in place and properly tested provides a sound understanding of the building blocks or components needed for the final product. And, having followed the RUP's iterative pro-

---

3. For a good discussion on this topic, see Kruchten 2000a.

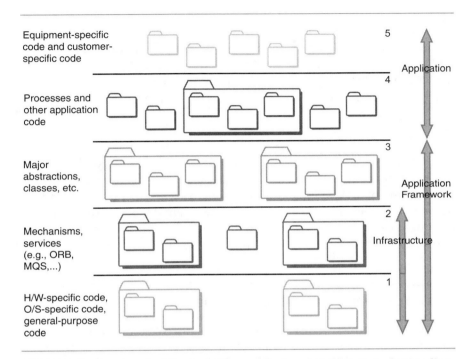

Equipment-specific code and customer-specific code

Processes and other application code

Major abstractions, classes, etc.

Mechanisms, services (e.g., ORB, MQS,...)

H/W-specific code, O/S-specific code, general-purpose code

Application

Application Framework

Infrastructure

FIGURE 2.5 A System Architecture. *The architecture provides an understanding of the overall system and a skeleton structure for the application. It includes, among other things, the subsystems and their interfaces and the most common components and their interfaces.*

cess, your team will already have gained some valuable experience in doing analysis, design, implementation, and testing, so you will usually have a firm grasp of what it will take to complete the system. Baselining an executable architecture also lays the groundwork for more accurate assessments of how many resources are needed and how long it will take to complete the project. Early understanding of this enables you to optimize your resource profile and manage scope to best address your business needs.

When the architecture is in place, you have addressed many of the most difficult parts of building the system.

When the architecture is in place, you have addressed many of the most difficult parts of building the system. It is now much easier to introduce new members to the project; boundaries are provided for additional code through the definition of key components and base-lining of interfaces, and the architectural mechanisms are ready to be used, providing ready-made solutions to common problems.

Summary

The architecture is the system's skeleton structure. By designing, implementing, and testing the architecture early in the project, you address major risks and make it easier to scale up the team and to introduce less-experienced team members. Finally, since the architecture defines the system's building blocks or components, it enables you to more accurately assess the effort needed to complete the project.

Build Your System with Components

One aspect of functional decomposition[4] is that it separates data from functions. One of the drawbacks to this separation is that it becomes expensive to maintain or modify a system. For example, a change to how data is stored may impact any number of functions, and it is generally hard to know which functions throughout a given system may be affected (see Figure 2.6). This is the major reason the Y2K issue was so difficult to address.

On the other hand, component-based development encapsulates data and the functionality operating upon that data into a component. When you need to change what data is stored, or how the data can be manipulated, those changes can be isolated to one component. This makes the system much more resilient to change (see Figure 2.7). Components can be implemented using object-oriented techniques or other techniques such as structured programming, and can be used

---

4. In functional decomposition, complex functions are recursively broken down into smaller and simpler functions, until you have functions that can be implemented easily. You also separate the data from the functions, which gives you a many-to-many dependency mapping between functions and data.

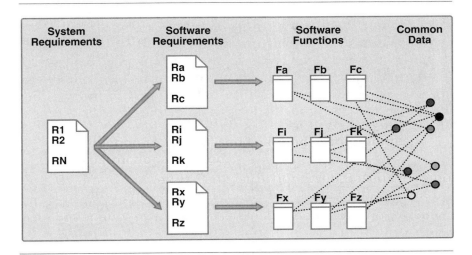

FIGURE 2.6 A Functional Decomposition Architecture. *Functional decomposition has the disadvantage that changes, for example, to how data is stored, may impact many functions, leading to systems that are both highly difficult and expensive to maintain.*

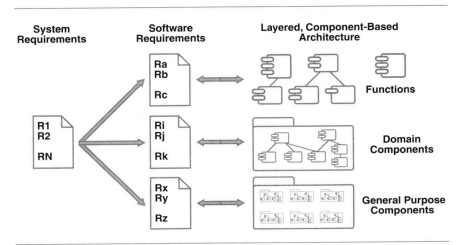

FIGURE 2.7 A Component-Based Architecture. *Component-based development leads to systems that are more resilient to changes in requirements, technology, and data.*

for developing a wide array of systems including legacy systems re-engineering, new application development, or package deployment.

To communicate with a component, and hence take advantage of all its capabilities and code, you need to know only the component's **interface.** You don't need to worry about its internal workings. Even better, a component can be completely rewritten without impacting the system or system code, as long as its interface does not change. This is an important feature of component-based development called **encapsulation,** which makes components easy to reuse.

A component can also be assembled by other components, thereby allowing it to provide many advanced capabilities. The combination of encapsulation and the availability of large components radically increases the productivity associated with reuse when developing applications.

Component technology is the basis for Web services initiatives.

Component technology is also the basis for the Web services initiatives recently launched by all the major platform vendors on both J2EE and .NET platforms, and it is why Web services may well be "the next big thing" in software development. In short, Web services are "Internet-enabled" components. Think of them as components on steroids. Like all components, they have a well-defined interface, and you can take advantage of all their capabilities simply by knowing that interface. As long as the interface does not change, you are unaffected by changes to a Web service. The major difference is that whereas a normal component typically limits you to communicating with components developed on the same platform (and sometimes only with components compiled on the same system), a Web services architecture allows you to communicate independently of the platform by exposing component interfaces over the Internet.[5]

Summary

Component-based development relies on the principle of encapsulation and enables you to build applications that are more resilient to change. Components also enable a higher degree of reuse, allowing you to build higher-quality applications faster. This can radically

---

5. For more information on Web services for the .NET platform, see Thai 2001.

decrease system maintenance costs. Component-based technology is the basis for Web services offered on J2EE and .NET platforms.

Work Together as One Team

People are the project's most important asset. Software development has become a team sport, and an iterative approach to software development impacts the ways in which you organize your team, how you should communicate within a team, the tools your team needs, and the values of each team member.

Traditionally, many companies have had a functional organization: All the analysts are in one group, the designers are in another group, and testers are in yet another group—maybe even in another building. Although this organizational structure builds competency centers, the drawback is that effective communication among the three groups becomes compromised. Requirements specifications produced by analysts are not used as input by developers or testers, for example. This leads to miscommunication, extra work, and missed deadlines.

Many companies have a functional organization.

Even worse than a functional organization are matrix organizations, where, for example, an analyst works on several different projects at the same time and is not really a full part of a team. This leads to considering your most valuable asset, people, as interchangeable parts.

Even worse than a functional organization are matrix organizations.

Functional organizations may be acceptable for long-term waterfall projects, perhaps as long as 18 months or more. But as you move toward iterative development and shorter projects of nine months, or even two to three months, you need a much higher bandwidth of communication between teams. To achieve this, you must

- Organize your projects around cross-functional teams containing analysts, developers, and testers.
- Provide teams with the tools required for effective collaboration across functions.
- Ensure that team members have the attitude of "I'll do what it takes to get high-quality working software," rather than "I'll do my small part of the lifecycle."

Let's take a closer look at each of these points.

The project team should consist of analysts, developers, testers, a project manager, architects, and so on. You might say that this works for small projects, but what happens when projects become bigger with, say, 50 people involved? The answer is to organize around the architecture,[6] to group what we call "teams of teams" (see Figure 2.8). Have an architecture team that owns the architecture; the architecture team decides on the subsystems and the interfaces between them. Then, for each subsystem, have a cross-functional team consisting of analysts, developers, and testers who work closely to ensure high-bandwidth communication and fast decisions. They communicate

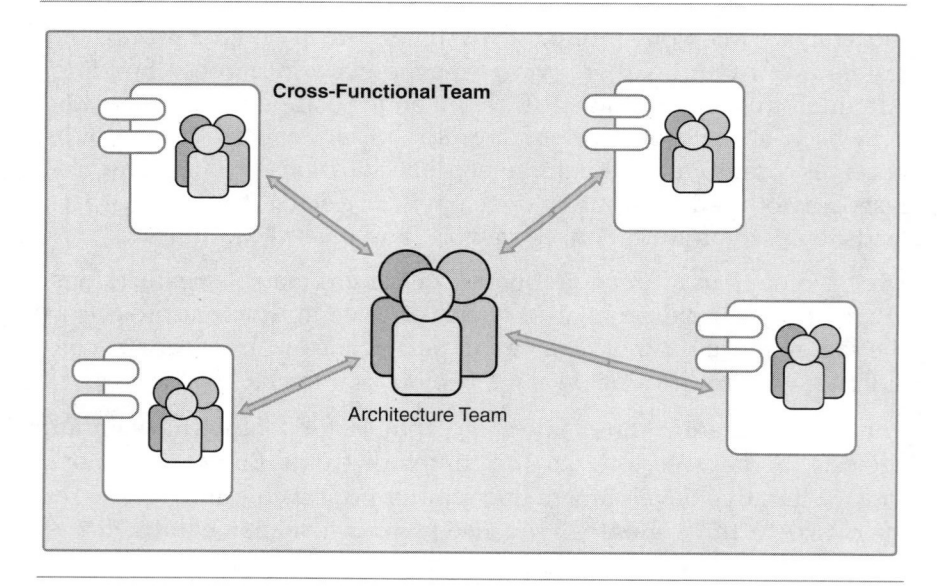

FIGURE 2.8 Teams Organized Around Architecture. *If the project is too big to have everyone on one team, organize teams around the architecture in "teams of teams." An architecture team owns the subsystems and their interfaces, and a cross-functional team is responsible for each of the subsystems.*

---

6. For more information on how to organize your team and other management issues, see Royce 1998.

with other teams primarily through the architecture and the architecture team.

For a team of analysts, developers, and testers to work closely together, they need the right infrastructure. You need to ensure that all team members have access to the requirements, defects, test status, and so on. This, in turn, puts requirements on the toolset your team will need to use. Communication between the different team members must be facilitated through integration between their tools. Among other things, this increases the return on investment in tools, allowing round-trip engineering and synchronization of requirements, design elements, and test artifacts.

You should also streamline the process, that is, reduce the amount of documentation to the extent possible, thus reducing the time spent on producing and maintaining documentation. In order to do this, you must replace their communicative value. One way to do this is through increased face-to-face communication. Consider having more team meetings, encourage direct communication rather than communication by e-mail, and co-locate team members whenever possible.

Working together as a team also enforces joint ownership of the final product. It eliminates finger-pointing and assertions such as *"Your requirements were incomplete"* or *"My code has no bugs."*[7] Everyone shares project responsibility and should work together to solve issues as they arise.

Working together as a team enforces joint ownership of the final product.

Summary

An iterative approach increases the need for working closely as a team. Avoid functional organizations, and instead use cross-functional teams of generalists, analysts, developers, and testers. Ensure that the tool infrastructure provides each team member with the right information and promotes synchronization and round-trip engineering of artifacts across disciplines. Finally, make sure that team members take joint ownership of the project results.

---

7. For more on this topic, see Kruchten 2000a.

Make Quality a Way of Life, Not an Afterthought

One of the major benefits of iterative development is that it allows you to initiate testing much earlier than is possible in waterfall development. Already in the first phase, Inception, you test some of the functionality captured in prototypes, providing you with valuable feedback on key use cases. In the second phase, Elaboration, executable software is up and running, implementing the architecture (see Figure 2.9). This means you can start testing to verify that the architecture really works. You can, for example, do some simple load- and performance-testing of the architecture. Gaining early feedback on this (perhaps one-third of the way into the project) may result in significant time and cost savings down the road.

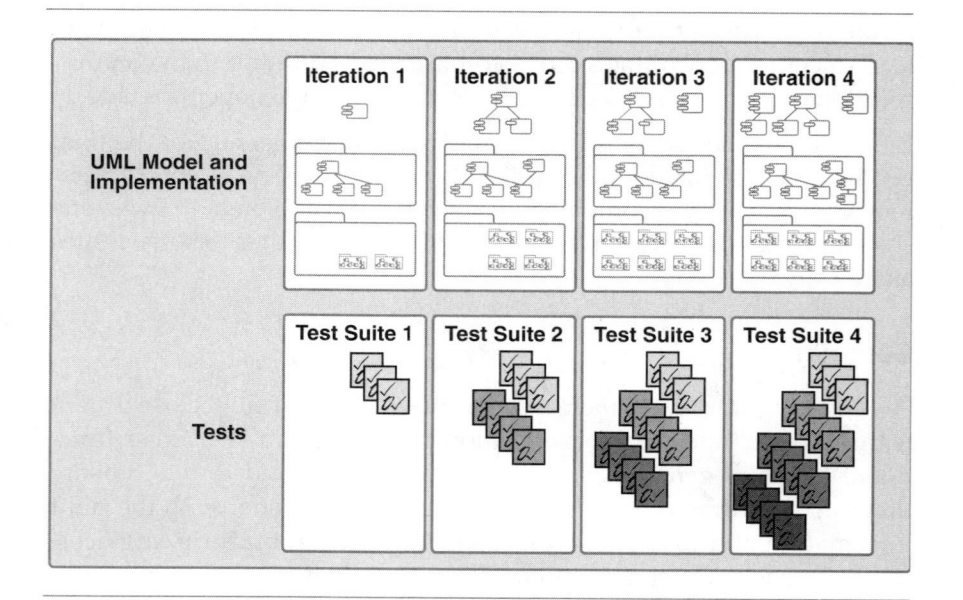

FIGURE 2.9 Testing Is Initiated Early and Expanded Upon in Each Iteration. *The RUP promotes early testing. Software is built in every iteration and tested as it is built. Regression testing ensures that new defects are not introduced as new iterations add functionality.*

In general, the RUP requires you to test capabilities as you implement them. Since the most important capabilities are implemented early in the project, by the time you get to the end, the most essential software may have been up and running for months and is likely to have been tested for months. It is not a surprise that most projects adopting the RUP claim that an increase in quality is the first tangible result of the improved process.

Another enabler is what we call "Quality by Design." This means coupling testing more closely with design. Considering how the system should be tested, when you design it can lead to greatly improved test automation because test code can be generated directly from the design models. This saves time, provides incentives for early testing, and increases the quality of testing by minimizing the number of bugs in the test software. (After all, test scripts are software and typically contain a lot of defects, just like any other software.)

Iterative development not only allows earlier testing, it also forces you to test more often. On the one hand, this is good because you keep testing existing software (so-called regression testing) to ensure that new errors are not introduced. On the other hand, the drawback is that regression testing may become expensive. To minimize costs, try to automate as much testing as possible. This often radically reduces costs.

Iterative development forces you to test earlier and more often.

Finally, quality is something that concerns every team member, and it needs to be built into all parts of the process. You need to review artifacts as they are produced, think of how to test requirements when you identify them, design for testability, and so on.

Summary

Ensuring high quality requires more than just the participation of the testing team. It involves *all* team members and *all* parts of the lifecycle. By using an iterative approach you can do earlier testing, and the Quality-by-Design concept allows software designers to automate test code generation for earlier and higher quality testing, thus reducing the number of defects in the test code.

Conclusion

We have examined the fundamental principles that represent "the Spirit of the RUP." Understanding them will make it easier for you to adopt the RUP properly. Don't focus on just producing a certain set of artifacts or carrying out a certain set of activities described in the RUP. That approach would likely get you lost in the wide set of available activities and artifacts that the RUP offers. Instead, let the "spirit" guide you, and adopt only the activities and artifacts that will best help your project adhere to these principles.

Now that you have an idea of "the Spirit of the RUP," go to the next chapter to learn how the RUP compares to other processes, how much you want to iterate, and what degree of formality you need.

CHAPTER 3

Comparing Processes: The RUP, Agile Methods, and Heavyweight Government Standards

In this chapter, you'll get a better understanding of how you should apply the Rational Unified Process. We'll discuss characteristics and differences between the RUP approach and

- Other **agile approaches** such as Extreme Programming (XP),[1] Scrum,[2] Dynamic Systems Development Method (DSDM),[3] Crystal,[4] and Adaptive Development.[5]

- **Process assessment frameworks** such as the Software Engineering Institute (SEI) Capability Maturity Models (SEI CMM and SEI CMMI) and ISO/IEC 15504.

- More **heavyweight development** approaches often linked to standards such as DOD-STD-2167a and MIL-STD-498.

---

1. See Beck 2000.
2. See Schwaber 2002.
3. See Stapleton 1998.
4. See Cockburn 2002.
5. See Highsmith 2000.

These processes and process assessment frameworks are compared using a "process map" with two dimensions: Low Ceremony/High Ceremony and Waterfall/Iterative. We'll use this map to understand what you should strive for in terms of process improvements, so that you can apply the RUP with the right amount of Ceremony and with the right level of iterative development to fit the specific needs of your project or organization.

How Can We Compare Processes?

How can processes be compared? We have characterized them by looking at the two dimensions discussed below and shown in our process map (see Figure 3.1).

- **Low Ceremony/High Ceremony**[6] on the horizontal axis. **Low Ceremony** produces minimum supporting documentation and has little formalism in the working procedure; **High Ceremony** has comprehensive supporting documentation and traceability maintained among artifacts, Change Control Boards, and so on.

- **Waterfall/Iterative** on the vertical axis. **Waterfall** is a linear approach with late integration and testing; **Iterative** is a risk-driven development approach with early implementation of an architecture and early integration and testing.

Agile Development: Low-Ceremony, Iterative Approaches

The Agile Development Movement has become increasingly popular, especially among individual developers and small teams, and is growing in popularity. Some of the agile approaches are XP, Scrum, and Adaptive Development. Note that we purposely left the RUP approach out of this list—we will come back to the RUP later in this chapter.

---

6. Alistair Cockburn refers to "Ceremony" as "Methodology Weight." See page 123 in Cockburn 2002 for an interesting discussion on this topic.

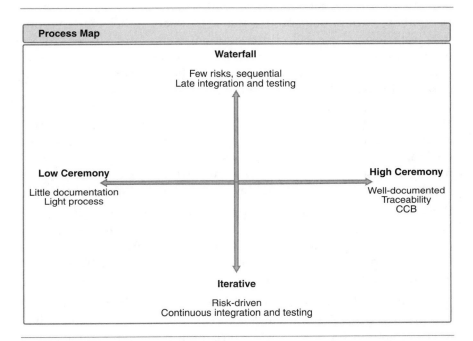

Process Map

Waterfall

Few risks, sequential
Late integration and testing

Low Ceremony

Little documentation
Light process

High Ceremony

Well-documented
Traceability
CCB

Iterative

Risk-driven
Continuous integration and testing

FIGURE 3.1 Process Map for Process Comparison. *By organizing processes and process assessment frameworks along two dimensions—Low Ceremony/High Ceremony and Waterfall/Iterative—you can compare them and analyze which are the most suitable for your project or organization.*

Agile development makes some sacrifices in terms of ceremony and rigor, in return for flexibility and the ability to adapt to evolving business environments. It places greater value on producing working software rather than creating extensive and comprehensive documentation. Instead of working from a rigid development plan, one of agile development's main tenets is **respond to changes that occur during the process**. This doesn't mean that plans and documentation are unimportant—they just aren't as important as ensuring that the software works or adapting plans to reality and changing needs.

XP, Scrum, Crystal, and Adaptive Development grew popular in the late 1990s, but they are primarily built on best practices that have been

Agile development makes some sacrifices in terms of ceremony and rigor, in return for flexibility and the ability to adapt to evolving business environments.

around for many years, such as iterative development, continuous integration, strong focus on executable software rather than byproducts, refactoring, use of coding standards, and user stories. As an example, iterative development has been around since the mid-1980s,[7] and for many years Rational Software has actively promoted[8, 9] iterative development with a strong focus on executable software rather than byproducts. The Agile Movement has done an excellent job promoting and popularizing these best practices and has introduced some of its own such as **pair programming** and **test-first design**. The Agile Movement has also done an excellent job of minimizing the ceremony surrounding software development, making sure that the primary focus is on software and not on supporting artifacts.

Perhaps one of the Agile Movement's most significant contributions has been the acceptance of concepts such as "process" and "best practices."

Perhaps one of the Agile Movement's most significant contributions has been the acceptance of concepts such as "process" and "best practices" by development camps that previously frowned upon them! Process has become "cool," and developers acknowledge the value of learning from others' experiences.

So where do agile processes fit on our process map? Figure 3.2 places all agile processes in the lower left quadrant because they are iterative, low-ceremony approaches that produce minimal documentation.

Since the Agile Movement is only a few years old, many of the agile approaches are new and unproven and don't yet provide much guidance on practical implementation. Consequently, many organizations struggle with effectively applying these methods.

Some agile processes, such as XP, Scrum, and Crystal[10] are now being used for bigger and more complex projects. As project sizes increase, more and more guidance is required for successful project execution. If we translate this onto our process map, we see that using agile processes for increasingly complex projects requires additional guidance

---

7. See Boehm 1986.
8. See Booch 1996.
9. See Kruchten 1996.
10. Crystal is a family of processes. Figure 3.2 shows where Crystal Lite is on the map, and the arrow indicates where higher ceremony versions of Crystal reside on the map. Crystal is one of several agile processes moving toward higher ceremony versions.

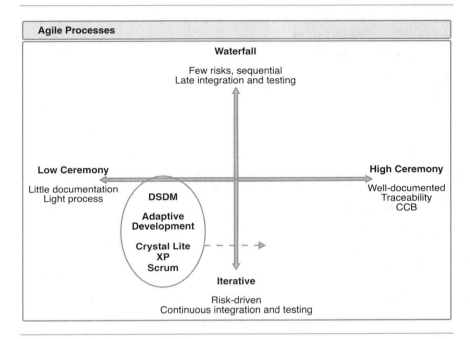

FIGURE 3.2 Agile Processes on the Process Map. *Agile development processes are characterized by a highly iterative approach using a minimum of documentation and formalism, which makes them ideal for smaller, less-complex projects. Some agile approaches have additional guidelines for more complex projects, making them higher ceremony.*

and more ceremony, thus shifting the process to the right, which corresponds with high ceremony (see Figure 3.2).

SEI CMM, SEI CMMI, ISO/IEC, DOD-STD, MIL-STD: High Ceremony Striving for Higher Predictability

Parallel to the Agile Movement is a strong trend toward high-ceremony approaches to software development. This trend includes software assessment frameworks such as SEI CMM, SEI CMMI, and ISO/IEC and processes such as DOD-STD and MIL-STD. Companies increasingly see software as strategic business investments and can no longer afford unpredictable results in terms of cost overruns and quality issues. As a result, many organizations have become aware of the importance of using a well-defined and well-documented software development process to facilitate success of their software projects.

Characteristics of a high-ceremony project include the following:

- Thorough plans are carefully documented.
- Many artifacts related to management, requirements, design, and testing are produced.
- Management, requirements, design, and testing artifacts are detailed, documented, and put under version control.
- Traceability links between requirements, design elements, and test artifacts are created and maintained.
- Change Control Board approval is required for changes.
- Inspection results are carefully recorded and tracked.

High-ceremony approaches are appropriate for complex systems development, large teams, and distributed teams.

High-ceremony approaches are appropriate for complex systems development, large teams, and distributed teams. Such approaches often produce quality systems that are easy to maintain, but the cost of producing them is typically higher, and time to market is slower than for low-ceremony approaches. If time-to-market is a primary concern, high-ceremony approaches may actually lead to lower quality, because there just isn't enough time to "do the job" prescribed by the process properly.

SEI CMM: Process Assessment Framework

The CMM is not a process— it is an assessment framework.

In the quest for better predictability and higher quality, organizations first need to understand how good their current process is, and what they should look for in a future process to reach a higher level of process maturity. The Capability Maturity Model,[11] developed by the Software Engineering Institute, is designed to do exactly this. The CMM is not a process—it is an **assessment framework** used to determine an organization's process maturity on a scale of 1 to 5. CMM does not tell you how to develop software—for that you need a process, such as the RUP, XP, or MIL-STD-498.

---

11. See http://www.sei.cmu.edu/cmm.

The CMM provides a very detailed outline of everything that could (not necessarily "should"—that would depend on project and organization specifics) be part of a software development or acquisition process for a mature organization. Unfortunately, many organizations and CMM assessors interpret this to mean that the more artifacts and activities used (equating to high ceremony), the better the process. But adding unnecessary artifacts and activities to your process, just to reach a higher process maturity rating on the SEI CMM scale, results in an overweight process—one that is cumbersome and ineffective. By having an overly strong focus on peer reviews, inspections, traditional quality assurance activities, and detailed planning, CMM also has the undesired effect of encouraging waterfall development rather than iterative development[12] by not forcing the identification of issues through early and continuous integration and testing.

Adding unnecessary artifacts and activities to your process just to reach a higher process maturity rating on the SEI CMM scale results in an overweight process.

SEI CMMI: Process Assessment Framework

To address this issue, SEI introduced **SEI CMMI**,[13] which more effectively accommodates modern best practices such as risk-driven and iterative development. Rather than encouraging an organization to create more ceremony (as CMM does), CMMI encourages users to focus selectively on the individual areas for improvements that best meet the organization's business objectives and mitigates the organization's areas of risk. Figure 3.3 shows where CMM and CMMI fit onto our process map.

CMMI more effectively accommodates modern best practices such as risk-driven and iterative development.

ISO/IEC 15504: Process Assessment Framework

Similar to CMMI, **ISO/IEC 15504** is a framework that assesses the maturity of software processes on a scale of 1 to 6; it was derived from the Software Process Improvement and Capability Determination (SPICE) project. ISO/IEC 15504 has many similarities with SEI CMMI, including selective assessment of only the process areas that are the most valuable for your organization. ISO/IEC 15504 can be placed roughly at the same place on our process map as CMMI.

Similar to CMMI, ISO/IEC 15504 is a framework for assessing the maturity of software processes.

---

12. See Royce 2002.
13. See http://www.sei.cmu.edu/cmmi/general/genl.html.

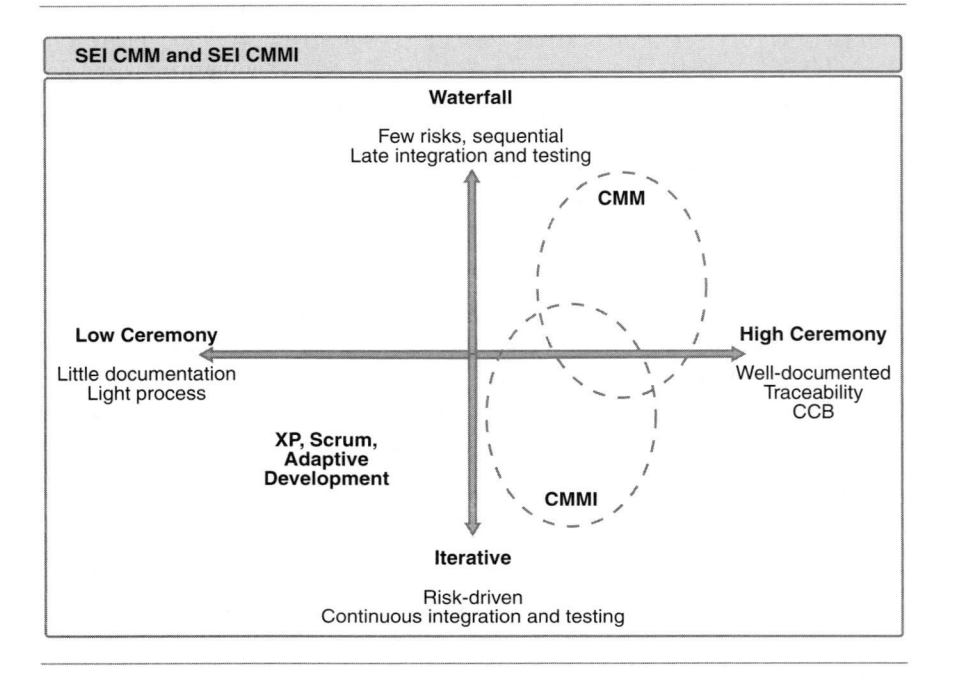

FIGURE 3.3 SEI CMM and CMMI on the Process Map. *SEI's CMM and CMMI both advocate high-ceremony approaches to software development. CMM has a slight bias toward waterfall development, while the newer CMMI has a slight bias toward iterative development.*

DOD-STD and MIL-STD: High-Ceremony Processes

Standards that provide a high-ceremony software development approach in an attempt to minimize cost and schedule overruns are DOD-STD-2167, DOD-STD-2167A, MIL-STD-1521B, and MIL-STD-498—all developed by the U.S. Department of Defense (DOD). These standards drive users toward a high-ceremony approach, with the exception of MIL-STD-498, which stresses that users should produce only artifacts that are necessary for their specific project. The authors of 2167 and 2167A went through some trouble explicitly to avoid a default waterfall interpretation, but unfortunately these standards were normally combined with MIL-STD-1521B, which prescribed a sequence of high-ceremony reviews (requirements review, preliminary design review, critical design review, and so on) that were so expensive to perform they made anything but a waterfall approach impractical. MIL-STD-498 is slightly more open to using iterative development, but it still does not go far enough (see Figure 3.4). Interestingly, the DOD now encourages the use of iterative development.

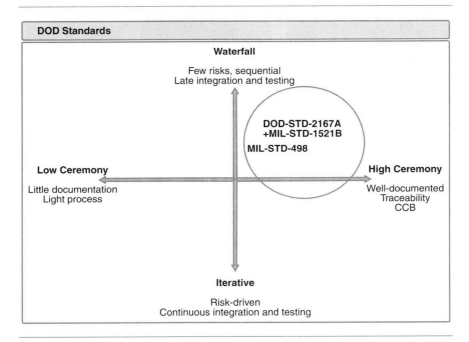

FIGURE 3.4 Various Military Standards for Software Development on the Process Map. *DOD-STD-2167 and 2167A, combined with MIL-STD-1521B, provide a very high-ceremony, waterfall approach to software development. MIL-STD-498 promotes a slightly more iterative approach to software development.*

The RUP: An Iterative Approach
with an Adaptable Level of Ceremony

RUP Configu-rations can fit anywhere on the Low Cere-mony/High Ceremony scale.

The Rational Unified Process is a customizable process framework that allows users to produce a wide variety of processes, or **RUP con-figurations** (described in Chapter 10). These configurations can fit anywhere on the Low Ceremony/High Ceremony scale, depending on project needs. Figure 3.5 shows where different RUP configura-tions would fit on the process map. The RUP strongly promotes an iterative, risk-driven approach to software development with continu-ous testing and integration. There is, however, some flexibility along

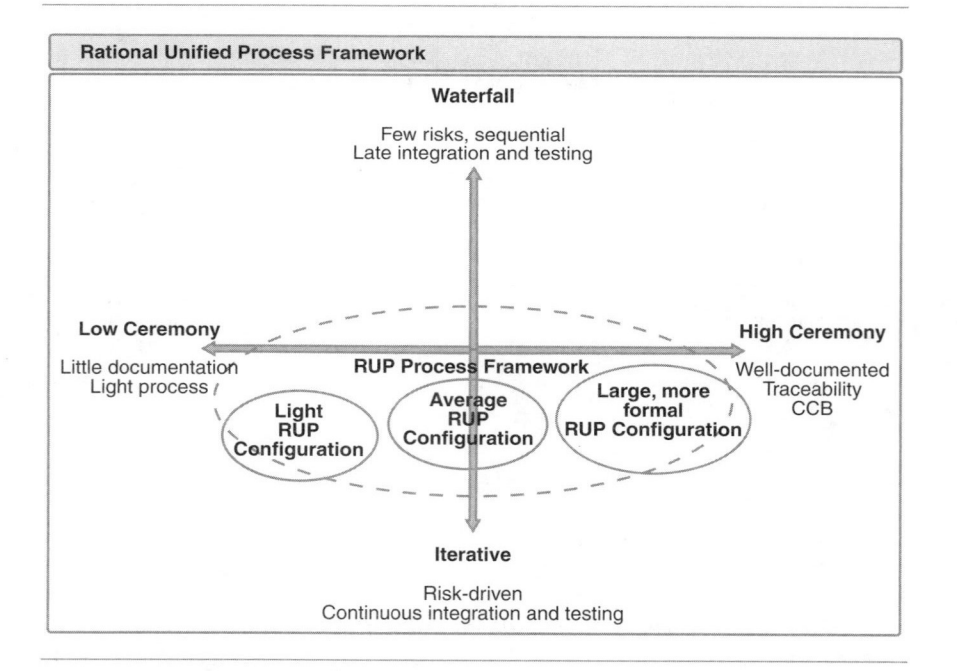

FIGURE 3.5 RUP Configurations on the Process Map. *The RUP framework allows you to produce a variety of process configurations from very low- to very high-ceremony processes.*

the Waterfall/Iterative axis, and some companies apply the RUP in a waterfall manner—something we generally advise against.

How Iterative Do You Want to Be?

There is a fairly large consensus among software industry leaders[14] in support of the benefits of iterative and risk-driven development (many of these benefits are discussed in detail in Chapter 2). Using such an approach typically has substantial benefits, with fewer cost and schedule overruns than waterfall approaches. Predictability is enhanced, allowing the identification of cost or schedule overruns in time to allow for scope cutting, making it possible to deliver at least a reduced set of the most essential capabilities on time and on budget.

But what prevents organizations from using a highly iterative, risk-driven approach with continuous integration and testing? Know-how, good process support, and good tool support.

- It may be hard for an inexperienced team to adopt a highly iterative approach. Such teams, unless they have good mentoring support, may start by experimenting with only a few iterations in their first iterative project.

- Good process support is required because iterative development introduces a lot of new challenges, especially for project managers and architects. The process needs to guide these and other team members in how to mitigate key risks early on, how to introduce the right Configuration and Change Management practices, and how to produce an executable architecture early on.

- Good tool support is also crucial. It is very difficult to do iterative development without good support for automated testing and Configuration and Change Management, among other things. Chapter 11 discusses the relationship between automation and iterative development.

Because of the benefits of iterative development, projects should strive to go far down on the Waterfall/Iterative axis. However, project

---

14. See Gilb 1988, Boehm 1996, Highsmith 2000, and McCormack 2001.

teams may find that they need to gain experience, process support, and enhancements of their tool environment in order to get there.

How Much Ceremony Do You Want?

We know that iterative and risk-driven development is desirable relative to waterfall development, and therefore projects should be on the lower half of the Waterfall/Iterative axis. Less certainty exists as to where projects should be on the scale of Low versus High Ceremony.

In "Get Ready for Agile Methods, with Care,"[15] Professor Barry Boehm describes how the need for rapidly adapting to evolving business environments should be balanced with the need for predictability and discipline by choosing the right level of ceremony to fit project-specific needs. (Boehm used the term "agile" versus "disciplined" to mean roughly the same thing we do with low versus high ceremony.)

Project factors favoring a lower ceremony approach include operating in a rapidly changing marketplace, co-located teams, small teams, and less technical complexity. Using a low-ceremony approach means reduced system documentation, for example, not documenting and tracking changes to requirements, designs, or test cases. Limited documentation means fewer updates are required when changes are made, thereby saving time and reducing the cost of change, which may be very important for a company operating in a rapidly changing marketplace.

Large-scale development, distributed development, technically complex projects, and complex stakeholder relationships are factors that drive toward higher ceremony.

Factors driving a project toward higher ceremony include large-scale development, distributed development, technically complex projects, and complex stakeholder relationships. For many such projects, lack of proper documentation can be very costly since it can prevent effective communication, and make it very hard and expensive to maintain technically complex or large software systems.

It should be noted that in some cases proper automation can accomplish the benefits sought by adopting a higher ceremony approach, without bearing the costs of document overhead. Examples of such tool technologies are

15. See Boehm 2002.

- Configuration and Change Management solutions that can simplify life for developers and hence provide them with a "lighter" process.
- Visual modeling support providing synchronization between requirements, design, and implementation, also known as round-trip engineering.
- Automated metrics collection tools that can simplify reporting for developers and analysis for managers.

All of these technologies come with an infrastructure overhead cost in terms of setting up and managing the necessary tool environment, but they can make the actual development effort much more efficient.

What Kind of RUP Configuration Meets Your Process Needs?

All of the above creates some important questions for determining what kind of RUP configuration is needed: Where should a project be on the process map? How much should it favor an iterative approach? How much ceremony is needed? To answer these questions, let us look at four different projects.

Project Deimos: Team of One

Project Deimos is a one-person project, developing a fairly simple application under the harsh time constraints of one week. Project Deimos is further described in Chapter 4.

Placement on the process map: The extremely small size, short duration, and relatively low complexity all indicate that the project should use an extremely iterative, flexible process (see Figure 3.6).

Project Ganymede: Small Project with Tight Timeline

Project Ganymede is a four-person project developing a database-centric, hosted business application. The team is working under tough time constraints and must deliver a first version of the application in three months. To make things worse, the team expects the requirements to change somewhat during the project due to the rapidly changing business environment. Luckily, several team members have built similar systems before.

Placement on the process map: The small size, harsh time constraints, changing requirements, hosted environment allowing rapid deployment of fixes, and experienced team all indicate that the project should use a highly iterative, flexible process (see Figure 3.6).

Project Mars: Average-Size Project without Iterative Development Experience

Project Mars is a 15-person project developing a Web-centric application. This is the third Web-based application the project team has developed on a J2EE platform. None of the team members has done iterative development, and there is no funding for iterative development training or mentoring. The team is using a very simple tool environment, including a low-end Configuration and Change Management system. The team knows that the system will be around for a number of years, so it needs to develop a robust system. To make things worse, the team has to develop the system under great time constraints, creating a difficult balance between making a system that is easy to maintain and doing it quickly.

Placement on the process map: The medium-sized project, as well as the balance between speed and system maintenance, indicate that the project should be somewhere in the middle of the Low Ceremony/ High Ceremony axis. Considering the severe time constraints and the need to get the architecture right, the team would benefit from using a highly iterative approach, but the lack of experience, training, and mentors, as well as the inadequate tool environment, all suggest the team would not be able to manage too many iterations in their first iterative project. They should be just below the center on the Waterfall/Iterative axis (see Figure 3.6).

Project Jupiter: Large Distributed Project

Project Jupiter is a large, 150-member project, distributed over three sites on two continents—a time zone difference of 11 hours complicates communication. The project has complex stakeholder relations, and some

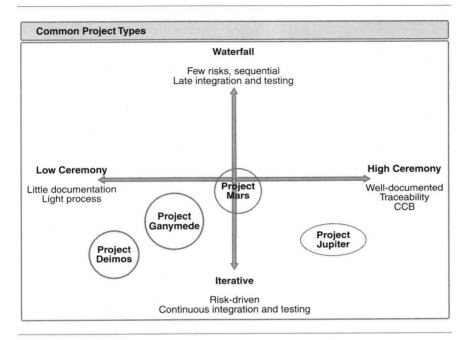

FIGURE 3.6 Example Projects on the Process Map. *Different projects require different process configurations, as shown with these four RUP projects. Project Deimos, a one-person, one-week project; Project Ganymede, a small project under harsh time constraints; Project Mars, an average-sized project with no experience in iterative development; and Project Jupiter, a very large project challenged by complex stakeholder relations and complex technology.*

stakeholders require good visibility in the project. This project will develop version 2 of a technically very complex system. The system will need to be maintained for many years. Additionally, quality is a major concern. Luckily, there are some very experienced team members, including top-notch project management and architecture teams.

Placement on the process map: Size, technical complexity, complex stakeholder relationships, long-lived system, quality concerns, and an experienced team all indicate that the project should use a highly iterative, high-ceremony process (see Figure 3.6).

Conclusion

Many projects can benefit from taking an iterative approach and using a RUP configuration that is low on the Waterfall/Iterative scale. To accomplish this, teams need to gain experience with iterative development; have good process support, mentoring, and training; and enhance their tool environment. The benefits of moving toward iterative development are often significant, but know-how, good process support, and good tool support are limiting factors.

The amount of ceremony required varies from project to project, depending on project size, technical complexity, contractual and regulatory considerations, automation, system life, and team distribution.

The "old school" of process improvement focused on moving projects toward higher ceremony.

The "old school" of process improvement focused on moving projects toward higher ceremony. An undesired side effect of many such attempts, such as MIL-STD-1521B and SEI CMM, was the tendency to drive projects toward waterfall development due to costly inspections and document-centric approaches. There were improvements to project quality and predictability, but often at a price—huge cost increases and an inability to adapt rapidly to changes. Newer efforts such as SEI CMMI lead project teams primarily toward high-ceremony approaches while also encouraging iterative development.

The "new school" of process improvement focuses on moving projects toward iterative and risk-driven development approaches, with continuous integration and testing.

The "new school" of process improvement focuses on moving projects toward iterative and risk-driven development approaches, with continuous integration and testing. This movement provides many benefits, with the main drawback being the need for additional education and improved process and tool environments. Many, but not all, projects would benefit also from moving slightly toward a lower ceremony development approach. This approach normally decreases development cost but could, at least for complex projects, come at the price of reduced quality. However, using an iterative approach, as well as investing in the right tool environment, can more than compensate for this issue. Among the new school of process improvement, we consider the RUP and other agile processes such as XP, Scrum, and Adaptive Development. Project teams should, however, be conscious about optimal positioning along the Low Ceremony/High Ceremony axis. Moving too far toward High Ceremony may increase development cost and decrease flexibility with limited gains, while moving too far toward Low Ceremony may cause quality and communication issues, especially for larger and more complex projects.

The Rational Unified Process is a process framework that allows you to produce customized process configurations that are iterative and risk-driven, with continuous integration and testing. The RUP configurations can be placed almost anywhere on the Low Ceremony/High Ceremony axis. Projects should first decide where they want to be on this axis before customizing the RUP product.

Projects should first decide where they want to be on this axis before customizing the RUP product.

When reading this book and working with the RUP product, it is important to remember the flexibility that the RUP provides you with in terms of placement on the process map. Chapter 2 describes the core principles of the RUP approach that apply for more agile as well as high-ceremony adaptations of the RUP. Chapter 4 walks through an extremely low-ceremony and agile implementation of the Rational Unified Process. Chapters 6–9 describe the RUP with a balance between low- and high-ceremony development, and Chapters 10 and 11 describe how to customize and implement the RUP product to find the right balance between low and high ceremony.

We've seen that the RUP can be configured to suit a variety of project sizes and requirements. In the next chapter we will see how it can be used in the most simple implementation, Project Deimos.

CHAPTER 4

The RUP for a Team of One: Project Deimos

We've talked about where different RUP configurations can fit on the process map. But how do you implement the RUP? Before we delve into detailed explanations of the RUP's phases and how to do iterative development, let's go through the simplest implementation possible—the RUP for a team of one: Project Deimos. This example will give you a basic idea of how to use the process and its underlying principles and will give you a feel for iterative development.

For some, the phrase "software engineering process" evokes an image of a huge set of dusty binders full of policies, directives, and forms, all saturated with administrative jargon. But these are materials that would probably be used only by very large companies that deliver software at a snail's pace to government agencies and Fortune 500 companies—software developed by armies of programmers aligned in giant cubicle farms and herded by "pointy-haired managers," like the one in the famous Dilbert cartoons by Scott Adams.

The purpose of a software engineering process is not to make developers' lives miserable or to squash creativity under massive amounts of paperwork. Its only real purpose is to ensure that a software development organization can predictably engineer and deliver high-quality software that meets all of the needs and requirements of its users—on schedule and within budget.

The purpose of a software engineering process is not to make developers' lives miserable or to squash creativity under massive amounts of paperwork.

In this chapter, we will see that a software engineering process does not need to be such a monster. We will explain how "the Spirit of the RUP" (see Chapter 2) can be applied to a very small project by following the work of Nick, a fictitious software engineer with 12 years of development experience. Although Nick prefers to work alone, he deliberately and conscientiously follows a well-defined process. Let's take a look at the diary he kept of a one-week project that he recently completed for Gary, an old friend of his.

A Solo Software Project: Project Deimos

The Seminal Idea (Saturday Night)

Tonight, I met my friend Gary in our favorite watering hole. He's the software development manager in a small company. As part of an effort to improve their process efficiency and predictability, some company employees recently took the Personal Software Process training course.[1] But Gary has a problem: A key element of the approach is that individual developers keep track of the time they spend on each type of activity, such as requirements capture, design, testing, and administration. Each of his developers uses a different tracking strategy, and at the end of the week, it is quite a nightmare to gather and consolidate all the data. An assistant has to go around gathering all the random Post-It notes, e-mails, and voice mails that team members use to estimate how they spent their time. This is discouraging because, for a software organization, accurate measurements of the effort expended on various activities are key for monitoring productivity, identifying potential areas for process improvement, and, above all, planning future projects effectively.

I suggested that Gary try automating the tedious job of tracking activity effort. Developers could have little timers on their screens that they could activate, associate with an activity name, suspend when they stop for lunch or some other interruption, resume when they return,

---

1. Humphrey 1997.

and close when the task is completed. The data would be stored somewhere safe and then retrieved and consolidated in a spreadsheet at the end of the week. "Great idea!" said Gary. "Nick, can you crank that out for me? It would save me a lot of hassle and therefore a lot of money. I'll pay you whatever you want. Well, sort of. How much do you want to develop this?" I told Gary that I needed to think about it. I had no engagement for the following week, so maybe I could crank out something in a few hours. But I quickly revised that: "Hmmmm, better make it a couple of days. Come to my office Monday around 11 A.M., and I'll have a proposal for you."

The Proposal (Monday Morning)

I thought about the timer project a few times over the rest of the weekend, and by the time I woke up this morning, I had a "mental concept" of it, as well as one or two possible implementation ideas. But this was a serious business proposition, so I needed a serious business case. What would I build, and how many resources would I need to throw its way? Mostly, this would require my time and maybe some software acquisitions. And finally, how much would I ask Gary to pay me? So I arrived here at my office early this morning, cleaned my desk, and laid out four sheets of paper. Then, at the top of each one, I wrote one of the following headings:

What would I build, and how many resources would I need to throw its way?

- Vision
- Plan
- Risks
- Business Case

The Vision

I start with the **Vision.** I need to describe, for Gary and myself, what exactly we want to achieve: the fundamental need he is trying to address, what the tool will look like, and how it will be used.

My first stab at it appears in Figure 4.1.

Personal Timer Tool: VISION

Problem
For Gary's organization, the inability to gather consistent data about time spent on various software development activities hampers the ability to monitor a project's progress against estimates, to invoice customers properly, to pay contractors, and, ultimately, to estimate work for future projects accurately.

Vision Statement
A Personal Timer Tool (PTT) that measures time spent and collects and stores this data for later sorting and extraction would (unlike Post-it notes and wild guesses) easily allow Gary's organization to make systematic, consistent assessments of where effort is spent, track actual time spent versus estimates for a project, and do a better job of estimating future development workloads.

Main Parties Involved
- Individual developers
- Administrative assistant
- Project managers

Use Cases
- Measure time for an activity
- Extract weekly time sheets
- Consolidate data for a project
- Set up tool and database for a project

FIGURE 4.1 Creating a Vision.

In the **Plan,** I'll sketch out a schedule for the next few days, mainly identifying major milestones—the points at which I'll have to make a decision, either on my own or, more likely, together with Gary.

At lunch today, I'll need to reach an agreement with Gary to go ahead and to get some commitment from him at least to start paying me for the job. I'll have to have him agree on the Vision, the Plan, and my estimate. For myself, I need a private **Business Case** (which Gary won't see), detailing how much time I need to spend on the project. If I can accomplish all this—getting agreement on an overall vision, a plan, and a price, and ensuring that I won't lose money—then I'll achieve my first milestone, the Lifecycle Objective Milestone—and bring the Inception phase to a close.

To make the pill easier for Gary to swallow, and also to cover myself in case I run into some unforeseen difficulty, I'll suggest that he commit only to paying me for producing a rough prototype, which I'll show him Tuesday evening. Only then, if he likes what he sees (and if I'm confident I can finish the project by Friday), will I ask him to commit to the total project amount.

The Plan

It's only 9:30 A.M., so I can work on the Plan. No need for heavy-artillery planning software to do a Gantt chart, but I want a rough plan that will distribute my time into major phases.

I want a rough plan that will distribute my time into major phases.

After sketching it out on a piece of paper, I decide to transfer it to my pocket agenda. My first-phase plan looks like Figure 4.2.

Personal Timer Tool: PLAN					
Monday	Tuesday	Wednesday	Thursday	Friday	Saturday
Inception Vision Plan Business Case Risks	Prototype Mitigate Risks	**Construction** Design Code Test	Design Code Test		
LCO: OK from G.	LCA: OK from G.		IOC: Show the first beta version		Sunday
Elaboration Prototype	Use Cases Tests	Design Code Test	**Transition** Improvements		
			Delivery		

FIGURE 4.2 The Plan.

Inception. I've been working on these activities since early morning and hope to wrap them up just after lunch with Gary. If I get his commitment to pay for a demonstration prototype, then this phase will represent a day of work on the project. If he won't commit, then we'll quit there and remain good friends.

Elaboration. I think I could conclude this phase by Tuesday lunch. I'll build a rough prototype that will allow me to "elaborate" on the requirements, the solution, and the plan, and to explore some of my ideas. Then I'll ask Gary again to validate everything with me over lunch. The prototype will give us several things:

- Something more concrete to show Gary so I can get more feedback from him on the requirements (you know, "I'll Know It When I See It"). So far all he'll have had to go on is a discussion in front of a glass of pale ale and some rough plans.

- More important for me, I can validate that I really have all the bits and pieces needed to do the job on my hard drive and that I do not underestimate the amount of effort. While shaving this morning, I thought I had an idea for an architecture and the various parts I would use, but now I am less sure. Can I use this little database I used on a previous project, and will I be able to interface it with a Java applet? Where did I put the user's guide for the API? Will that run on their OS?

- More information to create a much better plan and a more detailed schedule.

- A starting point for building the real thing, with a chance to scrap everything I did wrong.

- An opportunity to refresh my database definition skills, as well as my Java style.

I think of this crucial Tuesday lunch as the Lifecycle Architecture Milestone. At that point, both Gary and I will have the option to bail out, significantly recast the project, or go ahead with confidence.

Construction. I figure that if Gary gives me his go-ahead, helped along by a fine Beaujolais, then on Wednesday morning I'll start early to build the real thing, all neat and clean, and thoroughly test it. Then I'll ask Gary to come around 2 P.M. on Thursday and bring one of his programmers to try it out on *his* laptop. That will give me the afternoon to fix whatever they don't like.

I think of this Thursday session as the Initial Operational Capability Milestone because it will be the first time that actual users will try the software.

Transition. This will be the last run, and I hope it will last just a couple of hours. It'll conclude with a release—I'll probably e-mail the software to them—accompanied by my invoice, all by close of business Thursday.

The Risk List

I've already mentioned that I have a few doubts and worries. Rather than burying my head in the sand, I'll jot them down on that piece of paper headed **Risks.** I'll include anything I can think of that might make this little project fail, become delayed, or go over budget. And I'll use a pencil, because a Risk List always requires reorganization and sorting out again and again.

I'll include on the risk list all I can think of that might make this little project fail, become delayed, or go over budget.

What's on my list appears in Figure 4.3.

Personal TImer Tools: RISKS

- License for the development tools I need has expired.

- Database is too expensive.

- Mechanism for internode communication is not supported in Gary's organization.

- Some of Gary's programmer machines not connected to the Net.

FIGURE 4.3 Assessing Risks.

The Business Case

It's now 10:30 A.M., and I have all the information I need to build my initial **Business Case,** so I can begin filling in that last piece of paper. I've already estimated that the project will take four days of my time. I might need to upgrade both my Java compiler and the database software, so I'll mark those things TBD (To Be Determined). I figure that with my usual loading factor and a bit of padding for any bug fixes that might come later, it should be a reasonable deal.

If Gary is reluctant, I could even build a convincing business case from his perspective. If he were to free up a half-hour per week per developer, plus two hours of data entry and consolidation time for his administrative assistant, he would get his money's worth in less than six months. (I'm even thinking about how I could sell this little program to others through a profit-sharing scheme with Gary, but I'll focus on this some other day. Time is short.)

The Architecture

Since Gary has not shown up yet, I go a step further. On a fifth sheet of paper labeled **Architecture,** I do a quick pencil diagram of the major components of the timer software: Java applet, browser, database, and data extractor. It looks like Figure 4.4.

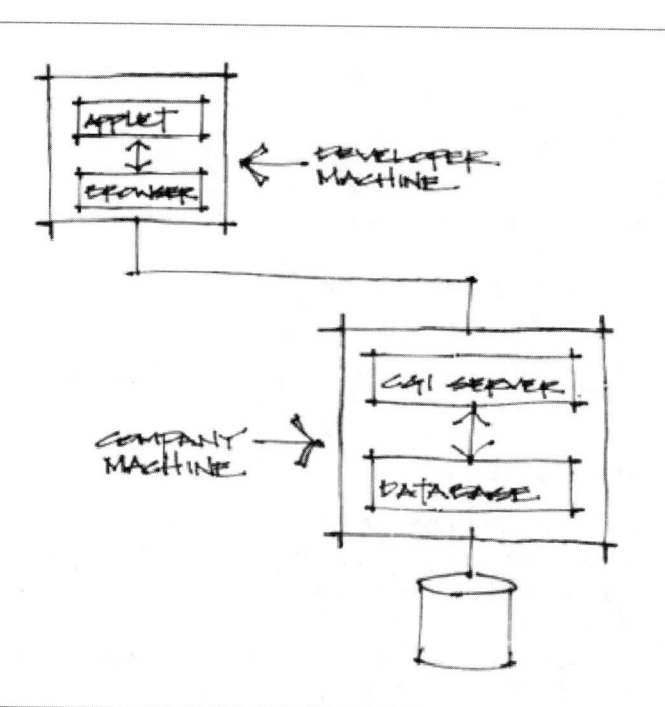

FIGURE 4.4 Sketch of Sample Architecture.

Then I add a couple of other components, using the UML. Since the diagram looks interesting, and since Gary is himself somewhat software-literate, I'll show it to him, too.

The Commitment (Monday Lunch)

To make a long story short, Gary likes it. He pays for lunch. I've brought my five sheets of paper (and my pocket agenda), and we scribble while waiting for the main course.

The bad news is that I did not completely understand the requirements. Gary wants all of his developers to accumulate data in a single database, over their local area network; he doesn't want to have each of them accumulate data in his or her own database because it's not that easy to merge the data. Also, they don't always work from the same machine, especially when they do testing. We make a few other touch-ups and clarifications to the requirements, but that network feature has me worried. It has consequences for my architecture and requires much more setting up and testing. Plus, we have identified the need for an administrator to maintain the database.

So, more or less on the fly, I adjust the documents that I prepared this morning.

The Vision, Take Two

I fix the Vision, adding that network feature. I also add a couple of ideas for future development that we discussed when I touched on the idea of making a business of this. Although I won't implement them in this round, they might constrain some design choices.

The Plan, Take Two

I decide not to take too many chances. To mitigate the big architectural risk, I shift the LCA Milestone (end of Elaboration) to dinner on Tuesday. I plan to do Construction over two days, with two iterations. For the first iteration, on Wednesday, I'll test and make sure the "single-person" version works fine, and on Thursday I'll develop the client/server feature over the network and test that. This will shift Transition to Friday for a final product delivery Friday evening. Gary also wants me to come to his office Friday morning to install the beta version and try it in situ.

Personal Timer Tool: PLAN, v2					
Monday	Tuesday	Wednesday	Thursday	Friday	Saturday
Inception Vision Plan Business Case Risks	Prototype Mitigate Risks	**Construction:** Single Person Design Code Test	**Construction:** Client/Server Design Code Test	**Transition** Improvements?	
LCO: OK from G.				IOC: Show the first beta version	Sunday
Elaboration Prototype	Use Cases Tests	Design Code Test	Design Code Test	**Delivery**	
	LCA: OK from G.				

FIGURE 4.5 Modified Plan.

The Risk List, Take Two

Now there are five new risks to add:

Personal Timer Tool: RISKS, v2
• Synchronization of updates to the database.
• Consistency of activities, projects, and users across multiple machines.
• Access rights policy for administrator and regular users.
• Same user connected from two different machines: Can it occur? What are the consequences?
• Dialog with one user dies for some reason and locks out all other users.

FIGURE 4.6 Assessing Risks, Take Two.

My biggest risk? If things go wrong, I'm jeopardizing the hiking trip I've planned for this weekend.

The Business Case, Take Two

Now we're talking about a full week of work, so I raise my estimate. Gary will have a return on his investment in only eight-and-a-half months, but he thinks a reasonable commitment is to pay me two-fifths of the project fee if I get to the LCA Milestone by Tuesday night. He promises to send me a purchase order for the Elaboration phase as soon as he is back in his office.

Digging In (Later Monday)

Back in my office, I start looking at more details for the two major use cases:

- Timing an Activity
- Getting a Tally of the Data

I expand them a bit on two other sheets of paper and build a sequence diagram on my whiteboard.

I'm also starting to get an idea of how I'll design the code in the applet, using three classes. I draw a sketch of what the timer will look like on the screen:

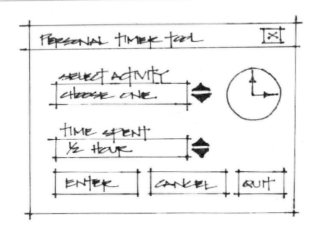

FIGURE 4.7 Sketch of Product Interface.

And as I go, I think of more and more questions and issues: Is the activities list predefined and static? (Probably not.) Can each developer create a new list, or only access an existing list? Gary is unavailable, and I can only get hold of his voice mail, so I write down my questions for tomorrow.

By evening, I've built an applet that looks like this on the screen:

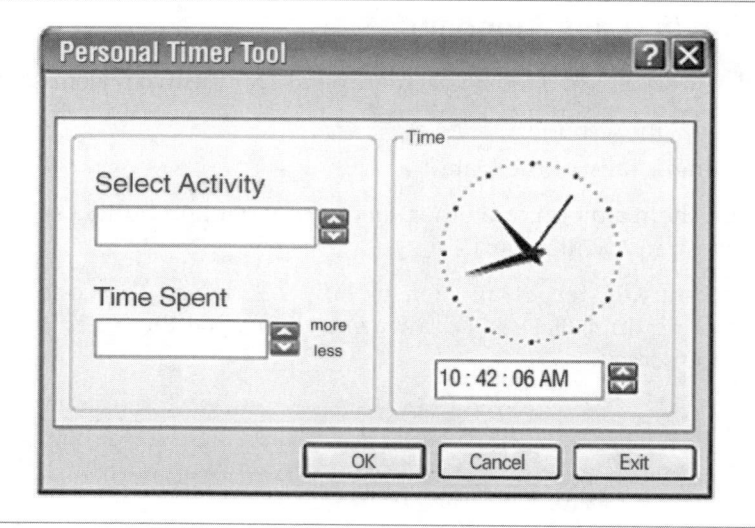

FIGURE 4.8 Screen Shot of Completed Product Interface.

I've also succeeded in writing some data for an activity on a text file, with all the testing I could think of (in true XP style). Not too bad for a single day of work.

Pressing On (Tuesday)

This is a real "cold shower, hot shower" day. Every time I cross one risk off my list, I have to add two more. I've made quite a few discoveries today. For lunch I decided to continue work; I stay in and order a pizza because I can't interface with the database. The thing crashed because my version of the database software is too old. Also, I didn't read the

API specification carefully enough. I lost an hour with tech support, then downloading the right version, then studying the documents.

I haven't made much progress, and I'm starting to think the whole thing was a bad idea. There are so many things that can go wrong, even with such a ridiculously small app!

I have built a UML model, though. Just a single class diagram and two collaboration diagrams. While I was at it, I also built a component diagram based on my architecture sheet, which I can discard now. I pin all my remaining sheets on the wall.

Since my Risk List was starting to look like a mess, I put it on my PC in an Excel worksheet.

I am not changing the Vision, but it is now accompanied by 17 Post-It notes, all with questions and issues. I start adding constraints, such as

- The code shall run on Windows NT or UNIX.
- The database runs under Windows NT 4.0 or above.

When Gary arrives for dinner with his colleague, Eric, I am putting the latest touches on a not-too-unreasonable prototype. All the data is canned; there is only one user ("Gary") and one activity ("Think"), and I was able to do an on-the-fly "suspend and resume" as an extension to the Timing an Activity use case. The database runs on my desktop with the applet on my laptop through the Net. My Risk List is now down to a few simple risks.

We spend about five minutes playing with the prototype until Eric crashes it. He's shocked, but I explain that robustness and completeness were not the objectives. Then we discuss the look and feel of the applet and reorganize the fields a bit. We look at my list of questions. Eric is very concerned about losing data if someone has to reboot a machine while a counter is running. I promise to look into it, although I was hoping he would say to forget it. Maybe I shouldn't have brought up the issue.

I end up adding a couple of new risks to my Risk List and half a dozen more requirements to my Vision Document, but that is not too bad. I decide to leave the Plan as is. To the Vision, I add more use cases for System Administration:

- Clean Up the Database
- Add a User
- Clean Up the Activity List

The good news is that Gary is happy with what he saw, and he says to move ahead with the whole project. He does not object to the constraints.

More Progress, More Changes (Wednesday)

I have found a solution to Eric's problem. Yes!

As I work, I put all my code and tests in a Configuration Management tool because I'm afraid I'll make a mistake and lose track of my changes. The plan is simple: Take a complete snapshot of each iteration.

Also, from the use cases I make a more complete list of tests to run.

I now work on a dialog for extracting the data, sorting it, and presenting it in a way that can be digested by Excel to make nice graphs.

Around 11:30 A.M. Eric calls. He forgot one requirement: A person may be working on more than one activity and need to have several counters active at the same time.

Ouch. Change the Vision. This one may be difficult, so I add it to the Risk List.

Nearing Completion (Thursday)

Testing. Do the network thing. Problems.

I renegotiate requirements with Gary, trading the new one Eric dropped on me yesterday for another one that was on my list. I *have* to do activity+project, because most of Gary's people do work on several projects at a time.

Based on the use cases, I start building a little Web-based user's guide in HTML.

I have so many little things to fix that I need to get better organized. I make a list so I can sort them out. I merge the Change Requests from Gary and Eric and also add several ideas for improvement.

More testing. First I try capacity testing. No problem. Then I try some concurrency: updating the database from two machines at once. Not good. Synchronization needs some serious rethinking. Error: Same user from two machines on same activity+project; there is one entry missing.

Late at night I find the problem. Now, almost everything works.

Beta and Ship (Friday)

In the morning, I go to Gary's company with my first beta version. We install it on several machines, I set up the database and brief his people, and they start playing with it. I run from one to another with my clipboard, writing out suggestions for improvements.

I add to my bug list two major problems and 12 minor ones (mostly matters of taste).

At lunchtime I'm back in my office. I fix all the critical problems and ignore three minor ones. I find another four issues myself, mostly through systematic testing. Finally, the next release is ready. It is numbered 0.9 in my Configuration Management system. It looks like I will have to go through 0.91 and 0.92. I start to despair.

Late at night, I take a break to write some Release Notes and prepare a little installer tool. By 1:00 A.M. I am done. I burn a CD-ROM and scream, "Ship V1.0!!"

I open a pale ale (there's no champagne in the fridge).

The End. Well, for this round anyhow.

Conclusion

The story about Nick and his one-week project shows that a well-defined process can also be applied to very small projects. Nick

Nick applies only the parts of the RUP that are relevant in the context of his one-week project.

follows "the Spirit of the RUP," and applies only the parts of the RUP that are relevant in the context of his one-week project.

Nick is very aware of **risks,** both technical (technologies, languages, interfaces, and performance) and business (schedule, expenditure, and missed expectations). He uses an **iterative process** to mitigate these risks, rapidly trying out ideas to validate them, to get feedback from his customer, and to avoid painting himself into a corner. He also sets up a **plan** with a few well-defined milestones, although the project is only one week long.

Nick has a simple **business case** for embarking on this project, with reasonable estimates for both his expenditures and the potential revenue. He revises this business case when he discovers that the basic requirements have changed.

Nick develops a **design,** beginning with an overall **architecture,** which he tries out very early. He also does more detailed design in areas where the direction may not be obvious. Nick tries to make sure he fully understands Gary's needs and vice versa. He tries to ensure that Gary knows exactly what he will get. Rather than jumping right into what he *thinks* Gary needs, Nick dedicates some time to writing down **requirements,** features, and constraints. Then, he validates this with Gary several times to make sure they share the same **vision** of the product.

Nick tries to spend his time on the highest priority tasks, and he sees that no issue is left aside or ignored for too long. Whenever he finds a problem with the product through a failed test, or whenever Gary comes back with a new request or a better idea, Nick captures this in the form of a **change request,** and he keeps managing and reprioritizing the change requests to drive his hourly schedule.

Besides the **code** of the product, early on Nick develops a set of **test cases** that match many of the requirements, and thanks to the iterative process he uses, many of these tests are matured, refined, and improved over time, as he develops the product.

To avoid losing some code by accident (for example, through a disk crash) or under pressure through his own mistake, Nick uses a simple strategy to manage the software, keep a history of versions of his files, and make snapshots of the version sets he tests. He tracks the evolutions and changes that he makes relative to these versions, so he can backtrack to a known **configuration** if he makes a mistake.

Finally, Nick writes simple **user documentation,** with a section that describes the release, how to install it, and its known limitations—one with the **release notes** and one describing how to use the product—that is, a **user's guide.**

This is the essence of the very lightweight engineering process Nick uses and which he affectionately refers to as his "Personal Unified Process"—PUP, for short. It is a low-ceremony process that focuses only on a small number of artifacts or workproducts. It does not involve a huge amount of paperwork, since many of the artifacts are stored in various development tools: the Configuration Management tool, the design tool, office tools, and so on. These few development artifacts produce value not only during the initial product development but also later on for additional releases. If Gary were to come back in three months asking Nick to develop a version 2, these artifacts would provide Nick with invaluable information to help him do a better job this time. They'll offer him important cost estimates, partial design or code to reuse, and a few lessons learned, mistakes he can avoid repeating.

In the next chapters, we will see how this unrolls for more serious endeavors.

PART II

The Lifecycle of a Rational Unified Process Project

CHAPTER 5

Going Through the Four Phases

A RUP development cycle goes through four phases: Inception, Elaboration, Construction, and Transition. This cycle ends with the release of a complete software product. What do you do during each of the various phases of the RUP? What happens during Inception, Elaboration, Construction, and Transition? What are you trying to achieve in each phase? What artifacts are produced? What activities are executed? The next four chapters will give you a sense of the dynamics of a RUP project. Each chapter is dedicated to a phase. But before you dive into these chapters, a few words of caution are necessary.

A Major Misconception

Although the four phases of a RUP project (Inception, Elaboration, Construction, and Transition) are run sequentially, remember at all times that the RUP lifecycle is fundamentally **iterative** and **risk-driven.** There is a big misconception that we would like to push aside very early in our discussion: The various phases are not simply a renaming (to sound fancy or different) of the classical phases of a waterfall process. From practitioners making their first acquaintance with the RUP, we have frequently heard, "Oh, I get it! In Inception you do all the requirements, in Elaboration you do the high-level

The RUP phases are not simply a renaming (to sound fancy or different) of the classical phases of a waterfall process.

design, in Construction you write the code, and you finish the testing in Transition."

In trying to match the RUP to their current practice, they completely miss the point of iterative development. Yes, in the early weeks or months of a project the emphasis is very likely to be more on requirements and during the final weeks or months to be more on testing and polishing. This change in focus across the lifecycle is precisely what is hinted at by the "humps" on the lifecycle iteration graph (see Figure 1.3); the height of the humps varies across the cycle. But inside each phase, you plan **iterations** (see how in Chapter 12), and each of these iterations includes many of the software development activities to produce tested code as an internal—and later external—release.

Major Milestones

What you need to achieve in each phase is mostly driven by risk.

The purpose of the RUP phases, therefore, is not to partition the activities by type: analysis, coding, and so on (this is what you achieve with the concept of disciplines). Rather, the purpose of a phase is to do just enough of any activity required to meet the objectives of this phase by the time you meet the milestone that concludes it. And what you need to achieve in each phase is mostly driven by **risk.** In other words, the phases define project states, whereas the states are in turn defined by the particular risks you are mitigating, or the questions you are answering.

- In the Inception phase (see Figure 5.1), you will focus on handling the risks related to the business case: Is this project financially worthy? Is it feasible?
- In the Elaboration phase, you will focus mostly on the technical risks, examining the architectural risks, and maybe revisiting the scope again, as the requirements become better understood.
- In the Construction phase, you will turn your attention to the "logistical" risks and get the mass of the work done; this is the phase where the project reaches its maximum staffing level.
- In the Transition phase, you will handle the risks associated with the logistics of deploying the product to its user base.

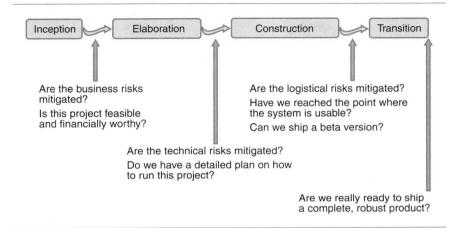

FIGURE 5.1 Major Milestones. *The major milestones of the RUP are not expressed in terms of completing certain artifacts or documents, like many other methods, but mostly in terms of risk mitigation and completion of the product.*

These major milestones are key business-level decision points for the project, where major decisions must be made about the continuation of the project and its scope, funding, strategy, delivery, or schedule.

Also, since the phases are not associated with one kind of role, a RUP project is not executed in a pipeline fashion by having a crew of analysts throw requirements over the wall to a team of designers, who throw a design to a bunch of developers, who pass it to the poor testers to take all the blame. A RUP project is a collaboration among all these people, from business analysts to testers. All the RUP roles are involved throughout most of the cycle (except maybe the very early startup of a brand-new project).

No Fixed Workflows

What remains constant across all RUP projects are these major milestones. What you must achieve by the end of each phase should be

The RUP does not define a fixed workflow, a fixed "recipe," or a predefined set of activities that must be run in each phase.

every team member's main concern. This does not mean that there is in the RUP a fixed workflow, a fixed "recipe," or a predefined set of activities that must be run in each phase. The RUP offers a palette of possibilities, but the context of your project will determine what you will actually use during the phase to achieve its objectives. From one development cycle to another, or from one project to another, the context will be different, and the risks will be different; so which artifacts you start with, the size of the project, its duration, and the number of involved parties will all play a role in dictating what must actually be executed and which artifacts must be produced or revisited.

Of course, in the RUP there are some common process fragments that are replicated across the lifecycle:

- Activities to start and close a project, a phase, or an iteration, and reviews
- Activities related to the detailed design, coding, testing, and integrating of software
- Activities related to Configuration Management, production of releases, and Change Management

These, however, are ancillary to what you need to achieve in that particular project phase.

The worst situation is the case of a project team trying to run the whole RUP and blindly developing all possible artifacts and executing all activities. By forgetting to tailor the RUP product to suit their context exactly, the team is running a high-overhead project, is overburdened very early, and is at risk of failing. You must streamline the RUP to be as low ceremony as suitable for your project (see Chapters 3 and 10).

No Frozen Artifacts

To simplify planning and to give a feeling of achievement or progress, there is also a temptation to try to *complete* a RUP artifact (model, document, code) in one shot, within one phase, or even within one single iteration, and to freeze it. "Let's build the requirements, have them 'signed off,' and be done with it." Or "The design is now complete."

There is nothing wrong with doing a perfect job early and not having to revisit an artifact. It is good that some artifacts become stable as you progress. But the objectives of the phases are not described in terms of *finishing* an artifact, but bringing it to the right level of maturity to be able to make the correct decisions about it. As the project evolves and more is understood about the objectives, as difficulties are discovered, and as external changes are introduced, artifacts have to be revisited, updated, and corrected. Therefore, activities that have already been run have to be re-executed. And having gone much too far in polishing an artifact too early may actually lead to much rework later on.

The objectives of the phases are not described in terms of finishing *an artifact, but bringing it to the right level of maturity to be able to make the correct decisions.*

The Vision and the Business Case will be developed during Inception and hopefully will be stable through the end of the cycle. The requirements are built gradually over Inception and Elaboration and should be complete by the end of the Elaboration phase. The architecture will be designed or selected gradually and should be stable enough by the end of the Elaboration phase. But these artifacts are not sacred and untouchable. You may have to alter the Vision, modify the requirements, or change the architectural design in later phases.

And as we wrote earlier, although all the artifacts described in the RUP could potentially play a role in a project, you do not need to develop *all* the artifacts in your project. Moreover, for a specific kind of artifact, use cases (UCs), for example, you may choose to develop some completely because they are delicate and risky, but not others, which can remain in the form of short descriptions because they are trivial or very similar to existing ones. For example, not all use cases are equally important and critical for the success of the project, and you may decide not to fully develop the description of minor ones.

You do not need to develop all *the RUP artifacts in your project.*

Three Types of Projects

In the next four chapters, to give you a better feel of the activities that can take place in each phase, we will use three different examples of RUP projects:

- Project Ganymede, a green-field[1] development of a small application. The **initial development cycle** of a brand-new application where everything, including the requirements, have to be designed from scratch.

- Project Mars, a **green-field development** of a larger system so that we can articulate the major difference with the first example.

- Project Jupiter, an **evolution cycle** of an existing large application (the "version 2.0"); this is more representative of a large number of RUP projects, which only evolve existing systems and do not create them from scratch.

There are many more types of projects; the combinations are infinite, but these three types should suffice to give you an idea about the evolving dynamics of a RUP project through its cycle.

When diving into the next four chapters, remember that the focus of each phase is to achieve some key milestone. These milestones have more to do with mitigating risks and achieving some concrete and objective progress toward the delivery of high-quality software than simply completing a wide range of artifacts and to "tick the box" on some arbitrary, predefined checklist.

---

1. "Green-field" development refers to developing a new application. The alternative to green-field development is to develop a new version of an existing application ("brown-field").

CHAPTER 6

The Inception Phase

In this chapter, we'll provide a basic understanding of what Inception, the first phase of the RUP lifecycle, is all about. Many newcomers to the RUP approach get lost in the rich set of activities and guidelines that it provides and often lose perspective on what they are trying to achieve. The RUP approach is actually quite simple: Make sure you have a clear picture of the objectives for each of the four phases (see Figure 6.1) and imagine what these concrete objectives mean for your situation. Understanding what you want to achieve in a phase will help you apply the RUP approach to your projects more effectively;

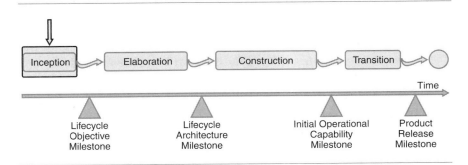

FIGURE 6.1 The Inception Phase. *Inception is the first phase of the RUP lifecycle; it has a well-defined set of objectives and is concluded by the Lifecycle Objective Milestone. Use these objectives to help you decide which activities to carry out and which artifacts to produce.*

you will select and perform only those activities that will contribute to achieving the objectives of a particular project.

As you read this chapter, it is important to remember what we discussed in Chapter 3 about low-ceremony and high-ceremony developments. We describe here an approach to software development that should help you develop better software, and we describe what types of artifacts you need to produce. As you apply these guidelines to your project, you need to decide how formally you want to capture artifacts: This could be done in your head, on a whiteboard, or in a model or document. How formally do you want to review these artifacts? We will try to point out obvious shortcuts you can make if you work in small projects or low-ceremony projects, but in the end, nothing can replace common sense, and you will need to make a judgment call as to what fits your project best. Also remember what we discussed in the previous chapter regarding RUP not having fixed workflows and avoiding frozen artifacts.

Objectives of the Inception Phase

Inception is about understanding the project scope and objectives.

Inception is the first of the four lifecycle phases in the RUP. It is really all about understanding the project scope and objectives and getting enough information to confirm that you should proceed—or perhaps convince you that you shouldn't. The five basic objectives of the Inception phase are

1. **Understand what to build.** Determine the vision, the scope of the system, and its boundaries, that is, what is inside the system and what is outside. Identify who wants this system and what it is worth to them.
2. **Identify key system functionality.** Decide which use cases (which ways of using the system) are most critical.
3. **Determine at least one possible solution.** Identify at least one candidate architecture.
4. **Understand the costs, schedule, and risks** associated with the project.
5. **Decide what process to follow and what tools to use.**

Note that the numbering of the objectives does not indicate priority, nor that they be addressed in any specific order. Quite the opposite: You will address all the objectives in parallel. In this chapter we will describe how to proceed to achieve each of these five objectives.

Inception and Iterations

Most projects have one iteration in the Inception phase. Some projects may, however, need more than one iteration to accomplish the objectives (see also Chapter 12 on the planning of an iterative project).

Most projects have one iteration in the Inception phase.

Among the reasons for multiple iterations, you find

- The project is large, and it is hard for the project team to grasp the scope of the system.
- The system is unprecedented, and it is difficult to pinpoint what the system should do.
- There are many stakeholders, and stakeholder relations are complex, such as difficult contractual negotiations.
- It is difficult to get the business case right in one shot or to develop an optimal balance between the scope of the project and the required investment. This is often the case when building new commercial applications.
- There are major technical risks that need to be mitigated by a prototype, or you need to build a proof-of-concept before you get buy-in from your sponsors. In particular, you may need to prototype your candidate architecture to get a better understanding of its performance, cost, and other characteristics.

If you have more than one iteration, the first iteration typically focuses primarily on objectives 1–3 (the "what" to build), while the latter iterations focus more on objectives 4 and 5 (the "how" to build it).

For each of our three example projects, you would typically have the following iterations pattern:

- Project Ganymede, a small green-field project: Since the application is small, you can typically understand what you need to build in a fairly short time frame. You likely need only one iteration.

- Project Mars, a large green-field project: Since the application is more complex and you have never built this type of system before, you need to take some time to get buy-in of what you are trying to achieve from all stakeholders. You probably need two iterations in Inception.

- Project Jupiter, a second generation of a large project: You are starting with an existing system, whose characteristics are understood, and you have a very good idea of what needs to be developed in this second generation. You have a number of use cases, extensions of existing ones or new ones, and some nonfunctional requirements, as well as a number of defects of the first system that you know you want to address. You still need to create an inventory of what to do so you do not miss any high-priority enhancements. It should be sufficient to do one iteration, and that iteration can probably be slightly shorter than most other iterations in your project.

Objective 1: Understand What to Build

All stakeholders must agree on a common definition of success.

This may sound strange, but the fact is that in many projects there is no common understanding of what needs to be built. Although all team members may think they know, often each one has a completely different understanding than the next. If you want to succeed, all stakeholders must agree on a common definition of success. You need to make sure that customers, management, analysts, developers, testers, technical writers, and other key people involved agree on what system to build.

To ensure a common understanding, you need to

A. **Agree on a high-level Vision.**

B. **Provide a "mile-wide, inch-deep" description** of the system. Briefly describe what the system should do, without providing so much detail that you get bogged down or that some stakeholders, such as customers or management, lose sight of what is being built because key information is hidden in a mass of requirements documentation.

C. **Detail key actors and use cases** so that all stakeholders can easily understand them and team members can use them as direct input for their work.

Produce a Vision Document

To address item A, you produce a **Vision Document.** For very small projects, this could be an informal document, maybe even an e-mail message capturing a previous whiteboard discussion. For average-sized projects, you might write a Vision Document of a few pages. No matter what the format is, a Vision should clarify to stakeholders

- The benefits and opportunities that will be provided by building the application.
- The problem(s) the application will solve.
- Who the target users are.
- At a very high level, what the product will do, expressed as high-level features or in terms of outlining a few key use cases.
- Some of the most essential nonfunctional requirements, such as supported operating systems, database support, required reliability, scalability, and quality, as well as licensing and pricing, if that is relevant.

The Vision creates the foundation for a common understanding of the motivation for building the system, as well as a high-level definition of the system to be built. The Vision should be complete and stable at the end of Inception, but you will continue refining it throughout the project, especially in Elaboration and early Construction (if there is a significant change of scope). It is important that the Vision is public, shared, and constantly reviewed, so that no one can say he or she didn't know or understand it. The widely used Statement of Work (SOW) is somewhat analogous to parts of the Vision.

The Vision creates the foundation for a common understanding of the system.

For more information, see the section Develop a Vision, in Chapter 15.

Generate a "Mile-Wide, Inch-Deep" Description

As item B specifies, you need to provide a good description of the system's scope without going into too much detail. The description requires two basic activities:

- **Identify and briefly describe actors.** Identify typical users for your system, and classify them based on what they do and what services they expect. Identify also other systems with which yours will interact. Capture these user types and external systems as **actors.**
- **Identify and briefly describe use cases.** Identify and describe **how each actor will interact with the system.** If the actor is a human, then describe typical ways the actor will use the system. Descriptions of these typical interactions with the system are called **use cases.**

A description a couple of paragraphs long is sufficient in Inception for most use cases.

At this stage, do not get into too many details: A description a couple of paragraphs long is sufficient for most use cases. However, you could spend a little more time on the use cases you identify as the most critical (and they should not be more than 20 percent of the total number) so that you have a solid understanding of them.

Hold a Workshop or Brainstorming Session

So, how do you produce this mile-wide, inch-deep description? For small projects, you get your team, your customer, and maybe other stakeholders together for a brainstorming meeting of a few hours. For larger projects, you may do a two-day workshop that includes all key stakeholders: project manager, architect, lead developer, customer, and a couple of analysts. During this session, your goal is to complete the seven steps that follow. Note that you do the steps in an iterative fashion, meaning that you will revisit these steps several times in Inception. It is often useful to "time-box" each step, that is, assign a fixed amount of time you will dedicate to it. As you run out of time on a step, go to the next step, and revisit the previous steps at a later stage. This will prevent participants from becoming too involved in one issue, forgetting that you want to achieve breadth more than depth. Note that if you have a brainstorming meeting, you will spend less time on each step, especially step 4. Have people work on step 4 after the meeting, and then have a follow-up meeting where you revisit steps 4–7.

Step 1: Identify as many actors as you can (remember, actors represent both users and external systems with which the system interacts). Throughout Inception and Elaboration you will eliminate some actors that are not needed, merge some actors that have similar needs, and add some additional actors you forgot. Write a one-sentence description of actors.

Step 2: Associate each actor with use cases, capturing the actor's interactions with the system by providing a brief description of the use case.

Step 3: For each of the use cases, determine whether it requires interaction with other users or systems. This will help you identify additional actors. Continue to go back and forth between finding actors and use cases until you think you have identified enough to understand the scope of the system. You most likely have not gotten them all, but it is good enough at this stage.

When you've completed these first three steps, your results will probably look similar to those shown in the use-case diagram in Figure 6.2.

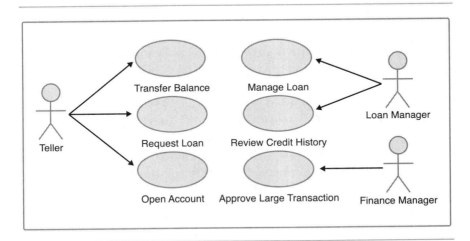

FIGURE 6.2 System Overview: User Kinds and Their Use Cases. *During a use-case workshop, capture (on a whiteboard) the user groups and systems (actors) that will interact with your system and the services (use cases) your system will provide to those actors.*

Step 4: Write a paragraph describing each actor and a couple of paragraphs about each use case. This can be done as a break-out session in which each person in the workshop is given two hours to describe, for example, one actor and two to three use cases. Make sure there is overlap; that is, the same use case and actors are given to several participants to describe. Then reassemble the group and review all descriptions. At this point you may encounter an interesting phenomenon: Although everyone agrees on the use-case names, each person has his or her own interpretation of what the use case entails. With detailed, written descriptions, these different interpretations become clear; by comparing them, you can see whether you need to come up with a few more use cases to cover all the functionality needed.

Step 5: Create a Glossary containing the key "items" the application deals with. For an insurance application, for example, you'd want to define things such as claims, different types of policies, and so on. Also add common terminology that is used in the domain and that the team or stakeholders may not be familiar with. This glossary should help the participants agree on a common terminology as this is often a cause of miscommunication and misunderstanding.

Step 6: Review key items that the system is dealing with, and make sure you have created use cases that detail how each key item is created, maintained, and deleted. Do you have a use case that describes how to set up a policy? How to make changes to a policy? How to cancel a policy? This is a great way of discovering holes in your use-case model, and spending only 30 minutes on this activity will often get you a long way.

Step 7: At this stage, you need to identify the most essential or critical use cases (maybe only one or two, and at most 20 percent of your use cases). See the section Identify Key System Functionality for more details.

For more information, see the section Describe Requirements "Mile-Wide, Inch-Deep," in Chapter 15.

Detail Key Actors and Use Cases

Another step in understanding what you must build is to refine some of the use cases. At the end of the workshop or brainstorming session, you assign one or several use cases to each analyst, who will describe in further detail essential or critical use cases identified in step 7. Typically, you'll generate a couple of pages for each one. The higher the ceremony, the more detailed the description.

For more information on detailing actors and use cases, see the section Detail Actors and Use Cases, in Chapter 15.

In parallel to writing the use-case descriptions, you should also develop user-interface prototypes. This allows you to visualize the flow of events, making sure that you, the users, and other stakeholders understand and agree on the flow of events. See the section Develop User-Interface Prototypes, in Chapter 15, for more information.

In parallel, you should also develop user-interface prototypes.

You should time-box the activities on use cases to avoid getting bogged down into too much detail. You should also focus on capturing the most essential flow of events and point out the existence of alternative flows of events (because it will help you to assess how complex the use case is to implement), rather than describing the details of each flow of events.

Especially for small projects, you often have the same person take on the role of analyst and developer, meaning that the person who describes a use case will also implement it. If so, you may want to spend less time on documenting the detailed requirements and come back to them as you implement the use case. It is still very useful to identify alternative flows of events, since this will be useful to you when you estimate the amount of work remaining.

For each of our three example projects, the teams do the following:

- Project Ganymede, a small green-field project: The project manager/architect spends a day writing a three-page Vision Document. The team spends half a day in a brainstorming session to come up with an initial set of actors and use cases. Thirteen use cases are found, and each team member takes four to five use cases, spending 30 minutes to detail each use case. Then they get

together and realize that they need another four use cases. They merge two use cases and eliminate one. They spend another two hours describing each of the four most critical use cases (see the section Objective 2: Identify Key System Functionality).

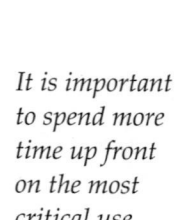

- Project Mars, a large green-field project: In the first iteration, the analysts, involving key stakeholders as necessary, spend roughly a week writing a first-draft Vision of eight pages. A lot of time is spent getting buy-in from all stakeholders. The team spends two days on a use-case workshop with eight key stakeholders, allowing them to come up with a good first-draft use-case model and glossary. In the second iteration, the team refines the Vision, which will be further refined later in the project, especially in Elaboration. They spend roughly four hours describing each of the nine most critical use cases (see the following section, Objective 2: Identify Key System Functionality). In conjunction with doing that, they make a number of updates to the use-case model.

- Project Jupiter, a second generation of a large project: The team makes some updates to the existing Vision, clearly labeling what will be accomplished in the second generation, which is done in a day or two. Most of the time is spent on making an inventory of additional capabilities to implement and the known problems in the first system that must be fixed. The team tries to identify use cases that need to be added, and the most critical of the new use cases are detailed, with the team spending two to four hours on each of them. Planned improvements to existing use cases are listed, but these improvements are normally not detailed at this stage.

Objective 2: Identify Key System Functionality

It is important to spend more time up front on the most critical use cases.

This is the second objective in the Inception phase, and you should work on it as you identify your use cases. It is important to decide which use cases are the most essential or architecturally significant to ensure that you spend more time up front on the most critical use cases.

The project manager and architect should work hand-in-hand on this activity, involving other stakeholders (such as the customer) as necessary, and using several criteria to determine which use cases are critical.

A. **The functionality is the core of the application, or it exercises key interfaces of the system,** and will hence have a major impact on the architecture. Typically an architect identifies these use cases by analyzing redundancy management strategies, resource contention risks, performance risks, data security strategies, and so on. For example, in a Point-Of-Sale system, Check Out and Pay would be a key use case because it validates the interface to a credit-card validation system—it is also critical from a performance and load perspective.

B. **The functionality *must* be delivered.** The functionality captures the essence of the system, and delivering the application without it would be fruitless. Typically the domain and subject-matter experts know what this functionality is from the user perspective (primary behaviors, peak data transaction, critical control transactions, and so on). For example, you cannot deliver an order-entry system if you cannot enter an order.

C. **The functionality covers an area of the architecture that is not covered by any other critical use case.** To ensure that you address all major technical risks, you need to have a good enough understanding of each area of the system. Even if a certain area of the architecture does not seem to be of high risk, it may conceal unexpected technical difficulties that can be exposed by designing, implementing, and testing some of the functionality within that part.

Items A and C will be of greater concern to the architect; project managers will focus mainly on items A and B.

For a system with 20 use cases, typically 3 to 4 of them are critical.[1] During Inception, it is important to understand *all* the critical use cases you identify and provide a fairly detailed description of them. However, you may postpone describing some of the alternative flows for these critical use cases until later in the project, as long as they do not have a major impact on the architecture.

For a system with 20 use cases, typically only 3 to 4 of them are really critical.

---

1. Note that for some systems, one or two use cases may constitute the core of the application, with a larger number of "supporting" use cases enabling execution of the core use cases. In this situation, fewer than 20 to 30 percent of use cases are architecturally significant, and we would typically implement several scenarios for each core use case.

The critical use cases are listed in the Software Architecture Document (SAD; see Chapter 16).

For each of our three example projects, you do the following:

- Project Ganymede, a small green-field project: The architect and the project manager is the same person. The architect/project manager suggests 4 of the 15 identified use cases as being critical. After discussion with the customer, a fifth use case is added. The architect/project manager gets the entire team together and spends an hour explaining why these are the most critical use cases. The team agrees, with potential changes made, and the architect/project manager documents the critical use cases in the SAD.

- Project Mars, a large green-field project: The architect proposes a list of 8 of the 40 use cases as being architecturally significant, strictly from a technical risk mitigation standpoint. The project manager suggests a set of 9 use cases that are critical to the stakeholders. The project manager would like stakeholder buy-in on the functionality of these as soon as possible. Five of the use cases overlap. After a few days of discussion between the architect and project manager, the project manager drops 2 use cases from the list (the project can delay getting feedback on those use cases from the users). The architect sees a way to mitigate some of the risks in 8 of the use cases through some of the use cases the project manager added. They end up with a joint list of 9 use cases, which the architect documents in the SAD.

- Project Jupiter, a second generation of a large project: A lot of time will be spent on improving existing use cases, which means that fewer use cases will be critical than for green-field development. The architect identifies one of the existing use cases as critical because it involves using some unexplored new technology. The architect also identifies 2 of the 9 new use cases as being architecturally significant. The project manager identifies one additional use case as critical from the user perspective. The architect documents the 4 critical use cases in the SAD.

Objective 3: Determine at Least One Possible Solution

Since the overall goal of Inception is to determine whether it makes sense to continue with the project, you need to make sure that there is at least one potential architecture that will allow you to build the system with a sensible amount of risk and at reasonable cost. As an example, you may consider three options for a client/server architecture (see Figure 6.3). By analyzing desired functionality (in the first version, as well as future versions of the application), compatibility with other applications, and requirements on operations and

Make sure that there is at least one potential architecture that will allow you to build the system with a sensible amount of risk and at reasonable cost.

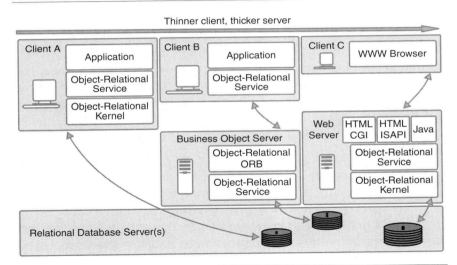

FIGURE 6.3 Three Options for a Client/Server Architecture. *During Inception, identify the type of architecture you intend to have and make implementations of necessary elements to the architecture to understand what risks you are facing. Here you see three options for a client/server architecture, each with vastly different requirements for tooling, competency, and complexity, and with different ability to address existing and future requirements on functionality, operation, and maintenance cost.*

maintenance, you may conclude which of these three options are viable. As you explore options, ask the following questions:

- What other, similar systems have been built, and what technology and architecture did you use? What was your cost?
- In particular, for an evolution of an existing system, is the current architecture still satisfactory, or does it need to evolve?
- What technologies would you have to use within the system? Do you need to acquire any new technologies? What are the costs and risks associated with that?
- What software components are needed within the system (database, middleware, and so on)? Can they be purchased? Can they be reused from another in-house project? What are the estimated costs? The associated risks?

In some cases, you may need to acquire or implement some key elements of the architecture, or different suggested architectures, to better understand the risks you are facing and the options you have. For applications where stakeholders might find difficulty envisioning the end product, you should also spend time on implementing some functional prototypes, sufficiently rich to verify that the Vision makes sense.

At the end of Inception, you should have a rough idea of what risks you are facing.

At the end of Inception, you should have a rough idea of what risks you are facing, especially in the areas of acquisition of technology and reusable assets, such as architectural framework, packaged software, and so on. During Elaboration, you may come up with a better architecture, and that is fine. It is during Elaboration that you will address the vast majority of the architecture- and technology-related risks you identified during Inception.

For each of our three example projects, you do the following:

- Project Ganymede, a small green-field project: The team builds a functional prototype of the use case that is considered the most critical. The functional prototype identifies some key architectural components, including one that you need to purchase. The team builds bits and pieces of functionality to understand how some new technology can be used, allowing you to better understand what can be delivered.

- Project Mars, a large green-field project: The team builds a conceptual prototype in the first iteration. This helps the interaction between the team and the customer, so the team can do a better job documenting what the customer wants. The second iteration focuses primarily on understanding what technology to use and associated risks. Some of the key building blocks are outlined, and fragmented implementations of a couple of the critical use cases are done to better understand what technology choices to make.

- Project Jupiter, a second generation of a large project: The team makes mock-ups of two of the four critical use cases identified. Half of this code is throw-away, but the mock-up convinces the team that it will be able to implement the use cases, and it gets some experience with some of the new technologies it will use. The team demonstrates the mock-ups to the customers and gauges the reactions of the audience to determine their expectations.

Objective 4: Understand the Costs, Schedule, and Risks Associated with the Project

Understanding what to build is key, but determining how to build it and at what cost is also crucial. To determine whether you should continue with a project, you need to understand roughly how much the project will cost. Most of the costs are related to what resources you will need and how long it will take to complete the project. Combine all of this knowledge with an understanding of the required functionality and its value to the users, and you can build a **Business Case** for the project. The Business Case documents the economic value of the product, expressing it in quantitative terms such as, for example, return on investment (ROI). The Business Case is the instrument you use to obtain adequate project funding. It also outlines the major unmitigated risks and therefore the level of uncertainty that remains within the project.

The Business Case documents the economic value of the product.

In many organizations, especially internal IT departments, the budget has already been set before the project gets to the IT department. In this case, you determine what can be delivered within the budget and the schedule.

For organizations developing software using a low-ceremony approach, the business case may take the form of a short memo or e-mail message, while high-ceremony projects require quite extensive business cases.

For each of our three example projects, you do the following:

- Project Ganymede, a small green-field project: The project manager/architect writes up a two-page memo, which functions as a business case, to the project sponsor. This provides the sponsor with sufficient information to understand the value of the expected investments.

- Project Mars, a large green-field project: The project manager produces an 8-page Business Case and a 12-page Software Development Plan (SDP), referencing project plans, risks lists, and other key management artifacts. The project manager arranges a half-day review meeting with key stakeholders to walk through the Business Case, risk list, Vision, and Software Development Plan (see the section Project Review: Lifecycle Objective Milestone that follows).

- Project Jupiter, a second generation of a large project: Compared to the first iteration, there is typically less business risk involved in developing the second generation of an application. Roughly the same process is followed as for the first project but with less rigor. The project manager writes a four-page Business Case and produces a Software Development Plan, referencing project plans, risk lists, and other key management artifacts. The project manager arranges a two-hour review meeting with key stakeholders to walk through the Business Case, risk list, Vision, and Software Development Plan (see the section Project Review: Lifecycle Objective Milestone that follows).

Objective 5: Decide What Process to Follow and What Tools to Use

It is important that your team shares a common view of how it will develop software, that is, which process it will follow. You should make sure that you streamline the process to minimize unnecessary overhead and be sure that the process addresses the specific needs of your project. Small projects can make decisions on exactly what process to follow as they go along, but bigger projects may need to spend more time up front considering their process of choice.

Make sure that you streamline the process to minimize unnecessary overhead.

The idea is to come up with a process and tool environment you think works in your first iteration. You deploy the process and tools in the second iteration, and get immediate feedback on what works and what does not. Based on the feedback, you update your process and tool environment, roll it out in the next iteration, and keep on iterating until you are satisfied with your environment.

Many organizations go with a "gut feeling" when deciding what process to adopt. Often, they wind up applying Band-Aids to problems without addressing the source of the wounds. A better approach is to assess your organization to understand where you are now, define where you want to be, and then decide how to get there, incrementally. In Chapter 10, we describe how you can customize the RUP product to fit the specific needs of your projects and how you produce a **development case**, a customized guide for selecting which parts of the RUP product to use and how to use them.

Once you have decided on a process, you can choose what tools to use. In some cases, the tool environment may already be decided, through a corporate standard, for example. If not, then you need to choose which Integrated Development Environment (IDE), requirements management tool, visual modeling tool, Configuration and Change Management tool, and so on to use. As we mentioned before, it is important that the tools do a good job of automating the process you choose; this may require that you customize tools and templates, set up project directories, and so on.

You also need to implement the process and tools in your projects, which we describe in Chapter 11.

For each of our three example projects, you do the following:

- Project Ganymede, a small green-field project: The team gets together and spends an hour agreeing on how it should work at large. After the meeting, the project manager/architect produces a

RUP configuration that corresponds to what they agreed on and writes a one-page development case for the Inception phase, outlining which artifacts should be produced, what templates to use, and how to document the information. They decide to wait until the beginning of Elaboration to detail how to work in Elaboration. The project manager/architect, being more experienced, functions as a mentor for the rest of the team, helping them with the adoption of the process and tools.

- Project Mars, a large green-field project: The project manager and architect spend time with a mentor, who guides them in what process to use. Once the mentor understands the needs of the project, the mentor spends a few days producing a RUP configuration and writing a development case for the project. The development case covers the entire project (even though more detail is provided for the Inception phase). Once done, the mentor uses the development case to influence what is taught in the training delivered to the team.

- Project Jupiter, a second generation of a large project: Most of the team members were involved when developing the first version of the application. They were happy with the process and tool environment, but had suggested a few improvements, which were documented at the end of the previous project. These suggestions for improvements are now implemented and rolled out to the team.

Project Review: Lifecycle Objective Milestone

At the end of the Inception phase is the first major project milestone, called **Lifecycle Objective Milestone.** At this point, you examine the lifecycle objectives of the project. The project should be aborted or reconsidered if it fails to reach this milestone. If your project is doomed to fail, it is better to realize this early than late, and the iterative approach combined with this milestone may force such an early epiphany.

The Lifecycle Objective Milestone review includes the following evaluation criteria:

- Stakeholder concurrence on scope definition and an initial cost/schedule estimate (which will be refined in later phases)
- Agreement that the right set of requirements has been captured and that there is a shared understanding of these requirements
- Agreement that the cost/schedule estimate, priorities, risks, and development process are appropriate
- Agreement that initial risks have been identified and a mitigation strategy exists for each

The project may be aborted or reconsidered if it fails to reach this milestone.

Conclusion

Inception is the first of the four lifecycle phases in the RUP. It is really all about understanding the project and getting enough information to confirm that you should proceed—or perhaps convince you that you shouldn't. This translates into five basic objectives:

- Understand what to build.
- Identify key system functionality.
- Determine at least one possible solution.
- Understand the costs, schedule, and risks associated with the project.
- Decide what process to follow and what tools to use.

By focusing on these objectives, you can avoid getting lost in the rich set of activities and guidelines that the RUP provides. Use these guidelines to achieve the objectives and to avoid common pitfalls. Apply the guidance we provide in Chapter 3 to guide you in how much ceremony you want to apply to your project. Don't try to produce all artifacts in the RUP product; focus on those that will help you reach your objectives.

CHAPTER 7

The Elaboration Phase

This chapter provides a general introduction to Elaboration, the second phase of the RUP lifecycle. This is the phase in which the differences between the waterfall and iterative approaches are most apparent: In particular, there is a radical difference in the types of activities performed in each of the approaches. The major advantages of the iterative approach will become clear: It addresses major risks, builds an early skeleton architecture of the system, and refines and evolves the project plans that were produced in Inception. These plans will continue to be revised throughout the project. In short, iterative development allows your project to adapt to the discovery of new or unknown issues.

Elaboration addresses major risks, builds an early skeleton architecture of the system, and refines and evolves the project plans.

Rather than describe each possible activity you could undertake in the Elaboration phase, we will focus on what you want to achieve—that is, the objectives of the Elaboration phase—and then provide guidance on how to achieve it. This will help you to stay focused on the most essential activities in an actual project, making it less likely that the project will derail or become mired in "analysis-paralysis," that is, nonessential activities that prohibit real progress. Or worse, you could focus on developing the wrong artifact or useless artifacts, just because they are described in the RUP.

While you read this chapter, remember that you need to decide how formally you want to capture artifacts; this could be done in your head, on a whiteboard, or in a model or document. How formally do you want to review these artifacts? We will try to point out obvious

shortcuts you can make if you work in small projects or low-ceremony projects, but in the end, nothing can replace common sense, and you will need to make a judgment call as to what fits your project best. This is something that you have captured in your Software Development Plan in Inception.

Objectives of the Elaboration Phase

As Figure 7.1 shows, Elaboration is the second of the four phases in the RUP approach. The goal of the Elaboration phase is to define and baseline the architecture of the system in order to provide a stable basis for the bulk of the design and implementation effort in the Construction phase. The architecture evolves out of a consideration of the most significant requirements (those that have a great impact on the architecture of the system) and an assessment of risks.

This general goal translates into four major objectives, each addressing a major area of risk. You address risks associated with requirements (are you building the right application?) and risks associated with architecture (are you building the right solution?). You also address risks associated with costs and schedule (are you really on

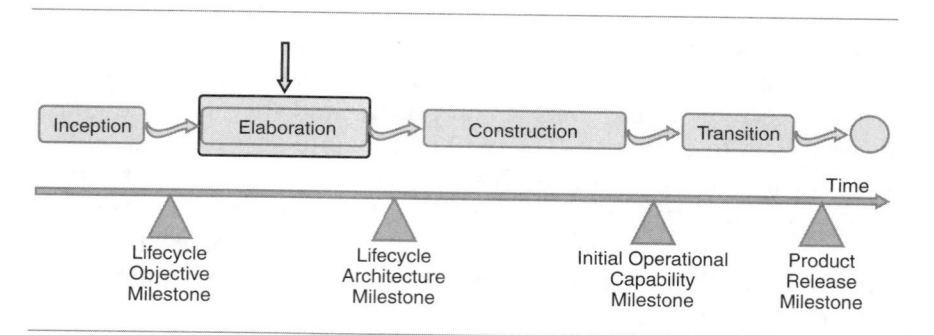

FIGURE 7.1 The Elaboration Phase. *Elaboration is the second phase of the RUP lifecycle; it has a well-defined set of objectives and is concluded by the Lifecycle Architecture Milestone. Use these objectives to help you decide which activities to carry out and which artifacts to produce.*

track?), and finally you need to address risks related to the process and tool environment (do you have the right process and the right tools to do the job?). Addressing these risks ensures that you can move into the Construction phase with a minimum of risk and issues.

1. **Get a more detailed understanding of the requirements.** During Elaboration, you want to have a good understanding of a vast majority of the requirements, since most of them are only briefly described in Inception. This will allow you to create a more detailed plan. You also want to get buy-in from key stakeholders to ensure that these are the correct requirements. And finally, you want to gain an in-depth understanding of the most critical requirements to validate that the architecture has covered all the bases, something that can be achieved only by doing a partial implementation of these requirements.

   You want to gain an in-depth understanding of the most critical requirements to validate that the architecture has covered all the bases.

2. **Design, implement, validate, and baseline the architecture.** You want to design, implement, and test a skeleton structure of the system. The functionality at the application level will not be complete, but as most interfaces between the building blocks are implemented during Elaboration, you can compile and test your architecture. This is referred to as "executable architecture" (see the section Objective 2: Design, Implement, Validate, and Baseline the Architecture that follows), to the extent that you can (and should) conduct some initial load and performance tests on the architecture. You make critical design decisions, including the selection of technologies, main components, and their interfaces; you assess the buy-versus-build options; and you design and implement architectural mechanisms and patterns.

3. **Mitigate essential risks, and produce more accurate schedule and cost estimates.** During Elaboration, you address major risks. Most will be addressed as a result of detailing the requirements and designing, implementing, and testing the architecture. You also refine and detail the coarse project plan for the project (see Chapter 12 for more details on planning).

   Many technical risks will be addressed as a result of detailing the requirements and designing, implementing, and testing the architecture.

4. **Refine the development case and put the development environment in place.** You refine the process you defined for Inception to reflect lessons learned. You also continue to implement the software development tools you need for our project.

Elaboration and Iterations

In the Elaboration phase, many risks are mitigated by producing an executable architecture, that is, a subset of the most essential aspects of the system that allow you to very concretely demonstrate key capabilities and therefore unambiguously assert that the risks are eliminated. If you've already built a system with the same technology that you're using in your project, then you can often achieve this objective in a single iteration because there is a limited amount of risk to address. You can reuse solutions from the past and thus make rapid progress.

But if you're inexperienced in the application domain, if the system is very complex, or if you're using new technology, then you may need two or three iterations to get the architecture right and to mitigate key risks. Other factors that will lead you to require multiple iterations include doing distributed development, having many stakeholders or complex contractual agreements, or needing to comply with safety regulations or other external standards.

For each of our three example projects, you would typically have the following iterations pattern:

-  Project Ganymede, a small green-field project: Because the application is small, you can typically get the architecture right in a short time. You probably need only one iteration, but if you have a lot of new technology and are building an unprecedented application, you may need two iterations.

-  Project Mars, a large green-field project: Because the application is more complex and you have never built this type of system before, you need some time to understand and mitigate technical risks and get the architecture right. You probably need two, or maybe even three, iterations in Elaboration.

- Project Jupiter, a second generation of a large project: You are primarily adding features and making bug fixes without making major changes to the architecture. You will use some new technology and develop some new subsystems, but one iteration should be sufficient. If you are not making anything but minor changes to the architecture, you may not have any iteration at all.

Assuming that our large green-field project would have two iterations, the general aim is to implement the use cases that are most essential to customers, as well as those associated with the most technical risk in the first iteration. Especially in the first iteration, and to some extent the second, start with only partial implementation of use cases (that is, implement only some of the scenarios within the use case) to quickly drive out as much risk as possible and to get a reasonable implementation before detailing the use cases. Each iteration could look as follows.

First Iteration in Elaboration

- Design, implement, and test a small number of critical scenarios to identify what type of architecture and architectural mechanism you need. Do this as early as possible to mitigate the most crucial risks.
- Identify, implement, and test a small, initial set of architectural mechanisms.
- Do a preliminary logical database design.
- Detail the flow of events of roughly half of the use cases you intend to detail in Elaboration, in order of decreasing priority.
- Test enough to validate that your architectural risks are mitigated. Do you, for example, have the right level of performance?

Second Iteration in Elaboration

- Fix whatever was not right from the previous iteration.
- Design, implement, and test the remaining architecturally significant scenarios. The focus in this iteration should be on ensuring architectural coverage (see the section Ensure Architectural Coverage later in this chapter for more information).
- Outline and implement concurrency, processes, threads, and physical distribution, as necessary, to address technically high-risk issues. Focus on testing performance, load, and interfaces between subsystems and external interfaces. (Note that planning *what* is done *when* is based on mitigating top risks early in the project. For some systems, resolving concurrency, processes, threads, and so on

may entail very high risk. If that is the case, then you should already have started addressing these issues in the first iteration in Elaboration.)

- Identify, implement, and test remaining architectural mechanisms.
- Design and implement a preliminary version of the database.
- Detail the second half of the use cases that need to be specified in Elaboration.
- Test, validate, and refine your architecture to the point where it can be your baseline. A baseline means that you use the architecture as a stable reference point. You can still make changes to it, but you want to avoid major rework except to resolve critical problems. If you cannot reach a sufficiently stable state on your architecture, you should add another iteration to Elaboration. This is likely to delay the project, but it will cost you even more to continue building on quicksand, that is, to invest further in an architecture that keeps going through major changes.

Objective 1: Get a More Detailed Understanding of the Requirements

By the end of Inception, you should have produced a good **Vision** as well as a **detailed description of the 20 percent or so most essential use cases,** at least of the architecturally significant portions of these use cases. You also have a brief description (maybe two to three paragraphs) of the remaining use cases.

By the end of Elaboration, you will want to complete the description of a majority of use cases.

By the end of Elaboration, you will want to complete the description of a majority of use cases. Some use cases may be so simple, or so similar to other use cases but operating on other data, that you can comfortably postpone them until Construction, or even never formally describe them. Detailing them will not address any major risks. You should also produce a user-interface prototype for major use cases, if necessary, to make stakeholders understand what functionality the use case provides. Walk through and test each use case with a user, using the user-interface prototype to clarify what the user experience will be and what information is displayed and entered.

As you detail use cases, you are likely to find additional use cases, which then are added and prioritized.

You should also continuously update the glossary. In some cases, you may want to express graphically how different glossary items relate to each other. You do this by expressing the most important glossary items as "domain objects" in a small domain model (see Workflow Detail: Develop a Domain Model, in the RUP, for more information).

As we described in the section Detail Key Actors and Use Cases in Chapter 6, you typically want to "time-box" the activities dealing with use cases to avoid getting bogged down in too much detail. Also note that especially for small projects, you often have the same person take on the role of analyst and developer, meaning that the same person who describes a use case will also implement it. If this is the case, you may want to spend less time on documenting the detailed requirements and come back to them as you implement and validate the use case.

At the end of Elaboration, you will have detailed a vast majority of the requirements (probably about 80 percent). As more and more use cases are implemented during Construction, you will refine each use case as necessary. You may find additional use cases during Construction, but that should be more of an exception than the rule.

For each of our three example projects, you do the following:

- Project Ganymede, a small green-field project: The team finds another use case and another actor. They spend another two hours per use case describing 9 out of the 12 use cases not yet detailed (see the section Detail Actors and Use Cases, in Chapter 15).

- Project Mars, a large green-field project: In the first iteration, the team refined the Vision and found 3 more use cases, making the total number of use cases 43. They described in detail another 12 use cases, adding to the 9 they already created (see the section Detail Actors and Use Cases, in Chapter 15). In the second iteration, they found 1 more use case, but decided to make 2 of the current use cases "out of scope." They also described in detail another 13 use cases, adding to the 21 they already had done.

- Project Jupiter, a second generation of a large project: They updated the Vision, added a use case, and described in detail most of the use cases not yet detailed (see the section Detail Actors and Use Cases, in Chapter 15). They analyzed in detail fixes to major defects that must be corrected and analyzed the impact on the architecture.

Objective 2: Design, Implement, Validate, and Baseline the Architecture

Software architecture and the related artifacts and activities are also described in Chapter 16. For now, let us simplify architecture to a few key design choices that must be made:

- The most important building blocks of the system, and their interfaces, as well as the decision to build, buy, or reuse some of these building blocks
- A description of how these building blocks will interact at runtime to implement the most important scenarios you have identified
- An implementation and testing of a prototype of this architecture to validate that it does work, that the major technical risks are resolved, and that it has the proper quality attributes: performance, scalability, and cost

To validate an architecture, you need more than a review of a paper representation; you need an executable architecture that can be tested.

In the RUP, an architecture is not limited to a paper drawing or a set of blueprints. To validate an architecture, you need more than a review of a paper representation; you need an **executable architecture** that can be tested to verify that it will address your needs and that it constitutes the proper basis on which to implement the rest of the system.

An executable architecture is a partial implementation of the system, built to demonstrate that the architectural design will be able to support the key functionality and, more important, to exhibit the right properties in terms of performance, throughput, capacity, reliability, scalability, and other "-ilities." Establishing an executable architecture allows the complete functional capability of the system to be built on a solid foundation during the Construction phase, without fear of breakage. The executable architecture is built as an **evolutionary prototype,** with the intention of retaining validated capabilities and those with a high probability of satisfying system requirements when the architecture is mature, thus making them part of the deliverable system.

Note that in the layered architecture shown in Figure 7.2, the elements in the **lower layers** either already exist or will be built during Elaboration; the **application layers** will be fleshed out with production code during Construction, but will be only partially completed during Elaboration (perhaps only to the extent of constructing the subsystems

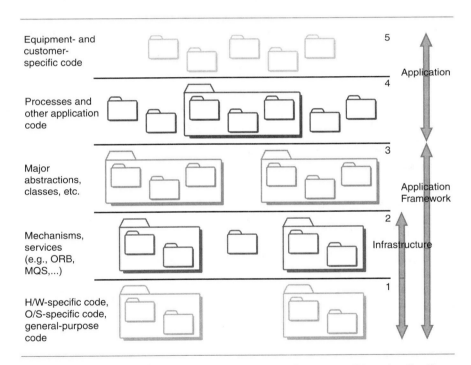

FIGURE 7.2 The Architecture Provides a Skeleton Structure of Your Application.
This figure shows one possible representation of the static structure of your system. The architecture consists of the most essential building blocks and their interfaces, and specifies common solutions to frequently encountered problems. It provides a skeleton structure of the application, leaving you to fill in the blanks within a stable and well-defined base.

shells). Nevertheless, you need to do performance- and load-testing of the critical scenarios by the end of Elaboration, and you should write "stubs" (if not actual application code) to enable this end-to-end testing.

At the end of the Elaboration phase, you baseline your architecture.

At the end of the Elaboration phase, you baseline your architecture, which means that you make your architecture a stable reference for building the rest of the system. From this point on, you should modify the architecture with care, and only if you have a good reason. This baseline provides some stability for the development team. Note that the larger your team and the more technically complex the project, the more important it is to baseline the architecture. The smaller the team and the less complex your architecture is, the more liberty you can take in modifying the architecture.

See Chapter 16 for more information on architecture.

Architecture: Defining Subsystems, Key Components, and Their Interfaces

At the end of Inception, you produced or at least identified one potential architecture that would allow you to build the system with a reasonable amount of risk and at a reasonable cost. In some cases, you also implemented key elements of the architecture, which we described in the section Objective 3: Determine at Least One Possible Solution, in Chapter 6.

At the end of Inception, you had a rough idea of what risks you were facing, especially in the areas of acquisition of technology and reusable assets, such as architectural framework, packaged software, and so on. You left the majority of questions unanswered; other answers were preliminary and left to be finalized during Elaboration.

Rather than inventing an architecture, you should first envisage using an existing architectural framework.

For all these reasons, early in the Elaboration phase you should have a fairly good understanding of what kind of system you are building. Rather than inventing an architecture, you should first envisage using an existing architectural framework to advance the architecture. Maybe there is a commercial framework available (for example, IBM's IAAA for insurance applications), or perhaps you have built this type of system before and can harvest the architecture from previous work.

If not, then you need to identify the major building blocks, that is, the subsystems and major components. Potential sources of input are the major abstractions captured in the domain object model or glossary (see Chapter 6). For example, an online transaction system typically requires a component or subsystem[1] that handles each major concept: Shopping Cart, Customer, and Price Promotions. For each identified subsystem or component, describe the key capabilities they need to offer, namely, their interfaces toward the rest of the system.

In parallel with identifying key components and subsystems, you need to survey available assets inside and outside the company. Can you acquire a set of components implementing the concept of Shopping Cart? Do those components satisfy your needs? What are the legal and financial implications? Will the components be maintained as technology and user requirements evolve? Do we have access to the source code to make necessary changes? Is the code properly documented with supporting guidelines about the components' design and how to use and test them?

Use Architecturally Significant Use Cases to Drive the Architecture

During Inception, you should have identified some use cases, perhaps 20 to 30 percent,[2] as being critical to the system (see the section Objective 2: Identify Key System Functionality, in Chapter 6, for more information). They are also likely to be significant in driving the architecture.

You also need to identify certain elements in the requirements—possibly nonfunctional requirements—that are difficult, unknown, or at risk, and find use cases (or fragments of use cases) that would illustrate the difficult points and whose implementation would force confrontation and resolution of the risk. These are the technical challenges often

---

1. A subsystem corresponds to a component or a collection of components.
2. Note that for some systems, one or two use cases may constitute the core of the application, with a larger number of "supporting use cases" enabling execution of the core use cases. In this situation, fewer than 20 to 30 percent of use cases are architecturally significant, and you would typically implement several scenarios for each core use case.

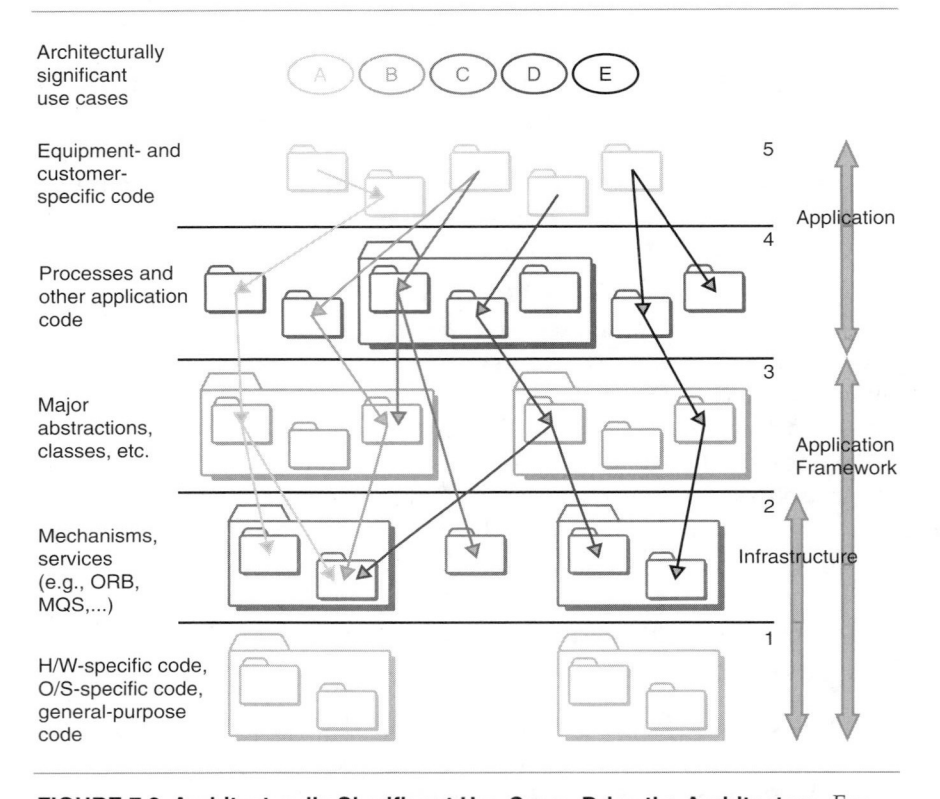

FIGURE 7.3 Architecturally Significant Use Cases Drive the Architecture. *For most systems, you can drive out a majority of technical risks and drive the implementation of the architecture by choosing the right 20 to 30 percent of use cases, and designing, implementing, and testing one or two scenarios for each use case. To implement a given use case, you need to identify which software elements are required to provide the functionality of that use case.*

relegated to the infrastructure part of the architecture. For example, if there is a very demanding response time requirement, or load requirements, identify one use case (or just one flow of events in one use case) that would illustrate this requirement, together with the expected performance requirement. Other examples would be an error recovery strategy or system startup.

Finally, you should identify some use cases that, although not critical nor technically challenging, address some parts of the system not yet covered, so that you will develop a good grasp over the whole architecture of the system by the end of Elaboration. For example, make sure that all your major "business entities" are exercised by at least one of your architecturally significant use cases.

You must ensure that the architecture will allow you to deliver all the architecturally significant use cases by designing, implementing, and testing as many of these use cases as necessary to mitigate the risks associated with them (see Figure 7.3). At the same time, you do not want to implement more capabilities than necessary to mitigate the risks, since that would take time from other activities related to **risk mitigation**, which is one of your primary objectives in Elaboration. This typically means that, in Elaboration, you should focus on only one or two scenarios or flows of events in a use case: Typically, you would choose the basic flow of events, or "Happy Day" scenario. If necessary, you may also need to implement some scenario(s) involving unexpected events. For example, you might implement one scenario to eliminate risk associated with exception handling, but there would be no point in implementing 10 scenarios to mitigate this same risk.

In Elaboration, you should focus on only one or two scenarios in a use case.

Design Critical Use Cases

The design representation of a use case is called use-case realization (see Figure 7.4). It describes how a particular use case is realized within the design model, in terms of collaborating objects. You can divide this work into an analysis section and a design section. The following provides an overview of the five most essentials steps when producing a use-case realization. It should be noted that these steps are helpful for all developers, but you need to determine from project to project how formally you want to document the results of each step, such as on a whiteboard or in a visual modeling tool. See the section Design Use-Case Realizations and Components, in Chapter 17, for a more detailed explanation of these steps.

1. **Make a preliminary outline of the analysis objects involved in the collaboration.** The RUP product provides some excellent

guidance to assist those developers inexperienced in object-oriented development in identifying good analysis classes.

2. **Distribute behavior to analysis classes.** That is, specify the overall responsibility of each analysis class so you understand how these classes together can provide the functionality of the use case.

3. **Detail analysis classes.** This helps you understand the responsibility of each analysis class. Review the analysis model to ensure that no two classes provide overlapping functionality and that the relationships between various classes make sense.

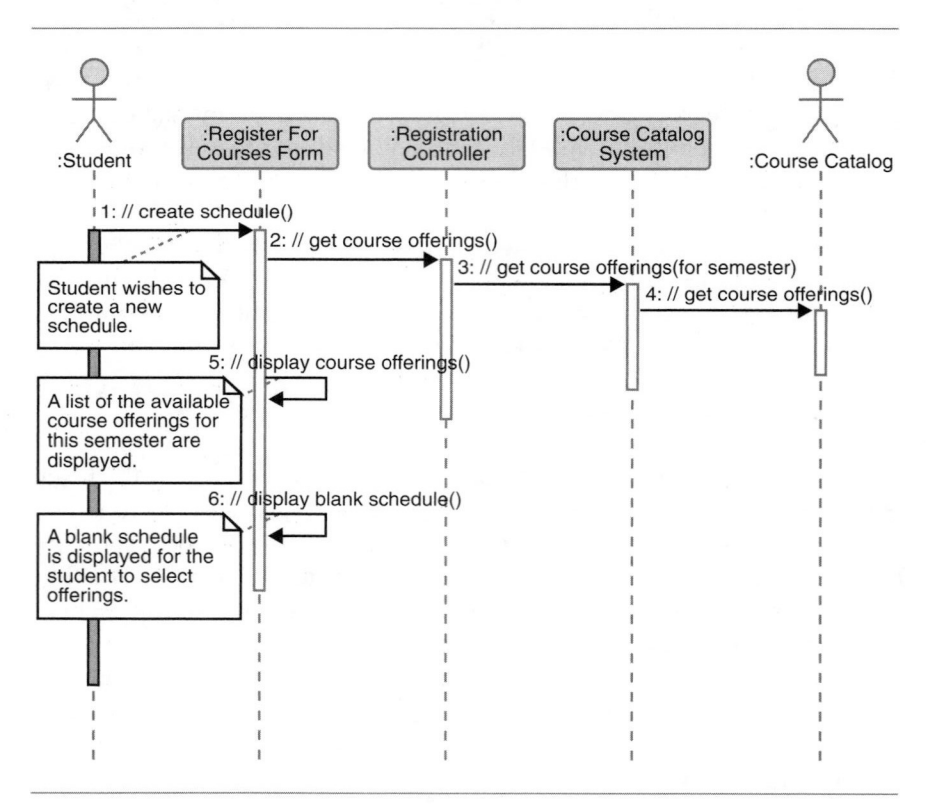

FIGURE 7.4 An Example Sequence Diagram. *A use-case realization shows how your design elements are collaborating to provide the functionality of the architecturally significant parts of the use case. One way to show this collaboration is through a sequence diagram.*

4. **Design use cases.** In other words, specify in exactly what order, and how, each design class will communicate with other design classes to provide the architecturally significant parts of the use-case functionality. This way of partitioning the functionality of a use case into a set of design elements that communicate with each other can be used for object-oriented or nonobject-oriented systems.

5. **Refine analysis classes into design classes.** In many cases, several design classes implement one analysis class. Detail each design class by specifying operations and attributes, review the design model to ensure that you have not duplicated functionality across several classes, and see that all relationships between classes make sense.

Simple use cases with limited sequencing, especially if implemented via a powerful programming language (such as Visual Basic or another fourth-generation language), typically do not require all these steps, especially step 4.

Consolidate and Package Identified Classes

The next step is to group the identified classes into appropriate subsystems. The architecture team will already have identified some of the subsystems (see the earlier section Architecture: Defining Subsystems, Key Components, and Their Interfaces). Some guidelines for packaging classes follow:

- **Localize the impact of future changes by grouping classes that are likely to change together into the same subsystem.** (See Figure 7.5.) For example, if you expect the interface for a certain actor to change radically, place all the classes implementing the interface for that actor in the same subsystem.

- **Enforce certain rules of visibility.** For example, enforce rules that define boundaries between the multiple tiers in a client/server application. You do not want to package classes from different layers into the same subsystem.

- **Consider packaging classes according to how you will configure the future application/product.** This means that you can assemble

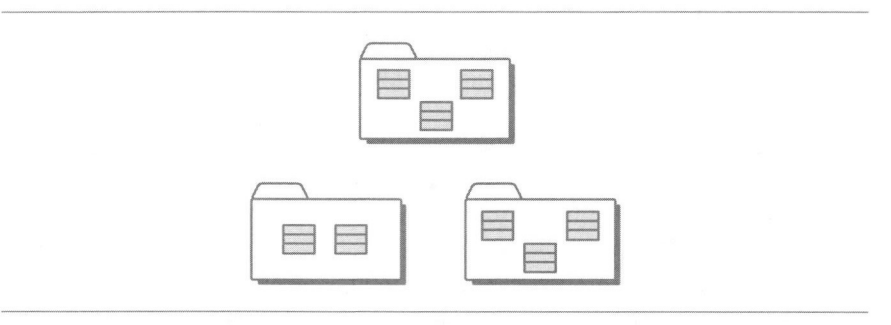

FIGURE 7.5 Packaging Should Localize Impact of Change. *You can localize the impact of change by placing all classes that are dependent on a certain database, or the interface for an actor, in the same subsystem.*

various configurations of the final application by choosing to include or exclude various subsystems.

For more considerations regarding how to package classes, see Guidelines: Design Package in the RUP product.

Ensure Architectural Coverage

One important objective in building the executable architecture is to ensure that it includes use cases touching on all major areas of the system. This ensures that a seemingly straightforward area of the system does not hide unexpected problems, an issue of particular importance when building unprecedented systems. Once you have consolidated the packaging and detailed the use-case realizations, you need to confirm that all areas of your system are covered. If, toward the end of Elaboration you discover "untouched" areas of the system, you should identify additional scenarios to implement in order to ensure architectural coverage (see Figure 7.6). This is part of your risk mitigation strategy to minimize unexpected issues later. A good coverage will also ensure that your estimates are valid.

Architectural coverage is typically more a concern for larger projects than for smaller projects.

Architectural coverage is typically more a concern for larger projects than for smaller projects and can often be disregarded by small projects.

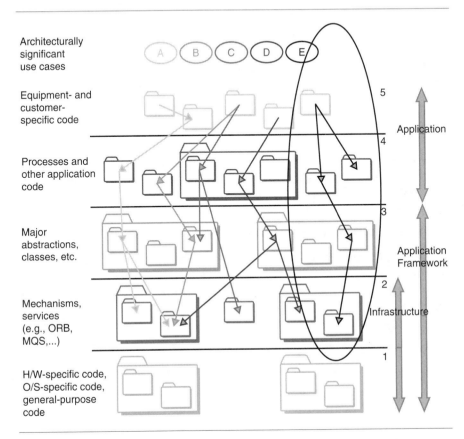

FIGURE 7.6 Architectural Coverage. *Use case E may not be considered architecturally significant, but it is added to the list of use cases to design, implement, and test to ensure that you have architectural coverage for otherwise untouched parts of the architecture.*

Design the Database

Many systems have a database, and you need to understand how persistent data is to be stored and retrieved. You can find comprehensive guidance within the Rational Unified Process in the area of database design (see the Database Design activity and the Data

Model guidelines in the RUP product). You can also find useful information in Ambler 2000.

Outline Concurrency, Processes, Threads, and Physical Distribution

Next, you need to describe the run-time architecture in terms of concurrency, processes, threads, interprocess communication, and so on. For distributed systems, you need to describe the distribution by outlining the physical nodes. This description includes defining the network configuration and allocating processes to nodes. We discuss this issue in more detail in Chapter 16.

Architectural mechanisms represent common concrete solutions to frequently encountered problems.

Identify Architectural Mechanisms

Architectural mechanisms represent common concrete solutions to frequently encountered problems (see Figure 7.7). They are architectural patterns, providing standard solutions to problems such as garbage collection, persistent storage, list management, "shopping

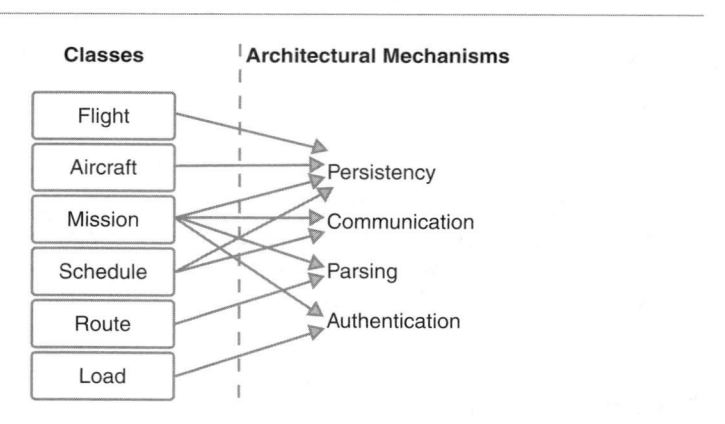

FIGURE 7.7 Architectural Mechanisms. *Architectural mechanisms provide solutions to common problems. You may have one or several mechanisms for persistency, communication, parsing, and authentication; each one may be used many times in the system.*

cart" implementation, or communication with external systems through a certain protocol.

By designing, implementing, testing, and documenting architectural mechanisms, you can solve the most common and difficult problems once, and then all team members can take advantage of these ready-made solutions whenever they need them. This approach allows developers to be more productive, and it greatly speeds up the work in the Construction phase, when typically more people join the project.

We also discuss architectural mechanisms in Chapter 16.

Implement Critical Scenarios

Each design class provides a specification for code. In most cases, implementing the class is done iteratively as the class is designed. You design a little, implement what you design, detect deficiencies, and then improve the design. As you implement components, you need to unit-test the component to ensure that it performs according to specifications and that you have not introduced memory leaks or performance bottlenecks (see the section Developer Testing, in Chapter 17, for more details).

When both designing and implementing a class, you need to consider how to test the system. You might also need to design and implement test classes representing test drivers and interfaces to automated test tools.

Integrate Components

When doing iterative development, it becomes increasingly complex to plan builds and integration testing. In parallel with identifying analysis classes, you need to determine in *what order* you will integrate *what components*, and as you do class design, you need to verify that you design and implement the functionality necessary to integrate and compile your evolving system for testing.

When doing iterative development, it becomes increasingly complex to plan builds and integration testing.

Integration is a continuous activity. If your iterations are four weeks long, for example, you should typically produce a build daily or at least twice weekly. As the size of your system and your team grow,

you may have to increase the interval between builds (as well as the iteration length). Note that the level of support you have for configuration management, including automated build management, highly impacts your ability to plan and frequently create builds.

Test Critical Scenarios

Testing is an extremely important aspect of Elaboration. The best way to verify that you have mitigated risk is to test the executable architecture. Among other things, you want to verify that

- **Critical scenarios have been properly implemented and offer the expected functionality.**
- **The architecture provides sufficient performance.** Typically there are a couple of scenarios critical to performance, and these need to be performance-tested. For an Online Transaction System, you might need to verify that the use case Check Out performs sufficiently. If it does not, then you may have to rework the architecture.
- **The architecture can support necessary load.** Usually, there is a small set of scenarios that are critical to load, and these need to be load-tested. For an Online Transaction System, you might need to verify that the use cases Browse Catalog, Put Item in Cart, and Check Out can carry a load of 1,000 simultaneous users. If it can't, then you might have to revisit various architectural decisions.
- **Interfaces with external systems work as expected.** Does the API work as expected? What about performance and synchronization issues?
- **Any other requirements in the supplementary specification (nonfunctional requirements) that are not captured above are tested.** Failover, reconfiguration, and recovery scenarios might fit into this category. The supplementary specification is an important source of requirements that need to be tested from an architectural viewpoint and might require you to construct special scenarios for effective testing.

Some of this testing can be automated with test tools, allowing you to see whether you lack the proper test tools or lack competency with the tools you have. In this way, the iterative approach forces you to "test" your test capabilities early on so that you can fix any issues before it is too late.

For more information on testing, see Chapter 18.

What Is Left to Do?

The list of activities we've just covered is quite comprehensive, so what is left to do? Well, keep in mind that although you have completed many types of project activities, you have only designed, implemented, and tested 10 to 20 percent of the system. You partially implemented only 20 to 30 percent of the use cases, and then implemented only one or two Happy Day scenarios for each of those use cases. You may also have implemented some architecturally significant alternative flows of events, among others, to test your exception mechanisms.

But overall, the majority of the coding effort for the project will deal with *alternative* or *unexpected* user interaction and exception handling. So, in Elaboration, you did a little of everything, but you still have roughly 80 percent of code left to do in the following lifecycle phases of Construction and Transition. On the positive side, however, the code you did implement and test represents the most difficult parts of the system, and it allows you to mitigate the vast majority of risks in your project.

In Elaboration, you did a little of everything, but you still have roughly 80 percent of code left to do.

For each of our three example projects, you do the following:

- Project Ganymede, a small green-field project: The team evolves the functional prototype built in Inception into a more complete executable architecture, allowing them to showcase some of the key functionality (when in the hands of developers, only certain very well-defined scenarios are supported) and, more important, confirm that the architecture supports the necessary performance, scalability, dependability, and so on. The architecture was tested and used as a baseline for further work.

- Project Mars, a large green-field project: The team evolved the conceptual prototype built in Inception into a more complete executable architecture, allowing them to showcase some of the key

functionality (when in the hands of developers, only certain very well-defined scenarios are supported) and, more important, to confirm that the architecture supports the necessary performance, scalability, dependability, and so on. Since performance and scalability were a big issue, a fair amount of time was spent on doing performance- and load-testing of the architecture. This exposed a number of issues with the architecture. A lot of rework was done, which saved a great deal of time down the road. The revised architecture was used as a baseline for further work. The architect walked through the architecture with the entire team to ensure that everybody understood the architecture.

- Project Jupiter, a second generation of a large project: The team could rapidly go through Elaboration because they did not face major technical risks. Technical risks were mitigated by implementing and trying out some of the new technology. Partial implementations of a few key use cases were done to verify that the new functionality would not regress the architecture.

Objective 3: Mitigate Essential Risks, and Produce Accurate Schedule and Cost Estimates

During Elaboration you mitigate the vast majority of technical risks—risks associated with understanding and getting buy-in on user requirements and risks associated with getting the project environment up and running. We discuss risk management in more detail in Chapter 14.

Plan the Project and Estimate Costs

Toward the end of Elaboration, you have more accurate information allowing us to update our project plan and cost estimate.

- You have **detailed the requirements** so you understand what system you are building. You update the Vision accordingly.
- You have **implemented a skeleton structure (executable architecture)** of the system, which means that you have solved many of

the most difficult problems; you are primarily left with filling in the holes within a large set of well-defined areas. (You should not underestimate the amount of work left, but at least you know what is left to do.)

- You have **mitigated the vast majority of risks.** This radically reduces the gap between lower- and upper-range estimates for schedule and cost.

- You **understand how effectively you are working with the people, the tools, and the technology at hand** because you have used all three to go through the full lifecycle at least once (once for each iteration in Elaboration).

See Chapter 12 for more information on planning a project.

For each of our three example projects, you do the following:

- Project Ganymede, a small green-field project: The project manager/architect spends a couple of hours updating the estimates on cost and schedule and writes a memo with risks and how to mitigate them. The project manager/architect spends 30 minutes with the team explaining the information and sends the information in an e-mail message to the project sponsor.

- Project Mars, a large green-field project: The project manager updates the Business Case, the Software Development Plan, with attached project plans, risks lists, and other key management artifacts. The project manager arranges a half-day review meeting with key stakeholders to walk through the Business Case, risk list, Vision, and Software Development Plan (see the section Project Review: Lifecycle Architecture Milestone, below).

- Project Jupiter, a second generation of a large project: The project manager updates the Business Case and the Software Development Plan with attached project plans, risks lists, and other key management artifacts. The project manager arranges for a two-hour review meeting with key stakeholders to walk through the Business Case, risk list, Vision, and Software Development Plan (see the section Project Review: Lifecycle Architecture Milestone, below).

Objective 4: Refine the Development Case, and Put the Development Environment in Place

During Inception, you defined what process to follow and documented your way of using the RUP approach in a **development case.** You also defined what tools to use and did necessary tool customizations. In Elaboration, you walked through the full lifecycle, doing some design, implementation, and testing of the architecture. You also put your code base under Configuration Management.

To support these activities, you complete the installation and rollout of the process and tools that you initiated, and as you walk through the lifecycle, you learn both what works well for your project and what does not work well. You understand how to improve the process and what tuning and further customizations are necessary for your tools. You update your development case accordingly and fine-tune your tool implementation.

For each of our three example projects, you do the following:

- Project Ganymede, a small green-field project: The team members get together and spend an hour discussing how they liked the process and tool environment used in Inception. After the meeting, the project manager/architect updates the development case to cover the Elaboration phase as well, outlining what artifacts should be produced, what templates to use, and how to document the information. Also in this phase, the project manager/architect functions as a mentor for the rest of the team, helping them with adopting the process and tools.

- Project Mars, a large green-field project: The mentor of the project talks with various team members to get some feedback on what worked well and what did not work well during Inception. Based on the feedback, the mentor updates the development case for the project. The mentor uses the development case to influence any training delivered during Elaboration.

- Project Jupiter, a second generation of a large project: The project manager talks with various team members to get some feedback on what worked well and what did not work well during Inception. Based on the feedback, the project manager updates the development case and walks through any updates with the team. Most team members are familiar with the process and tools, so no training is needed.

Project Review: Lifecycle Architecture Milestone

At the end of the Elaboration phase is the **Lifecycle Architecture Milestone.** At this point, you examine the detailed system objectives and scope, the choice of architecture, and the resolution of the major risks. If the project fails to reach this milestone, it might be aborted or at least seriously reconsidered, and it's better for this to happen early, rather than late. The iterative approach, in combination with this milestone, forces such a decision.

The Lifecycle Architecture Milestone review includes the following evaluation criteria:

- Are the product Vision and requirements stable?
- Is the architecture stable?
- Are the key approaches to be used in testing and evaluation proven?
- Have testing and evaluation of executable prototypes demonstrated that the major risk elements have been addressed and resolved?
- Are the iteration plans for Construction of sufficient detail and fidelity to allow the work to proceed?
- Are the iteration plans for the Construction phase supported by credible estimates?
- Do all stakeholders agree that the current Vision, as defined in the Vision Document, can be met if the current plan is executed to develop the complete system in the context of the current architecture?
- Are actual resource expenditures versus planned expenditures acceptable?

For large projects, this review may take the form of a one-day assessment, or it may be performed over several days. Smaller projects may do the assessment in a one-hour team meeting.

Conclusion

At the end of Elaboration, the second of the RUP approach's four phases, you can look back and see that you made considerable progress, compared to where you were at the end of Inception. Here are the major achievements:

- You moved from a high-level understanding of the most important requirements to a detailed understanding of roughly 80 percent of the requirements.

- You moved from a potential and probably conceptual architecture to a baselined, executable architecture. This means you designed, implemented, and validated the architecture—a skeleton structure of the system—then produced a baseline of it.

- You mitigated a majority of architecturally significant risks and produced more accurate schedule/cost estimates for the remaining lifecycle phases. You used the Lifecycle Architecture Milestone to decide whether you should move ahead with the project, cancel it, or radically change it.

- You refined the development case and put the development environment in place.

- You had a small team of your most skilled people tackle the most difficult activities; you laid the groundwork for successful continuation of the project and for scaling it up with a minimum of financial, business, and technical risks.

CHAPTER 8

The Construction Phase

This chapter describes what Construction, the third phase of the Rational Unified Process lifecycle, is all about (see Figure 8.1). While you read this chapter, remember that you need to decide how formally you want to capture artifacts: This could be done in your head, on a whiteboard, or in a model or document. Nothing can replace common sense, and you will need to make a judgment call as to what fits your project the best.

Elaboration ended with the internal release of a baselined, executable architecture, which allowed you to address major technical risks, such

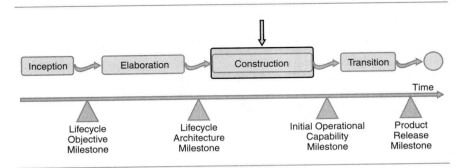

FIGURE 8.1 The Construction Phase. *Construction is the third phase of the RUP lifecycle; it has a well-defined set of objectives and is concluded by the Lifecycle Architecture Milestone. Use these objectives to help you decide which activities to carry out and which artifacts to produce.*

Construction focuses on detailed design, implementation, and testing to flesh out a complete system.

as resource contention risks, performance risks, and data security risks, by implementing and validating actual code. During the Construction phase, you focus heavily on detailed design, implementation, and testing to flesh out a complete system.

So what is left to do? Actually, the vast majority of the work. Many use cases have not been implemented at all, and the ones that have are typically only partially implemented—just enough to validate some hypothesis or to mitigate a risk. Subsystems have been defined and interfaces implemented, but only a very small subset of the underlying code (handling the business logics, the alternative flows of events, and error handling) has been implemented. As you implement more and more functionality, you will fine-tune the requirements. So, among other things, there is a lot of requirements tuning and detailed design, implementation, and testing to be done in Construction (see Figure 8.2).

In fact, the Construction phase is typically the most time-consuming. As we will discuss in more detail in the section Staffing the Project, in Chapter 12, on average, 65 percent of overall effort and 50 percent of overall schedule time are spent in Construction (note that these figures can vary greatly from project to project).

Even though most major technical risks were addressed during Elaboration, new risks will continually pop up in Construction, which you need to address. In general, however, these risks should have a smaller impact on the overall architecture. If not, it indicates that you did not do a good job during Elaboration.

Ensuring architectural integrity, parallel development, Configuration and Change Management, and automated testing become primary skills to ensure success.

During Construction, you focus on developing high-quality code cost-effectively. You take advantage of architectural mechanisms to accelerate the production of code. Especially for larger projects, ensuring architectural integrity, parallel development, Configuration and Change Management, and automated testing become primary skills to ensure success. You leverage the baselined architecture that you produced in Elaboration to allow you to scale up the project and add additional people as required.

As you design, implement, and test more and more functionality, you will continuously renegotiate especially detailed requirements to

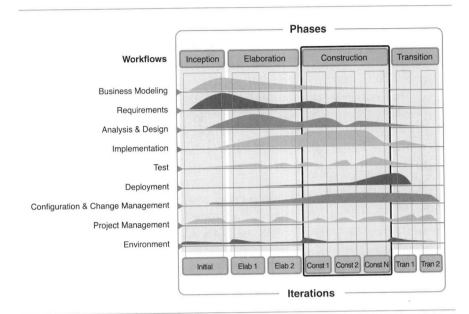

FIGURE 8.2 Work Distribution over the RUP Phases. *In Construction, the emphasis shifts toward requirements tuning and detailed design, implementation, and testing. You also have a strong focus on deployment toward the latter part of the phase. Configuration and Change Management are now used routinely on all aspects of the project.*

determine what is the right functionality to deliver. You will increasingly focus on what is the right balance between quality, scope, time, and "feature polishing" (choosing the right balance between producing barely usable features and perfecting a solution that already is good enough—also referred to as "gold plating").

Objectives of the Construction Phase

Construction is really about cost-efficient development of a complete product—an operational version of your system—that can be

deployed in the user community. This translates into the following objectives:

1. **Minimize development costs and achieve some degree of parallelism** in the work of the development teams. Optimize resources and avoid unnecessary scrap and rework. Even smaller projects generally have components that can be developed independently of one another, allowing for natural parallelism between developers or teams of developers (resources permitting).

2. **Iteratively develop a complete product that is ready to transition to its user community.** Develop the first operational version of the system (beta release) by describing the remaining use cases and other requirements, filling in the design details, completing the implementation, and testing the software. Determine whether the software, the sites, and the users are all ready for the application to be deployed.

Construction and Its Iterations

The number of iterations required for Construction varies from project to project, but in most cases Construction has more iterations (usually two to four) than any other phase (see the section Determining the Number of Iterations, in Chapter 12).

Iteration planning is largely driven by the parts of use cases that should be implemented because they are most essential to customers or are associated with risks.

So what goes into each of the iterations? Iteration planning is largely driven by the parts of use cases that should be implemented. You want to implement the use cases that are most essential to customers, as well as those associated with the most technical risk. Especially in the first iteration, and to some extent the second, start with only partial implementation of use cases (that is, implement only some of the scenarios within the use case) to drive out quickly as much risk as possible and to get a reasonable implementation before detailing the use cases. Once you have decided which use cases to implement, or partially implement, identify which components need to collaborate to provide the use-case functionality; these are the components that must be further designed, implemented, and tested within that iteration. This identification provides you with a better understanding of the time required to implement the use cases and whether, based on available resources, the scope of work needs to be changed for the given iteration.

Let's assume that you have 15 use cases and your project has three iterations in Construction. How do you proceed? Table 8.1 shows a possible plan, starting with what has been achieved coming into Construction (results at the end of Elaboration) and what is done in each of the three Construction iterations.

TABLE 8.1 Progress Made Prior to and Through Construction Iterations. *The requirements, components, and the testing of the system evolve in each iteration. By the end of the Construction phase, you have the first operational version (beta release) of the system.*

Requirements	Components	Tests
End of Elaboration		
• 15 UCs identified • 8 UCs described in detail, 4 with some depth, 3 just briefly	• 18 main components identified • 4 have 50% of the code implemented, including all interfaces • 10 have interfaces plus minimal logic implemented (approximately 10–20% of final code) • Lower layers in a layered architecture have been almost completely implemented • Implemented code has been unit-tested	• Initial performance- and load-test of architecture has been done, primarily driven by architecturally significant UCs • Functionality of 4 architecturally significant UCs has been properly tested
End of the first iteration in Construction		
• 12 UCs described in detail, 3 with some depth	• 18 main components identified (one was not needed due to elimination of a UC) • 10 have been almost completely implemented • 8 have 50% of the code implemented, including all interfaces	• Performance- and load-test of the system are continued to ensure architecture has not been compromised • Functional testing of UCs is done as they are completed *(continues)*

TABLE 8.1 Progress Made Prior to and Through Construction Iterations. *(continued)*

Requirements	Components	Tests
	• 8 have interfaces plus minimal logic implemented (approximately 10–20% of final code) • Lower layers in a layered architecture have been completely implemented • Implemented code has been unit-tested	
End of second iteration in Construction		
• 1 of the 3 UCs not yet described is scoped out due to time constraints • Other 14 UCs described in detail	• 18 main components identified (one was not needed due to elimination of a UC) • 10 have been almost completely implemented • 8 have 50% of the code implemented, including all interfaces • implemented code has been unit-tested	• Performance- and load-test of the system is continued to ensure architecture has not been compromised • Functional testing of UCs is done as they are completed
End of third and last iteration in Construction		
• 14 UCs described in detail	• 18 main components identified • System is fully functional; you have a beta release • All 18 components have been almost completely implemented (fine-tuning and bug fixing will take place during Transition) • Implemented code has been unit-tested	• Performance- and load-test of the system are continued to ensure architecture has not been compromised • Functional testing of UCs is done as they are completed

Objective 1: Minimize Development Costs and Achieve Some Degree of Parallelism

Developing software in a cost-effective manner is the objective of all phases. If you have only started to think about it in Construction, then you will fail to achieve it. However, if you have done Elaboration correctly—that is, if you have created a baselined, robust executable architecture—you can develop a more cost-effective software than would otherwise be the case. This is possible since you can reuse architectural mechanisms; you can work in parallel by organizing around the architecture (see the following section, Organize Around Architecture), and you will run into fewer unexpected problems since you have mitigated many major technical risks. In this section, we will look at some of the things that especially larger teams should consider in Construction (and possibly earlier) to ensure successful software development.

Organize Around Architecture

One of the many benefits of a robust architecture is that it clearly divides the system responsibilities into well-defined subsystems. You have an architect or an architecture team worrying about the architecture and how it all ties together, and individuals can focus primarily on their assigned subsystem(s). Developers still need to understand the overall system, but they can focus primarily on a subset of a system, that is, one or several subsystems assigned to them. Organizing around the architecture prevents people from stepping on each other's feet.

Organizing around the architecture prevents people from stepping on each other's feet.

Organizing around the architecture also helps with communication. Face-to-face communication is normally the most effective form of communication, but as projects grow bigger, you need to reduce the need for communication since the face-to-face method does not scale well. The upper half of Figure 8.3 shows how many possible communication paths there are among all team members (note that it grows geometrically with the size of the team). For a team of size N, the number of communication paths = N * (N–1) / 2. This means that a two-person team has 1 communication path, a three-person team has 3 communication paths, but a six-person team has 15 communication paths.

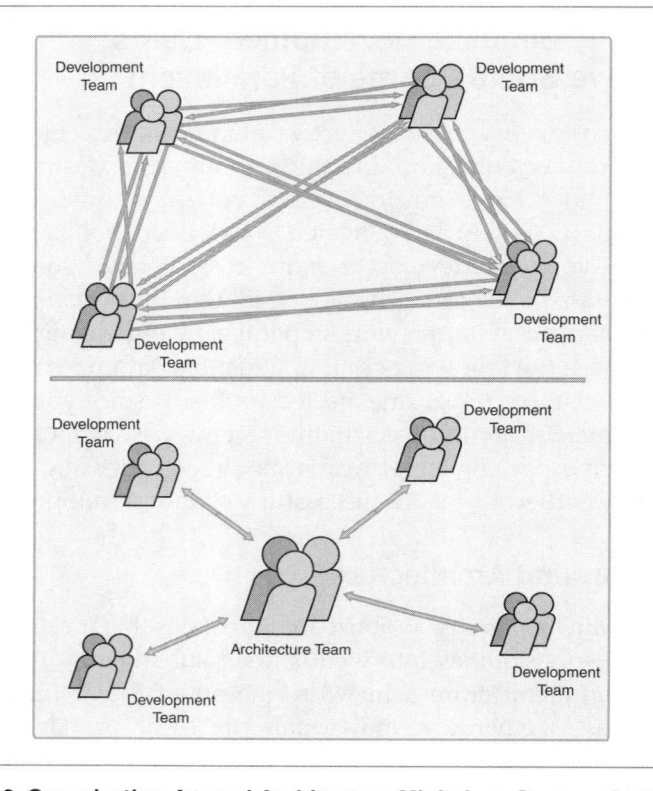

FIGURE 8.3 Organization Around Architecture Minimizes Communication Overload. *The possible communication paths between team members grows **geometrically** with the size of the team. Organizing around the architecture radically reduces the number of communication paths within a team. Issues regarding subsystem interaction are resolved by the architecture team, which owns the interfaces between subsystems.*

An increase in communication paths destroys project team efficiency, and you need to find better means of communication (other than everybody communicating with everybody). This can be achieved by having one team responsible for the architecture, and several small teams each responsible for one or several subsystems. Communication between these few teams is channeled through the architecture team to resolve issues around the overall solution and interfaces between subsystems. As you can see from the lower half of Figure 8.3, this leads to simplified communication, enabling effective communication even in large projects. For those same reasons, you should have one integration team.

Configuration Management

Configuration Management System

The Configuration Management (CM) system needs to be set up during Inception and refined in Elaboration when you baseline the architecture. Here, we describe why you need a CM system and how it benefits you during Construction.

As a project progresses, it becomes increasingly complex to track all versions of the many files being created and changed. Especially during iterative development, you are continually creating new versions of files, and you need help with, among others, the following tasks:

As a project progresses, it becomes increasingly complex to track all versions of the many files being created and changed.

- Iterative development means frequent builds, maybe even daily builds. You need to track which version goes into each build. Sometimes it is the latest version, sometimes an earlier version because the work on a new version has not been completed.

- Iterative development means that you will try out different solutions to see if you can improve upon what you have. You need to merge successful solutions into your mainstream development paths.

- As a project grows, it is essential to be able to hide changes made by one team from other teams so they will not be negatively impacted by code that is not yet working properly. Sometimes you want to make your work visible to the rest of the project several times a day, sometimes only every few days.

- For larger projects, you may also want to control who is allowed to make certain types of changes.[1]

---

1. Note that even though some industry leaders propose that anybody should be able to change any code or design in the system, our experience shows that this practice does not scale effectively as projects grow beyond 10 people.

- When you notice that you have introduced a defect, you want to be able to go back in time to understand when the defect was introduced. You may also need to be able to go back to old builds quickly to get hold of a build that works (for example, if last night's updates to your e-commerce site made your site crash).

The solution is to use a CM system that tracks all this. You need to set up "units of responsibility/visibility"[2] attributes in your CM system. A robust architecture helps here since "units of responsibility/visibility" are typically mapped to the subsystem structure. It is the configuration manager's responsibility to set up the CM system.

Once the CM system has been set up, team members can pay less attention to the thousands of code files, documents, and their versions, allowing them to focus more on core development tasks, thus increasing their efficiency.

Integration Planning

With iterative development, it becomes increasingly complex to plan builds and integration testing. Each iteration needs an Integration Build Plan specifying which capabilities should be testable in each build and which components need to be integrated to produce required capabilities, such as use cases, parts of use cases, or other testable functionality. The tests may include functional, load, stress, or other types of tests.

In many cases, a build is produced by incrementally integrating several smaller builds. This is typically done bottom-up in the layered structure of subsystems in the implementation model. For each build, define which subsystems should go into it and which other subsystems must be available as stubs (that is, as mock-up code emulating the required capabilities of the subsystem). Figure 8.4 shows three builds.

Enforce the Architecture

To benefit fully from the work done with the architecture, you need to actively enforce the architecture. Small teams should be able to

---

2. Rational ClearCase refers to these as Versioned Object Bases (VOBs).

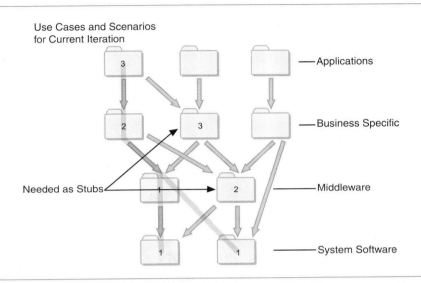

FIGURE 8.4 Incremental Builds Facilitate Builds for Large Systems. *Builds of large systems are often done by integrating several smaller builds, starting from the bottom. This figure shows an integration performed in three builds: build 1 and test, add build 2 and test, then add build 3 and test.*

achieve this by frequently discussing design options. Larger teams need to pay more attention to this problem.

You have defined architectural mechanisms—that is, reusable solutions to common problems, such as dealing with persistency or interprocess communication. You now need to prevent each developer from arbitrarily reinventing solutions for these problems. This can be done through training on the architecture and architectural mechanisms available, coupled with design reviews that include the architects and developers.

You also need to ensure that interfaces of subsystems are not arbitrarily changed and that any changes are properly communicated to other teams to minimize impact on them. This communication can be done through a Configuration Management system, where you, among others, put interfaces under CM.

Ensure Continual Progress

To ensure continual progress, you need to establish short-term goals and continually prove that you have achieved them. The following guidelines are proven recipes for success:

- **Create one team, with one mission.** You want to avoid functionally oriented teams, where analysts are organized in one team and throw the requirements over the wall to the developers who design and implement the requirements and in turn throw the code over the wall to the poor testers, who try to figure out what should be tested. Instead, you should have cross-functional teams, where each team member feels responsible for the application and for the team making progress. Having a quick daily meeting in which the team discusses status and decides what to focus on next can also facilitate team building.[3]

- **Set clear, achievable goals for developers.** Each developer should have a very clear picture of what to accomplish in a given iteration, if not within a portion of the iteration. The developers should agree that the expected deliverables are achievable.

Continual demonstration and testing of executable code is the only way to ensure progress.

- **Continually demonstrate and test code.** Measure progress primarily by looking at what code is compiled and tested. Do not be satisfied with statements such as "we are 90 percent done." Continual demonstration and testing of executable code is the only way to ensure progress.

- **Force continuous integration.** If possible, do daily builds. For large projects, or projects with poor or nonexistent CM systems, daily builds may not be feasible. Performing frequent builds ensures frequent integration testing, which provides feedback on the recent code that has been written since the last build. Continuous integration typically also reduces gold plating.

For each of our three example projects, you do the following:

- Project Ganymede, a small green-field project: As a major component was identified (already in Elaboration), the team decided who should be the main person responsible for its design, imple-

---

3. See Schwaber 2002.

mentation, and testing. Team members frequently get together to discuss architectural issues and to review each other's design and implementations. They set up a CM system in Elaboration, which they used to do daily builds.

- Project Mars, a large green-field project: The development group is organized as three teams, each with the responsibility for one or two of the major subsystems. Within the teams, it is also clear which person is responsible for the design, implementation, and testing of each component. The teams have weekly architecture meetings in which they discuss architectural issues, and the architect is consistently involved in reviewing the work of the various teams, resolving issues as they arise. They had set up a CM system in Inception, which they used to do biweekly builds.

- Project Jupiter, a second generation of a large project: The project staff is divided into three teams, each with the responsibility for one or two of the major subsystems that were added or had major changes made to it. Within the teams, it is also clear which person is responsible for the design, implementation, and testing of each component. The architect is consistently involved in reviewing the work of the various teams, resolving issues as they arise. Since they are building upon a stable architecture, there are few major architectural issues to resolve. A CM system was already in place when they started the project, which they used to do biweekly builds.

Objective 2: Iteratively Develop a Complete Product That Is Ready to Transition to Its User Community

Describe the Remaining Use Cases and Other Requirements

As you implement and test a use case, you often need to revisit at least some of the detailed requirements, and in many cases, you may even want to rethink the entire use case as you come up with better solutions. If the analyst and developer are different people, they need to

To build really great applications, it is important that there is an open dialog between analysts and developers.

discuss jointly how to interpret requirements if they are unclear or can be improved. Analysts should have a very good understanding of the business needs, but may have problems coming up with an optimal solution (they may be blind to how business is done today). Developers can in many cases come in with fresh eyes and find new, innovative ways to address identified business solutions. To build really great applications, it is important that there is an open dialog between analysts and developers to avoid losing the fresh perspective developers may provide.

Nonessential use cases and those with no major architectural impact are generally skipped in Elaboration. For example, if a general print feature has already been implemented and there is a use case for maintaining certain information, you can be fairly certain that adding a use case to print that information will not significantly impact on the architecture. Also, in some systems there are many similar use cases, having the same general sort of functionality, but for different entities or different actors, with different user interfaces. These types of use cases are often left to be detailed in Construction, along with partially detailed use cases—those use cases that have been detailed for the main flow, or a few, but not all, flows of events.

Many nonfunctional requirements, such as performance requirements or requirements around application stability, are essential to getting the architecture right, and most of them should have been properly documented by the end of Elaboration. You may, however, need to add to or detail some of these as you learn more about the system.

Fill in the Design

In Elaboration, you defined the subsystems and their interfaces, key components and their interfaces, and architectural mechanisms. If you have a layered architecture, you implemented or acquired the hard part of the lower layers—the infrastructure—and the architecturally significant use cases.

For each iteration in Construction, focus on completing the design of a set of components and subsystems and a set of use cases. For more information on use-case design, see Design Use-Case Realizations and

Components in Chapter 17. As you implement components (consisting primarily of interfaces and stubs), you will see the need to create additional supporting components as a result of better understanding the system. In the earlier Construction iterations, focus on addressing the highest risks, such as those associated with interfaces, performance, requirements, and usability. Do this by designing, implementing, and testing only the most essential scenarios for your selected use cases. In later Construction iterations, focus on completeness until you eventually design, implement, and test all scenarios of the selected use cases.

In the earlier Construction iterations, focus on addressing the highest risks. In later Construction iterations, focus on completeness.

Design the Database

During Elaboration, you made a first-draft implementation of the database. In the Construction phase, additional columns may be added to tables, views may be created to support query and reporting requirements, and indexes may be created to optimize performance, but major restructuring of tables should not occur (this would be a sign that the architecture was not stabilized and that the start of the Construction phase was premature).

Implement and Unit-Test Code

Iteration planning is primarily determined by deciding *which use cases* to implement and test, and *when*. Use-case implementation is done component-by-component. Generally, by the time you get to Construction, some of the components have already been implemented or partially implemented. And for layered system architectures, most of the components in the lower layers already are implemented. Figure 8.5 shows how the component implementations generally evolve over time.

Developers need to test their implementations continuously to verify that they behave as expected. To test component(s), you may need to design and implement test drivers and test stubs that emulate other components that will interact with the component(s). A visual modeling tool may be able to generate these test drivers and stubs automatically. Once you have the stubs, you can run a number of test scenarios. Usually, test scenarios are derived from the use-case scenarios in

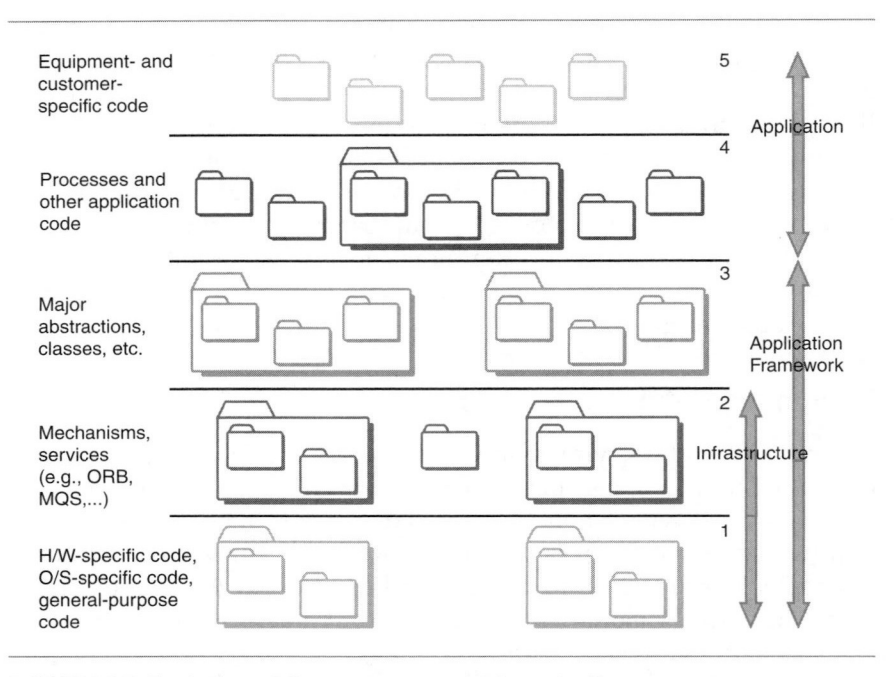

FIGURE 8.5 Evolution of Components over Time. *As time progresses, components become more and more complete, with lower layer components being finished more rapidly. Some higher layer components need to be implemented to drive requirements down to lower layers and to enable the effective testing of lower layer components.*

which the component(s) participate, since the use-case scenarios identify how the components will interact when the users are running the application. You also look at the nonfunctional requirements to understand any other constraints that need to be tested.

Do Integration and System Testing

When producing a build, components are integrated in the order specified in the integration build plan. Usually, the build is subjected to a minimal integration test by the integration team before being fully tested.

To increase quality, continuously integrate and test your system. To minimize testing costs, you need to automate regression testing so you can run hundreds or thousands of regression tests daily or weekly toward the current build, thereby ensuring that newly introduced defects are rapidly found. The following steps will help you in your testing effort:

To increase quality, continuously integrate and test your system.

- Identify the targets of testing by analyzing the iteration plan to make sure that you properly test what is produced in the current iteration.
- Identify testing ideas: an enumerated list of ideas identifying potentially useful tests to conduct. Testing ideas are identified from sources including the risk list, change requests, use cases, other requirements artifacts, UML models, and so on.
- Analyze the testing ideas and select a subset from which to produce test cases. Define inputs, outputs, execution conditions, and points of observation and control. By analyzing the sum of test cases, you identify the overall test automation architecture, including the overall structure of essential test components and test scripts. You also identify how tests (derived from test cases) should be structured into test suites.
- Implement tests (manual or automated) for each test case. Organize tests into test suites, and then execute them.
- Analyze test failures, and then file defects and change requests.

See Chapter 18 for more information on testing.

Early Deployments and Feedback Loops

Performing frequent builds forces continuous integration and verification that the code works. Integration and system testing also reveals many quality issues. Additionally, it is crucial to get early feedback on whether the application is useful and provides desired behavior, by exposing it to actual users. For example, maybe it is performing according to requirements, but the requirements do not quite make sense. This is especially important when developing unprecedented applications or applications in unfamiliar domains, where it is difficult to assess what the real requirements are.

It is crucial to get early feedback by exposing it to actual users.

Future users of the system often do not want to, or have the ability to, spend time on early versions of the application. It may, for example, be hard to convince any one user to spend time on providing you with feedback, since the benefits may not be obvious to the users. This is often the case when building commercial products, when the identity of future users is unknown. During early stages of Construction, the application may be hard to use, cumbersome to install, and filled with workarounds, so much so that it is difficult to put it in the hands of the target user group without active hand-holding.

Based on your needs for feedback and the availability of customers to provide it, you should choose the right approach for getting feedback, which provides value both to the development team and to the future users of the system. These approaches include

- Bringing a few users to your development environment and demonstrating key capabilities.
- Bringing a few users to your development environment and having them use the product for some time.
- Installing the software at a test site and sitting with the users as they are using the software.
- For hosted applications, providing some users with early access. You probably need to guide the user through the application, which may not be stable or intuitive to use at this stage.

Typical results of successful early deployments and feedback loops include verification of whether requirements are right or need to be modified, feedback on usability and performance, and identification of insufficient capabilities.

Testing in a development environment that is not equivalent to the target (production) environment may produce misleading results. Organizations that focus on tight quality control may need to invest in a separate environment that is equivalent to that of the target environment. This simulated environment enables frequent test builds and more accurate test results.

Prepare for Beta Deployment

A beta deployment is "prerelease" testing in which a sampling of the intended audience tries out the product. Beta deployment is done at the end of the Construction phase and is the primary focus of the Transition phase. A successful beta program needs to be prepared in Construction.

A beta deployment is "prerelease" testing in which a sampling of the intended audience tries out the product.

Beta testing serves two purposes: First, it tests the application through a controlled actual implementation, and second, it provides a preview of the upcoming release. The deployment manager needs to manage the product's beta test program to ensure that both of these purposes are served.

It is important to get a good sampling of the intended audience by making sure that you have both novice and experienced users and users in different environments and with different needs. This variety will help ensure that all aspects of the products are properly tested.

It is also essential that the product is complete, based on the scope management that has occurred during the iterations. Although all features should be implemented, it is acceptable to have some unresolved quality issues, such as an unstable element (as long as it does not cause data loss), or Help files or dialog boxes with less than optimal crispness in their guidance, or partial implementation of a rarely used function. You need to include installation instructions, user manuals, tutorials, and training material, or you will not get feedback on them from the beta testers. The supporting material is essential, but unfortunately it often is not included.

Prepare for Final Deployment

For many projects, you need to prepare for the final deployment in Construction (and sometimes earlier, during Elaboration). These activities typically include

1. **Producing material for training users and maintainers to achieve user self-reliability later.**
2. **Preparing deployment site and converting operational databases.** To get the new system up and running, you may have to

purchase new hardware, add space for new hardware, or convert data from earlier systems to the new system.

3. **Preparing for launch: packaging and production; preparing for rollout to marketing, distribution, and sales forces; preparing for field personnel training.** Especially when developing a commercial product, this range of activities should take place to ensure a successful launch.

We describe these and other activities related to the final deployment in more detail in Chapter 9.

For our three example projects, the work in Construction is not significantly different, with respect to coding, integration, and testing, except for the number of people involved. There are, however, differences in the activities related to deployment, which are outlined here:

- Project Ganymede, a small green-field project: The team works closely with the future users of the system and spends a fair amount of time demonstrating use cases to customers as they complete and test them; this interaction gives the team many ideas for how to improve the application. Since there would only be a handful of users of the system and the development team would be actively involved in the rollout and maintenance of the application, they spend almost no time on preparing for a beta or final release.

- Project Mars, a large green-field project: Since the product would be rolled out to the 37 offices worldwide, it is important to get input from a variety of offices. The team had identified eight people on three different continents representing large and small offices and who are treated as an extended part of the development team. Monthly, they walk through the progress that has been made and demonstrate new capabilities. This process provides valuable feedback, specifically in understanding how different the needs are for different offices in different countries. Toward the end of Construction, they also arrange for a week of training for the extended team so they get the skills to run a local beta program in each of their eight offices.

- Project Jupiter, a second generation of a large project: Since this is a commercial product, they need to interact closely with sales to identify a few key customers who would be willing to do a beta rollout of the product. Some of these beta customers were exposed to an internal version, which was facilitated by development team members who visited onsite to install the alpha release and help them get started. This allowed for some early and valuable feedback.

Project Review: Initial Operational Capability Milestone

The Construction phase ends with an important project milestone, the **Initial Operational Capability Milestone,** which is used to determine whether the product is ready to be deployed into a beta test environment by answering (among others) the following questions:

- Is this product release stable and mature enough to be deployed in the user community?
- Are all the stakeholders ready for the transition into the user community?
- Are actual resource expenditures versus planned expenditures still acceptable?

The Transition phase may have to be postponed by adding an iteration to Construction if the project fails to reach this milestone.

Conclusion

During Construction, the third of the four phases of the RUP, you make a lot of progress compared to where you were at end of Elaboration. In a successful Construction phase, you accomplish the following:

- **You develop software cost-effectively by taking advantage of the architectural baseline (including architectural mechanisms) created in Elaboration.** By aligning the organization in teams along the architecture, you achieve some degree of parallelism in the work of development teams.

- **You are able to scale up the project** to include more team members as necessary, by having a robust architecture baseline as a starting point and by organizing around the architecture.
- **You build and assess several internal releases** to ensure that the system is usable and addresses the user needs.
- **You move from an executable architecture to the first operational version of your system.** You have a fully functional beta version of the systems, including installation, supporting documentation, and training material.

CHAPTER 9

The Transition Phase

In this chapter, we introduce the fourth and final phase of the RUP lifecycle, the Transition Phase (see Figure 9.1). While you read this chapter, remember that you need to decide how formally you want to capture artifacts: This could be done in your head, on a whiteboard, or in a model or document.

You ended the Construction phase with the deployment of a fully functional beta version of the system, including the installer, supporting documentation, and training material. But you know that this beta

Transition is about fine-tuning of functionality, performance, and overall quality

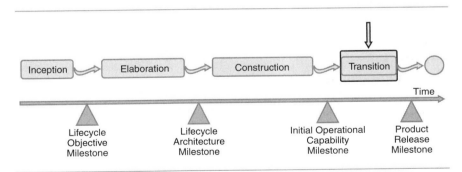

FIGURE 9.1 The Transition Phase. *The Transition phase is the fourth and last phase of the RUP lifecycle; it has a well-defined set of objectives and is concluded by the Product Release Milestone. Use these objectives to help you decide which activities to carry out and which artifacts to produce.*

version is not the final product and that it still requires fine-tuning of functionality, performance, and overall quality.

The focus of the **Transition** phase is to ensure that the software fully addresses the needs of its users. The Transition phase normally spans one or two iterations that include testing the product in preparation for release and making minor adjustments based on user feedback. At this point in the lifecycle, all major structural issues should have been worked out, and user feedback should focus mainly on fine-tuning, configuration, installation, and usability issues. More complex projects may have several iterations in Transition, with each iteration producing a more refined, deployable version of the system. Often in Transition you may have to complete some feature that had been postponed to meet some earlier deadline.

It should be noted that the Transition phase in the RUP approach differs radically from traditional development, primarily because you enter the phase with a reasonably stable, integrated, and tested version of the system. Conversely, in the traditional waterfall approach, the final integration phase often starts with major breakage—sometimes you cannot even compile the whole system, interfaces between subsystems are not compatible, or the system crashes frequently, resulting in major rework for your team and several weeks' delay before the system is up and running and ready to test. The introduced delays result in a large portion of management time being spent on resetting and renegotiating expectations from key stakeholders.

Objectives of the Transition Phase

The Transition phase has the following objectives:

1. **Beta test to validate that user expectations are met.** This typically requires some tuning activities such as bug fixing and making enhancements for performance and usability.
2. **Train users and maintainers to achieve user self-reliability.** These activities ensure that the adopting organization(s) are qualified to use the system and have moved any necessary data from earlier systems or taken any other measures required to operate the new system successfully.

3. **Prepare deployment site and convert operational databases.** To get the new system up and running, you may have to purchase new hardware, add space for new hardware, or convert data from earlier systems to the new system.

4. **Prepare for launch-packaging, production, and marketing roll-out; release to distribution and sales forces; field personnel training.** Especially when developing a commercial product, these activities should take place to ensure a successful launch.

5. **Achieve stakeholder concurrence that deployment baselines are complete and consistent with the evaluation criteria of the vision.**

6. **Improve future project performance through lessons learned.** This includes documenting lessons learned and improving the process and tool environment.

Transition Iterations and Development Cycles

Transition and Iterations

The Transition phase ranges from being very straightforward to extremely complex, depending on the kind of product (see Figure 9.2). A new release of an existing desktop product may be very simple, merely requiring some minor bug fixes that can be done in one iteration. The replacement of an air-traffic control system may be extremely complex, however, requiring several iterations in which additional features and integrations with other systems need to be added, and complex cutover activities need to take place to transition the business from using the old system to the new system. This transition can include running old and new systems in parallel, migrating data, training users, and adjusting business processes.

Transition can include running old and new systems in parallel, migrating data, training users, and adjusting business processes

Activities performed in Transition iterations depend on the project goal(s). Most projects have a reasonably simple Transition, working on fixing bugs; the primary focus is implementation and testing. Occasionally, new features may have to be added, and the iteration is then similar to a Construction phase iteration in that it requires some work on requirements, analysis and design, and so on.

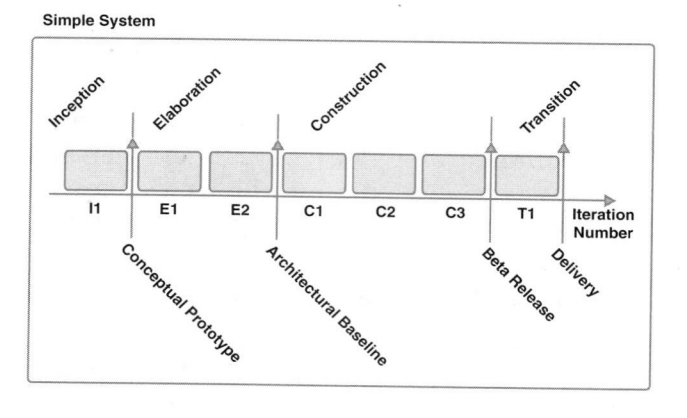

FIGURE 9.2 Number of Iterations in Transition. *The number of iterations required in Transition varies: For a simple system requiring primarily minor bug fixing, one iteration may suffice. For a complex system, such as an air-traffic control system, several iterations may be required to add features and perform complex cutover activities to transition the business from using the old system to using the new system.*

When developing commercial products, and sometimes applications for wide internal use, you have to address packaging, production, marketing, and potential rollout to a sales and support organization.

This is described in more detail in the section Objective 4: Prepare for Launch: Packaging, Production, and Marketing Rollout.

When developing applications that require a lot of new hardware, such as large financial processing systems, or require conversion of data from old to new systems, you have to address the activities described in the section Objective 3: Prepare Deployment Site and Convert Operational Databases.

Very complex projects may require an incremental delivery approach, each deployment providing an increasingly more complete and higher quality version of the system. This approach may be necessary if the only way to fine-tune the system is with feedback from actual system usage. This method is common for large-scale management information systems, or command and control systems, with distributed deployment and complex hardware requiring multiple systems to be integrated and fine-tuned together. Transition iterations for such projects would look very much like the final iteration or final two iterations in Construction (see Chapter 8), with the added complexity of having to manage multiple deployments. Describing the complexity of these types of projects is outside the scope of this book.

Very complex projects may require an incremental delivery approach, each deployment providing an increasingly more complete and higher quality version of the system.

Transition and Development Cycles

By the end of Transition, the phase objectives should have been met, and the project should be in a position to be closed. For some projects, the end of the current lifecycle may coincide with the start of another lifecycle, leading to the next generation of the same product. For other projects, the end of Transition may coincide with a complete delivery of the artifacts to a third party, who may be responsible for operations, maintenance, and enhancements of the delivered system.

One pass through the four RUP phases (Inception, Elaboration, Construction, and Transition) is a **Development Cycle:** At the end of Transition you have completed a development cycle (see Figure 9.3). Each development cycle produces a **generation** of the software. Unless the product "dies," it will evolve into its next generation by repeating the same sequence of Inception, Elaboration, Construction, and Transition

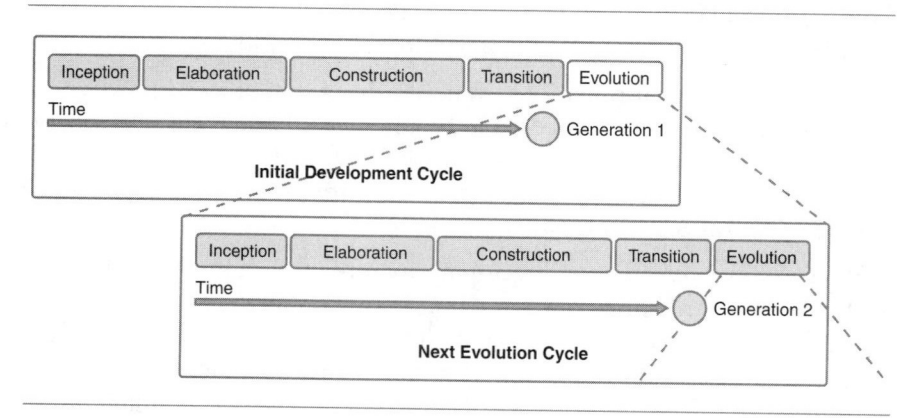

FIGURE 9.3 Development Cycles. *A Development Cycle consists of one pass through the four RUP phases, usually broken down into five to nine iterations, and followed by another Development Cycle (evolution cycle). In many cases, the Inception phase of the evolution cycle overlaps with the Transition phase of the existing cycle.*

phases, but with a different emphasis on the various phases, as required for the new project goals. These subsequent cycles are called **evolution cycles** (see also Chapter 12).

There is often an overlap between two development cycles, where the Inception phase of the next development cycle overlaps with the Transition phase of the existing one. You may choose not to have an overlap or to have a bigger overlap, but by starting the next development cycle much earlier than the current Transition phase, you introduce a substantial amount of complexity, requiring mature development organizations with advanced Configuration Management processes.

Whereas major evolution of a system should be undertaken as a project using a RUP lifecycle and its four phases, many systems simply enter into another mode in which operations, support, and routine maintenance are provided on an ongoing basis, mostly driven by external requests and not with any predefined phases and milestones. A bug-fix release can take the shape of a very simple iteration, similar to what you would do in Transition, running through a few of the RUP activities in implementation, testing, and deployment.[1]

Objective 1: Beta Test to Validate That User Expectations Are Met

Capturing, Analyzing, and Implementing Change Requests

The first operational version—the beta release—of the system was completed and deployed by end of Construction. During Transition you do the beta testing, which provides a lot of user feedback from the beta testers. To ensure that the feedback is useful, actively gather it through interviews, online queries, submitted change requests, or other means. You need to take the time to analyze the feedback, and submit and review change requests so you understand what changes are required before final product release.

Change requests (mainly defects and beta test feedback) are the major planning input for continuing development. Mostly, the change requests are only for minor system tweaking, such as fixing minor bugs, enhancing documentation or training material, or tuning the performance. Sometimes additional features must be added, requiring that you work with requirements, analysis and design, implementation, and testing (see the section Iteratively Develop a Complete Product That Is Ready to Transition to Its User Community, in Chapter 8).

It should be noted that adding features this late in the project could indicate failure in earlier phases, but could be well-motivated especially for very large and complex systems. In most cases you should refrain from adding new features and instead postpone them to the next development (evolution) cycle. In some cases, however, the system may not deploy successfully without the additional feature.

As you implement change requests, it is essential to have in place a good Configuration Management process as well as comprehensive regression testing. At this stage, builds with incorrect file versions or

---

1. See Kruchten 2000b.

missing files are common sources of defects. Good CM practices and tools radically reduce these types of errors, and comprehensive regression testing rapidly identifies any introduced defects.

During Transition, you need to spend a fair amount of time improving documentation, online Help, training material, user's guides, operational guides, and other supporting documentation. It is important that actual beta testers properly test these elements in the target environment.

Transition Testing

The focus of testing during Transition shifts toward improving quality and avoiding regression. Additionally, there is often a requirement for formal acceptance testing, which may involve a repeat of all or part of the system-level tests. In planning for Transition testing, you should provide effort and resources for the following:

- **Continued test design and implementation** to support ongoing development.
- **Regression testing,** which will require variable effort and resources, depending on the chosen approach; for example, retest everything or retest to an operational profile.
- **Acceptance testing,** which may not require the development of new tests.

As defects are fixed and beta feedback is incorporated, successive builds are tested using a standard test cycle:

- **Validate build stability.** Execute a subset of tests to validate that the build is stable enough to start detailed test and evaluation.
- **Test and evaluate.** Implement, execute, and evaluate tests.
- **Achieve your test objectives, or, in RUP parlance, achieve an acceptable mission.** Evaluate test results against testing objectives and perform additional testing as necessary.
- **Improve test assets.** Improve test artifacts as needed to support the next cycle of testing.

When the system is deemed fit to undergo acceptance testing, a separate testing cycle is performed focusing on executing tests and evaluating results.

Patch Releases and Additional Beta Releases

If serious defects that prevent effective beta testing are found, you may need to produce a patch release (special bug-fix release installed on top of the current baselined release) and make it available to beta customers for download. Often these patch releases may be available only to specific beta testers to address their special areas of concern or to block defects they are encountering (although sometimes they go to all beta testers).

As described in an earlier section, Transition and Iterations, there may be more than one iteration in Transition. If so, you typically produce a new release that is distributed to all beta testers, such as Beta 1, Beta 2, and so on. You need to ensure that enough beta testers are upgrading to the new release to provide sufficient feedback.

Metrics for Understanding When Transition Will Be Complete

It is not always obvious when you can end Transition. To help determine when Transition will be complete, you can analyze defect metrics and test metrics, among other things. This analysis can help you answer questions such as, "When will the quality be good enough?", "How many more defects can we expect to find?", and "When will we have tested all functionality?"

Let's look at a small sample set of metrics you may find useful: defect metrics and test metrics.

Defect Metrics

For defects, you should track

- How many new defects are *found* each day.
- How many defects are *fixed* each day.

The important thing is to focus on the *trend* rather than the actual number of defects. Figure 9.4 shows that the number of open defects increased until February 10, and as you moved more and more developers to fix defects, the code improved in quality. You closed more defects than you opened, leading to a rapid decrease in the number of open defects. Through trend analysis of this figure,

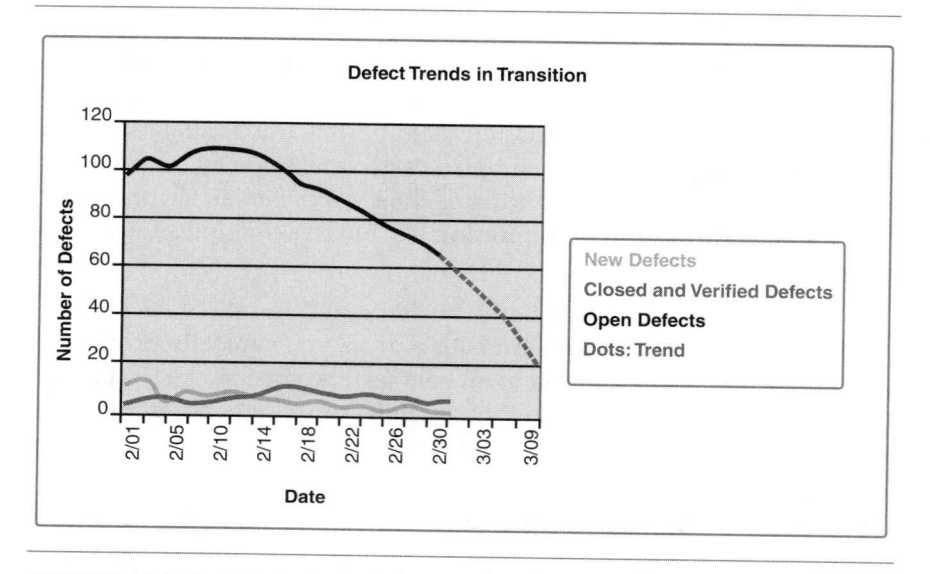

FIGURE 9.4 Trend Analysis of Defects. *By analyzing a defect* **trend***, you can predict when a certain threshold value of open defects will be reached. If you plan to release the product once there are less than 20 defects, the graph shows that this will likely occur around March 9.*

you can estimate that 20 open defects will be reached around March 9, and another week would be needed to come down to below 5 defects. However, it is common that as you approach 0 open defects, the defect-fixing rate will slow down—this needs to be factored into your estimates.

Test Metrics

Another important set of metrics of great value is **test metrics,** such as test completion. If, for example, only 60 percent of planned tests are completed, you should expect to find many more defects once testing is completed. You can predict how many new defects can be expected by determining how many defects are typically found per test case and multiplying that by the number of test cases yet to be executed and analyzed. This can be expressed with the formula:

$$D_{Remaining} = D_{Average} \times (TC_{Total} - TC_{Executed})$$

Where

$D_{Remaining}$ = number of defects yet to be found

$D_{Average}$ = average number of defects found per test case

TC_{Total} = total number of test cases

$TC_{Executed}$ = number of test cases executed so far

You do not want to deliver a system that has not been properly tested. By analyzing the trend of completed and successful test cases, you can predict when you will have completed the test effort, yet another data point allowing you to decide when it is appropriate to end Transition.

Objective 2: Train Users and Maintainers to Achieve User Self-Reliability

During Transition, make sure that all users, operational staff, and maintenance teams are given appropriate training. This training also allows you to do advanced beta testing of training material, user documentation, and operational manuals.

When you need to train a large number of users, such as when rolling out a new system enterprisewide, or you need high-quality training material, such as for many commercial products, you typically need to start this activity much earlier, in Construction (or often in Elaboration). You need to develop training material and train your instructors during Construction (and possibly have already started your planning in Elaboration). In conjunction with the launch of the beta release, you need to do test runs of the training sessions to make sure that the training does the job. For a commercial product, or other rollouts where you have to bring a large number of instructors up to speed on the material, you may need to run a number of "Train the Trainer" sessions in conjunction with the beta release.

Objective 3: Prepare Deployment Site and Convert Operational Databases

Making a smooth transition may be very complex when replacing an existing system. Data needs to be transferred, and the new and old systems may need to be run in parallel for some time to ensure accurate performance of the new system. This may lead to a lot of extra work in terms of entering information into both systems and verifying that the system functions match.

In some cases, you may need more room or bigger facilities to house new machines, you may need to arrange for a power supply or backup power, you may need to install networks and systems for backup, and so on. Turnkey systems may require rollout onto various desktops and servers.

It should be noted that for many complex deployments, you may need to start these activities much earlier (typically in Elaboration or in Construction).

Objective 4: Prepare for Launch: Packaging, Production, and Marketing Rollout

Although this section is primarily relevant for independent software vendors developing shrink-wrapped products, some of the activities that follows are useful for other developments, especially for applications rolled out to a large set of internal customers.

It should be noted that for many large rollouts of commercial products, you may need to start this activity much earlier (in Elaboration or in Construction).

Packaging, Bill of Materials, and Production

The Bill of Materials (BOM) uniquely identifies all the constituent parts of a product. The final packaged product will consist of the software on some storage media, some documents or manuals, licensing agreement forms, and the packaging itself.

You need to ensure that all the items for manufacturing are in their final approved state at the time of delivery to the manufacturer. The approved application and installation software will need to be checked for viruses and saved on a mass-producible storage medium (for example, a master CD). Manuals and printed materials need to be in "camera-ready" format. Once all the component parts are in place and complete, they can be handed over to the manufacturing organization for mass production and duplication.

Marketing Rollout

If you are building a commercial product, here are some of the artifacts you might want to consider:

- **Core Message Platform (CMP).** A one- to two-page description providing short, medium, and long descriptions of the product, its positioning, and key features and benefits. The CMP is the cornerstone in any successful launch and is used as a baseline or template for all internal and external communication related to the product.
- **Customer-consumable collateral.** Data sheets, whitepapers, technical papers, information on your Web site, prerecorded demos of the product, demo scripts, and multimedia presentations providing an overview of the product.
- **Sales support material.** Sales presentations, technical presentations, field training material, fact sheets, positioning papers, competitive write-ups, coaching on how to meet sales objections, references, success stories, and so on.
- **Launch material.** Press releases, press kits, analyst briefings, and internal newsletters.

Objective 5: Achieve Stakeholder Concurrence That Deployment Is Complete

Product Acceptance Test

Product acceptance testing is the final test action prior to deploying the software. The goal of acceptance testing is to verify that the

software is ready and can perform those functions and tasks it was built for.

There are three common strategies for acceptance test:

- Formal acceptance
- Informal acceptance
- Beta test

Formal acceptance testing is a highly managed process where there is a clear one-to-one supplier-acquirer relationship. It is often an extension of the system test. The tests are planned and designed carefully and in the same detail as system testing. The test cases selected should be a subset of those performed in system testing. It is important not to deviate in any way from the chosen test cases. In many organizations, formal acceptance testing is fully automated. Formal acceptance testing is most frequently performed by the supplying organization under control of the acquirer, by the acquirer itself, or by a third party appointed by the acquirer.

Informal acceptance testing has less rigorously defined test procedures than those of formal acceptance testing. The functions and business tasks to be explored are identified and documented, but there are no particular test cases to follow. The individual tester determines what to do. This approach to acceptance testing is not as controlled as formal testing and is more subjective than the formal one. Informal acceptance testing is most frequently performed by the end-user organization.

Beta testing is described in an earlier section, Objective 1: Beta Test to Validate That User Expectations Are Met.

Independent of the approach selected, you should agree on the test cases and how they should be evaluated *before* acceptance testing is implemented and executed.

Product acceptance testing often involves more than executing the software for readiness; it also involves all product artifacts delivered to the customer(s), such as training, documentation, and packaging. Evaluating the nonsoftware artifact(s) varies greatly depending on the artifact being evaluated (refer to the Guidelines and Checklists, available in the RUP product, for information regarding what and how to evaluate). For examples, see the Guidelines and Checklists for the artifacts Use Case and Software Architecture Document, in the RUP product.

Objective 6: Improve Future Project Performance Through Lessons Learned

At the end of each project, it is advisable to spend some time analyzing and documenting what worked well and what didn't. What refinements would you recommend for your process or development environment? What are other lessons learned? This is often done in a post-mortem assessment. Based on the results, you update your RUP development case and improve your development environment to reflect the lessons learned.

You should also determine whether any work can be reused for other projects. If so, make sure to remove any sensitive data and store the reusable assets in such a way that they can easily be found and used by other teams.

Project Review: Product Release Milestone

Transition ends with the fourth major project milestone, the **Product Release Milestone**, to determine whether the objectives were met and if you should start another development cycle. (Several development cycles may have been already planned during Inception.) In some cases this milestone may coincide with the end of the Inception phase for the next cycle. The primary evaluation criteria for Transition answers these questions:

- Are the users satisfied?
- Are actual resource expenditures versus planned expenditures acceptable, and, if not, what actions can be taken in future projects to address this issue?

At the Product Release Milestone, the product is in production, and a process of maintenance, operation, and support begins. This may

involve starting a new development cycle with new major enhancements or some additional maintenance release to fix found defects.

Conclusion

During Transition, the fourth and last of the RUP lifecycle phases, you ensured that the software addresses the needs of its users and can be successfully deployed in the target environment. You met the following objectives:

- You performed one or more beta tests of the new system with a small set of actual users and fine-tuned it as necessary.
- You trained users and maintainers to make them self-reliant.
- You prepared the site for deployment, converted operational databases, and took other measures required to operate the new system successfully.
- You launched the system with attention to packaging and production; rollout to marketing, distribution, and sales forces; and field personnel training. This is specifically a focus for commercial products.
- You achieved stakeholder concurrence that deployment baselines are complete and consistent with the evaluation criteria of the vision.
- You analyzed and used lessons learned to improve future project performance.

PART III

ADOPTING THE RATIONAL UNIFIED PROCESS

CHAPTER 10

Configuring, Instantiating, and Customizing the Rational Unified Process

In this chapter we will discuss how you can **configure** the RUP product for your organization or for your project. Configuring the RUP consists of two steps:

1. Producing a RUP Process Configuration, that is, deciding what parts of the RUP to use.
2. Producing Process Views, that is, producing role-based or personalized views into your RUP Process Configuration.

We will see that you can choose one of the ready-made RUP Process Configurations with their associated Process Views, or you can use RUP Builder to rapidly produce your own configuration and views.

We will also look at how you can effectively **instantiate** the RUP for your project by producing a development case—a brief description of how your project should use your RUP Configuration.

Finally, we will discuss how you can **customize the RUP,** that is, incorporate your own best practices to it so they can be seamlessly included into your RUP Configurations. As we explore how to configure, instantiate, and customize the RUP, we will describe in more detail the components and tools of the RUP Framework you will use.

Configuring the RUP

Producing a RUP Process Configuration

You need to specify a subset of the RUP framework to use for your project.

The RUP process framework contains a vast amount of guidance, artifacts, and roles. Because no project should use all of these artifacts, you need to specify a subset of the RUP to use for your project. This is done by selecting or producing a RUP Process Configuration, which constitutes a **complete process** from the perspective of a particular project's requirements. You can use one of the ready-made configurations as is or use a ready-made configuration as a starting point or create a process configuration from scratch.

To understand how to build a RUP Configuration, you need to understand the concepts of RUP Process Component, RUP Library, RUP Base, and RUP Plug-In.

- A **RUP Process Component** is a coherent, quasi-independent "chunk" or module of process knowledge that can be named, packaged, exchanged, and assembled with other process components.

- A **RUP Library** is a collection of Process Components out of which a set of RUP Process Configurations may be "compiled" with RUP Builder. New Process Components can be added to a RUP Library through the means of RUP Plug-Ins.

- A **RUP Base** is a collection of Process Components meant to be extended by applying plug-ins to generate RUP Process Configurations. It resides in a RUP Library.

- A **RUP Plug-In** is a deployable unit for one or several Process Components that can be readily "dropped" onto a RUP Base to extend it. A RUP Plug-In can be compiled into a single physical file (with extension ".cfu"), allowing it to be moved around and added to a RUP Library with a compatible RUP Base.

  To explain this via a simple analogy, a **RUP Plug-In** is a set of "precompiled" **RUP Process Components,** ready to be "linked" into a **RUP Base** to create one or more **RUP Configurations.**

A RUP Process Configuration is produced using RUP Builder. RUP Builder is shipped with a number of predefined configurations, and you can create additional configurations as needed (see Figure 10.1). Based on what plug-ins you choose, you can make the process smaller or bigger; and you can make it address the technology, domain, and tools relevant to your project or set of projects. You can also choose how formally you want to work, for example, whether to use more comprehensive document templates or lighter templates suitable for smaller teams. Once you have defined which plug-ins belong to a configuration, and which process components within those plug-ins and RUP Base you want to use, RUP Builder validates that the selected process components are compatible and publishes a RUP Configuration Web site from your configuration.

Using RUP Builder, you add more content to your RUP library by adding RUP Plug-Ins.

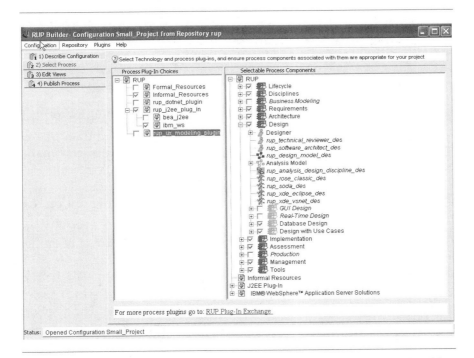

FIGURE 10.1 RUP Builder Publishes RUP Process Configurations. *RUP Builder allows you to make your process smaller or larger and of higher or lower ceremony. This is done by selecting which plug-ins and process components should be included in a RUP Configuration and then publishing your configuration.*

RUP Plug-Ins are available on RDN: http://www. rational.net.

Using RUP Builder, you add more content to your RUP library by adding RUP Plug-Ins. This content can then be used to build RUP Process Configurations that better fit the needs of your project. There are many companies packaging their know-how in RUP Plug-Ins and making them available to RUP users through the RUP Exchange, a subsite on the Rational Developer Network (RDN) where RUP Plug-Ins and other process-related material are made available to the user community. By visiting the RUP Exchange, you can download plug-ins of interest. You can also produce your own plug-ins, which we describe in the section Customizing the RUP, later in this chapter.

Producing a RUP Process Configuration takes only a few minutes. The tricky thing is to know what to select; understanding what is available for selection may take some time. As a first-time user, you should initially focus on reviewing the already-defined process configurations and use them as a starting point.

Producing Process Views

Your RUP Process Configuration contains the parts of the RUP Process Framework that is applicable to your project. More than likely, however, all of that content is not applicable to you as a project manager, analyst, architect, developer, tester, or configuration manager. For this reason, depending on your role and responsibilities, you will want your own window or view into your RUP Configuration, or what we call Process View.

A Process View is a role-based or personalized tree control.

A Process View is a role-based or personalized tree control containing links to desired elements in your RUP Process Configuration, as well as links to files or URLs external to your configuration. For larger projects, you typically create role-based process views, which team members may further personalize to their specific needs. For smaller projects, you may choose to create personalized views for various team members directly. Process Views are created in RUP Builder. Each team member can further personalize Process Views using MyRUP, that is, the Web browser used to browse RUP. Figure 10.2 shows Process Views in MyRUP (in this case, a personalized view created from a generic analyst view).

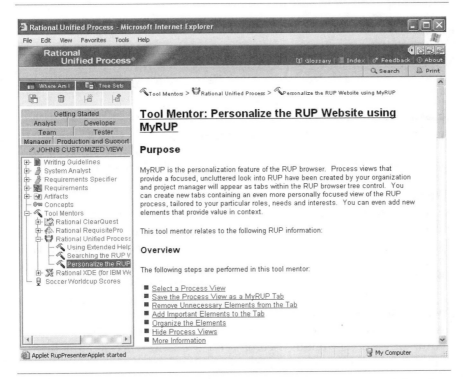

FIGURE 10.2 Process Views in MyRUP. *MyRUP allows you to have role-based or personalized Process Views. Process Views are created in RUP Builder or in MyRUP, and contain links to content in your RUP Configuration or external links based on your role, your interests, your current activities, or your taste.*

Remember, even though each team member may use a personalized view, the entire project team is still using the same process, that is, the same RUP Process Configuration. Each team member, however, can have his or her own personalized view into that common configuration. Each premade configuration in the RUP comes with role-based Process Views that you can use as a starting point for your own Process Views.

Each premade configuration in the RUP comes with role-based Process Views.

Customizing RUP Templates

You may also consider modifying the document templates provided by the RUP to suit the needs of your organization. At a minimum, you may want to include your own company's logo and perhaps remove sections that you do not believe will be useful for your projects.

Instantiating the RUP in a Project

Add just enough ceremony to ensure success, but not so much that it slows you down.

Each project needs to decide how to instantiate, that is, how their project should apply their RUP Process Configuration. Your RUP Configuration may contain more artifacts than you will produce in your specific project, and the project team needs to understand which of those artifacts to produce and how to capture the information—in a document, in a tool, or on a whiteboard as a throw-away artifact. This type of information is documented in a **development case.** Make sure that the process you instantiate is streamlined—that is, it is at as low a level of ceremony as is suitable for your needs (see Chapter 3). A common mistake is to instantiate a process at a level of ceremony that is too high, adding more formalism to your project than may be required. Add just enough ceremony to ensure success, but not so much that it slows you down.

A RUP Development Case

A development case provides specific process guidance for a project or group of similar projects.

A development case is an artifact that provides specific guidance for a project or for a set of projects with very similar characteristics, regarding exactly which artifacts your project should produce, which tools or templates will be used, when to produce them, and with what level of formality. A development case may also specify who in your project takes on what roles in the RUP approach, which can make the development case a key artifact supporting an effective instantiation of the RUP Configuration for your specific project.

Note that the development case does not contain any information on *how* to produce an artifact, thus repeating what is in the RUP. Rather, it links to the RUP Configuration used by your project, which in turn provides information on how to produce an artifact. This allows a development case to be quite brief (normally four to eight pages long) and therefore produced quickly. We recommend that your development case contain, at minimum, a brief list describing one stereotypical iteration for each of the four phases—Inception, Elaboration, Construction, and Transition—and that it indicate what artifacts are produced, their level of formality, and how they should be reviewed. Figure 10.3 shows an example of such a list, which indicates what artifacts should be produced and with what formality they should be reviewed. For guidance on what the artifact is and how to produce it, you follow the link, which will lead you to your RUP Configuration.

A development case specifies, in detail, which subset of artifacts within your RUP Configuration should be produced. For example,

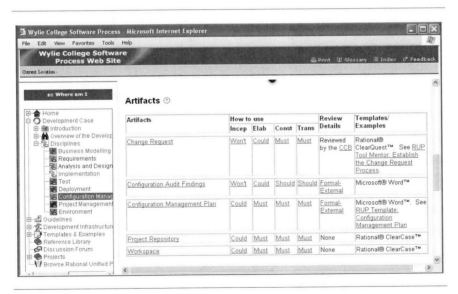

FIGURE 10.3 Development Case—Artifacts and Formality. *A development case is a project artifact specifying what artifacts to produce, at what time, and with what formality. It may also specify additional information such as what templates to use and how to review the artifact.*

A development case specifies which subset of RUP artifacts within your Configuration you will produce.

your RUP Configuration may provide guidance on two artifacts, Stakeholder Requests and Vision, but you may decide to use only the Vision document in your project. Your development case should specify that you produce a Vision document during Inception and list how formally it should be developed and by whom it should be reviewed. Since you do not plan to produce a Stakeholder Request document, the development case will not list it (optionally, you could have your development case specify that Stakeholder Request documents should not be produced).

Figure 10.4 presents another extract from a development case. It shows who is playing what role in the project. Again, when you click on a role, you are brought to your RUP Configuration Web site for a description of the different roles.

Member	Role	Allocation	Phone	Notes
Rick Bell	Project Manager	100 %		
Bob King	Business Modeling Team Lead	100 %		
Bill Collings	Business Process Analyst	25 %		
Glen Fox	Business Process Analyst	25 %		
Yee Chung	Business Designer	25 %		
Abu Zony	Business-Model Reviewer	10 % (*)		
Carol Ming	System Engineering Team Lead	100 %		
Sue Gamble	System Analyst	75 %		
Steve Johnson	Architect	100 %		
Diane NG	Software Engineering Team Lead	50 %		
Diane NG	Designer	50 %		
Simon Jones	Process Engineer	50 %		
Simon Jones	Configuration Manager	50 %		
Kerry Stone	Test Manager	75 %		

FIGURE 10.4 Development Case—Roles. *A development case may specify staffing information, such as who in the project takes on what role(s) in the RUP.*

You should consider doing a very simple development case for your first project; the greatest value normally comes from the initial four to eight hours of investment. The RUP provides templates allowing you to rapidly produce a development case for your project. There is also great value in doing frequent updates to the development case, perhaps at the end of each iteration, or at least at the end of each phase. This approach allows you to improve the process you follow based on experiences gained. At the end of each project, you should also consider updating a development case template to incorporate feedback from your project, for use on future projects producing similar development cases. Too often, we have seen process engineers spending weeks and weeks on a development case before they get started with the first project. Writing a good development case is like developing software: You will not get it right the first time, so make a small investment first, try it out, improve it, try it out again, and so on.

Naturally, there are some cases where it is well worth the investment to spend a few weeks to produce a good development case. In large projects, where confusion about what process to follow can be very costly, or for systems where a high degree of discipline is necessary to comply with regulations, or wherever quality is crucial—in these cases the extra time can yield high dividends downstream.

Project Web Site

All project members should have easy access to a development case. One way to achieve this is to have a project Web site providing one point of access for all your project information, including staffing information, meeting minutes, links to relevant information, links to artifacts that have been produced, information about when you are doing certain types of builds, and so on. We also recommend that the project Web site include your development case so it will be readily available for all project team members. And you should create a link to your project Web site in each team member's Process View. When developing a project Web site, you may want to use the Project Web Template that comes with the RUP product as a starting point.

Your project Web site should include your development case.

Alternatively, you should consider using Rational ProjectConsole, which is a Rational Suite component that will automatically extract

information from Rational tools and third-party tools to build a project Web site for you with information about all current artifacts. Rational ProjectConsole will also present advanced metrics, allowing you to analyze the data. It comes with suggested metrics and reports for each of the four phases in the RUP approach.

The project Web site will provide links to your RUP Configuration as appropriate. This allows you to change the underlying RUP Configuration with a minimum impact to the development case (see Figure 10.5). You may find that a few of the hyperlinks no longer work or that you need to add or remove a few artifacts in your development case to reflect the changed configuration, but typically these changes will

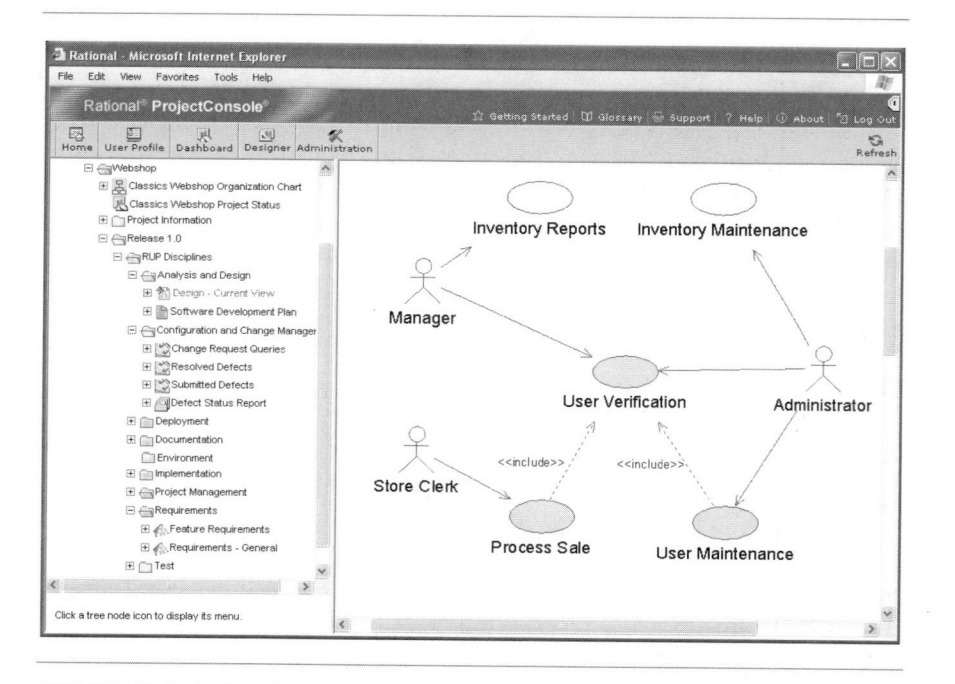

FIGURE 10.5 Project Web Site in Rational ProjectConsole. *Rational ProjectConsole can automatically generate a current project Web site, providing one point of access for all your project information, including development case, meeting minutes, and links to artifacts that have been produced.*

take only a few minutes to implement (assuming that your development case is not too extensive).

Alternatives to Producing a Development Case

Producing a development case ensures that your team members have a clear understanding of exactly which artifacts should be produced, when they should be produced, by whom, and how they should be reviewed. However, this information can be distributed in other ways. A project manager or mentor may tell project members what to do and how to review artifacts, or project members may consult the project plan to understand what they are supposed to deliver. They can then go to the RUP Configuration to understand how to do the work. Especially for smaller projects with an experienced mentor, these alternative approaches can work well.

Customizing the RUP

Some organizations may see the need to create RUP Process Configurations that are different from what can be produced with the RUP Plug-Ins available from IBM Software and its partners. These organizations can customize the RUP to accommodate the specific needs, characteristics, constraints, and history of its organization, culture, and domain. Maybe the organization needs to develop software according to a certain quality standard or management lifecycle. They can also customize the RUP to include examples or reusable assets from previous projects. Customizing the RUP should be done by creating RUP Plug-Ins; this enables you to create a different set of RUP Process Configurations. Plug-ins are very powerful and can be grouped into two major categories: Thin RUP Plug-Ins and Structural RUP Plug-Ins:

Customizing the RUP should be done by creating RUP Plug-Ins.

- **Thin RUP Plug-Ins—changing content files for existing process elements.** Plug-ins of this type allow customers to add, modify, or remove content files associated with existing process elements. This allows you, for example, to change the guidelines for how to produce a Vision Document based on experiences from previous projects, modify the templates for a certain artifact, add examples from your specific domain, or add reusable assets harvested from previous projects. These types of changes are done using a component of Rational Process Workbench (RPW) called RUP Organizer.

- **Structural RUP Plug-Ins—changing process elements and their relationships.** Plug-ins of this type allow process-mature customers who have developed process content outside the RUP to integrate that content into the RUP. You can add, modify, or remove process elements such as artifacts, activities, roles, disciplines, workflows, and tool mentors. This flexibility allows you to make major alterations to the RUP Library, for example, by adding your own process guidance on how to do package implementation or legacy system integration to the RUP. These types of changes are done using RPW. Modifications to the process elements and their relationships are done using an RPW component called RUP Modeler. Changes to the associated files for each model element are done using RUP Organizer.

You should avoid doing customizations of the RUP by modifying the RUP Base and the existing RUP Plug-Ins directly. If you make customizations in these tools directly, you will have to redo those customizations whenever new versions of the RUP product become available. By making customizations through the means of plug-ins, you can more easily migrate changes to future versions of the RUP. This strategy minimizes your maintenance costs since you do not directly modify the content that IBM Software and its partners produce; instead, you specify what changes to make to the content.

Rational Process Workbench and Process Engineering Process

You create RUP Plug-Ins by using Rational Process Workbench.

You create RUP Plug-Ins by using Rational Process Workbench, a process authoring tool that consists of the following:

- **RUP Modeler.** This tool allows a process engineer to visually model process elements such as **activities, artifacts, roles, disciplines,** and **tool mentors** and their relationships, and to compile them into **RUP Process Components.** RUP Modeler is an add-in to Rational XDE and works in conjunction with **RUP Organizer.**

- **RUP Organizer.** This tool allows you to associate content files to process elements such as **activities, artifacts, roles, disciplines,** and **tool mentors,** all of which comprise a Process Component, and to compile these **RUP Process Components** and create a **RUP Plug-In** with the new or modified files. The files can be examples, guidelines, or reusable assets (among others). RUP Organizer also allows you to modify **Extended Help.**
- **RUP Process Library.** This contains process models with all the process elements such as roles, artifacts, activities, and tool mentors defined in the RUP as well as related content files for each model element.
- **Process Engineering Process.** This provides process guidance for customizing, implementing, and improving the process, as well as templates for content authoring, such as HTML templates for descriptions and guidelines, a template for producing plug-ins, and all graphics needed for process authoring.

Most organizations should consider using RUP Organizer to augment the process continuously through Thin RUP Plug-Ins, thus incorporating experiences and assets from previous projects, but only process-mature organizations should build Structural RUP Plug-Ins using RUP Modeler and RUP Organizer because this undertaking requires a fair amount of expertise.

RUP Organizer allows you to associate content files with process elements.

Creating Thin RUP Plug-Ins Using RUP Organizer

RUP Organizer is an easy-to-use tool. You create content pages with your HTML editor of choice, create templates, and harvest examples and reusable assets. RUP Organizer allows you to associate these content files with the appropriate process elements in a process component by dragging and dropping them on a process element (see Figure 10.6). You can then create a Thin RUP Plug-In containing all the changes you have done to one or several process components. In this way, you can create a plug-in that consists of only a couple of files, or one that consists of a large number of files. In most cases, most of the time spent to create a plug-in involves editing the actual content files. Note that Thin RUP Plug-Ins will not change the structure of your process elements, that is, it will not change what artifacts, activities,

Thin RUP Plug-Ins will not change the structure of your process elements.

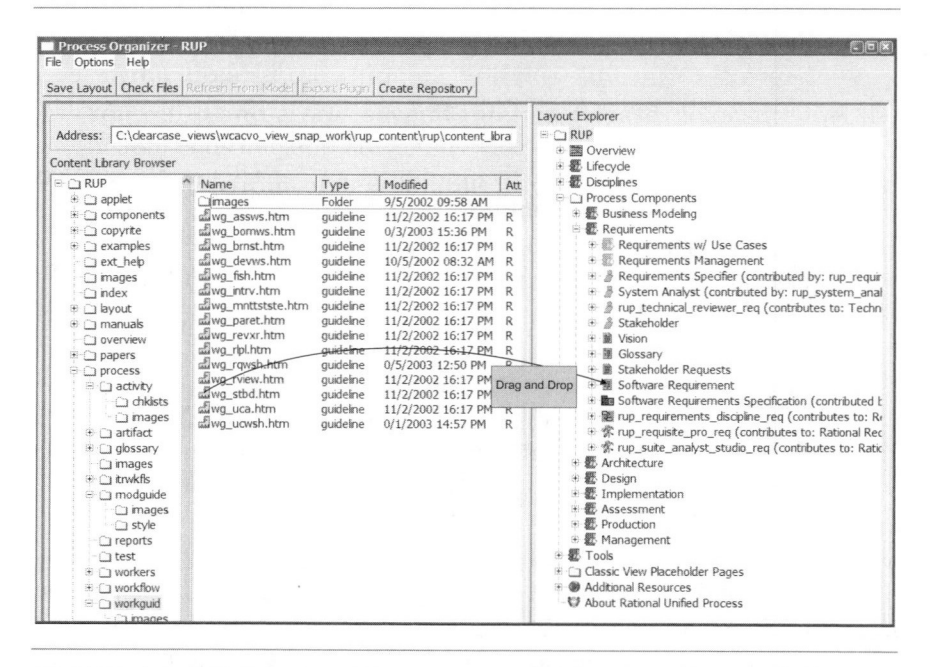

FIGURE 10.6 RUP Organizer AllowsYou to Build Thin RUP Plug-Ins. *RUP Organizer allows you to associate content files, such as examples, guidelines, templates, or reusable assets, to process elements and produce a Thin RUP Plug-In containing these changes. This allows you to rapidly include lessons learned in future RUP Process Configurations.*

roles, workflows, tools, or tool mentors you have—nor will Thin RUP Plug-Ins change their relationship to each other, such as which artifacts are input or output to which activities.

Creating Structural RUP Plug-Ins Using RUP Modeler and RUP Organizer

RUP Modeler is a tool for the advanced process engineer. This tool allows process engineers to create or evolve an object-oriented model of the process using UML. In particular, they can introduce new process elements—roles, activities, artifacts, and the relationships between these process elements:

- Which artifacts are input or output of which activities.
- Which roles are responsible for which artifacts (see Figure 10.7).
- Which guidelines, templates, and examples accompany artifacts and activities.

RUP Modeler allows you to define how these process elements should extend or override process elements in the RUP Base or other RUP Plug-Ins. It allows you to visualize the many thousands of links you may have among all of these process elements, which will be stored in the RUP Library. Later on, RUP Builder will use all this model information to automatically generate thousands of hyperlinks as it publishes the RUP Configuration.

RUP Modeler is a tool for manipulating the underlying object-oriented model of the RUP in UML.

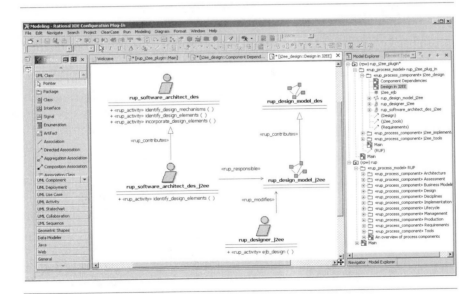

FIGURE 10.7 RUP Modeler Allows You to Visualize and Customize Your Process.
RUP Modeler is a process-modeling tool that brings the power of visual modeling and the UML to process modeling. It allows the advanced process engineer to make major alterations to RUP.

We recom-
mend you
use the RUP
in a few
projects before
attempting
to create
Structural
RUP Plug-Ins.

While process engineers who use RUP Modeler appreciate its power, using the RUP Modeler requires a certain level of expertise. You need to be familiar with object-oriented modeling, Rational XDE, and the RUP product to build a Structural RUP Plug-In. It can be quite time-consuming to produce a plug-in, so you should undertake this effort judiciously. We recommend you use the RUP in a few projects before attempting to create Structural RUP Plug-Ins; make sure that you understand what changes are necessary and what changes can be postponed or skipped completely.

Creating a plug-in with RUP Modeler and RUP Organizer may require anything from a couple of weeks to a few months, depending on available personnel and the complexity of the plug-in. Listed here are the basic requirements for producing these Structural RUP Plug-Ins:

- **Understand the RUP.** Make sure that you really understand what is already in the RUP product and how it is used in practice. If you do not have practical experience in using the RUP, you should consider working with somebody—ideally, a mentor—who has this experience. What is available in the RUP may not suit your needs perfectly, but the content may prove adequate compared to the effort and cost involved to change or extend it.

- **Understand what changes to make to the RUP.** Get a clear understanding of the process you would like to have your organization or project follow before you start doing the actual customization. Develop a clear mapping of your desired process to what is already contained in the RUP. Use the RUP Development Case template to help you with this mapping. Exactly what would you like to add, delete, or change? Is it crucial to make those changes immediately, or should you perhaps wait until you have first used the RUP on a few projects? Many people who are new to the RUP have a tendency to change a lot of things just because they are used to a different terminology or a slightly different set of artifacts or activities. However, the cost of making these changes can be very high, and the value of the changes can be relatively low. Consider instead doing a simple mapping of "old terminology, artifacts, and activities" to "new terminology, artifacts, and activities," and publish it in your development case.

- **Outline what process elements to add, change, or delete.** By producing a brief specification of which process elements (disciplines, roles, artifacts, workflow details, activities, tools, and tool mentors) to add, change, or delete, you will gain a better understanding of the scope of the customization effort. With this adjusted delineation of your elements, you can prioritize your changes and develop your content in iterations, as advocated by the RUP. You also need to decide whether you will be producing one or several process plug-ins. If more than one, you will typically want to develop one plug-in at a time, saving you from taking on too big a project all at once.

- **Produce the RUP Plug-In without the content.** Using RUP Modeler and the templates provided, create your new process elements, and describe how they should override the process elements in the RUP Base or other RUP Plug-Ins. Avoid making changes directly to the RUP Base or to RUP Plug-Ins provided by IBM Software or its partners. Otherwise, you will be forced to redo your customizations when there is a new release of the RUP Base or RUP Plug-Ins.

- **Develop your process content.** Developing (actually writing down) your process content is by far the most time-consuming task. There is a huge difference between knowing how to do something and providing a detailed and clear step-by-step guide on how to do it. If you already have the content written down in some form, such as whitepapers or technical notes, you will save a lot of time. You can write the process content directly in text format and then copy it over to the RUP HTML templates provided, or you can write it directly using your preferred HTML editor. Other content files may consist of examples from previous projects or reusable assets that you have harvested.

- **Update your plug-in with the created process content.** The next step is to tie the content pages to the right process element, using the drag-and-drop capabilities of RUP Organizer. You then need to do a thorough testing of your plug-in. RUP Modeler will verify that your plug-in is semantically correct. Using RUP Builder, you can try out your plug-in by creating a number of different RUP

Configuration Web sites and testing them to make sure that the content looks like you expect it to look.

Once you have created RUP Plug-Ins, you can import them into the RUP Builder and create RUP Configurations containing the content you have developed in-house.

Conclusion

An organization or a project manager should decide which RUP Process Configuration and initial set of Process Views to use.

An organization or a project manager should decide which RUP Process Configuration and initial set of Process Views to use. The RUP comes with several out-of-the-box configurations and views, and additional configurations and views can be created rapidly using RUP Builder and RUP Plug-Ins. You can find the current set of available RUP Plug-Ins through the RUP Exchange on the Rational Developer Network.

Most projects will benefit from the process engineer spending at least a few hours producing a development case, which provides a brief guide on how you should apply, or instantiate, your RUP Configuration in your project.

Most projects should consider building Thin RUP Plug-Ins using RUP Organizer. Thin Plug-Ins allow you to add, modify, or delete guidelines, examples, templates, and reusable assets.

Process-mature customers with specific needs may also take on the bigger effort of producing Structural RUP Plug-Ins using RUP Modeler as well as RUP Organizer. Structural Plug-Ins allow you to make major alterations to the RUP.

Plug-ins are imported into RUP Builder and are used to produce RUP Configurations.

CHAPTER 11

Adopting the Rational Unified Process

In this chapter, we will discuss the motivation for introducing the RUP, how to implement the RUP for a project, and different approaches and strategies for implementing the RUP across a series of projects within an organization.

The reason for introducing the RUP and supporting tools into your organization is to obtain business benefits measured in improved project results. To be worth the investment, process improvement through effective use of the RUP and associated technologies *must* ultimately lead to higher quality systems, lower cost, or shorter time to market. Time spent on process improvement easily becomes overhead unless these objectives are clear in everyone's mind. A common mistake is to roll out too "heavyweight" a version of the RUP, where you have too many artifacts that need to be produced by the project team. This may prevent you from reaching expected business results. Whenever possible, you should minimize the number of artifacts to be produced, without compromising on quality.

Time spent on process improvement easily becomes overhead unless the objectives are clear in everyone's mind.

Adopting the RUP means that you need to change the way you work, and change is difficult. You need to have a clear understanding of the motivation for change, what changes make sense, what changes are of lower priority, how to introduce change, and how to measure success in terms of improved project results.

To achieve improved project results, you often need to roll out not only an improved process, but also supporting tools. Organizations that do not understand the relationship between process and tools will likely fail to achieve any tangible benefits from their process improvement effort. There is only so much process improvement you can do without improved tool automation (see the section Achieve Effective Return on Investment Through Tool Automation, later in this chapter). If your project is a pilot project in a bigger rollout of a process and tools, you should also read the section Pilot Projects, below, for more specific guidelines.

Adopting the RUP in a Project

It is easier to implement the RUP at the beginning of a project to avoid adding the complexity of transitioning from your current process to the RUP in the middle of the project. The following five steps will help you when introducing the RUP product in the beginning of your project:

1. **Assess.** Assess what issues your team has been facing in the past, what impact they have on your business, and which issues are of the highest business priority to address for the future. Clearly articulate expected business benefits, ideally through a business case.

2. **Plan.** Plan the rollout activities, such as customization of the process, training (that is, structured lessons) and mentoring (that is, an expert project member working side-by-side with the project team doing on-the-job-training), and purchase of required tools. Focus on Just-In-Time (JIT) training to ensure motivated students, rather than broad rollout of training, since you learn faster if you know you will put the knowledge into practice soon.

3. **Configure and customize.** Do necessary configuration and customization of the process, tool environments, and training material. Do only customizations that are motivated from a business perspective, that is, are aligned with the business case.

4. **Execute.** Deploy the process and tools in your project, train and mentor project members, and run your project. Focus the team on

project results, and use mentors to ensure that usage of the process and tools are aligned with business objectives.

5. **Evaluate.** Evaluate project performance and compare it to expectations as expressed in the business case. Identify opportunities for future improvements.

Let's have a closer look at each step.

Assess

It is important to have a clear view of the objectives for change. Why are you introducing the RUP? To understand the objectives, make a prioritized list of the problems you currently are facing and their impact on your business, such as "requirements creep causes schedule slips," "unreliable build process reintroduces defects that already have been fixed," "brittle architectures make maintenance costs go up," "ad hoc and manual test processes lead to poor quality,"and so on. The better you can quantify the value of potential process improvements in terms of increased quality, reduced time-to-market, and lower cost, as well as the effect those improvements will have on the bottom line, the better you can focus your process improvements on the high-priority areas. It will help you in motivating people to change (since they will understand the benefits to them and the organization), in getting funds to make necessary investments (since management will see tangible improvements resulting from the investment), and in getting buy-in from key stakeholders (since they will see how it benefits the organization). It will also help you to determine and prioritize which process improvements to make, that is, what parts of the RUP to adopt in what order. Ideally, a RUP implementation should be motivated through a clear and concise business case.

Ideally, a RUP implementation should be motivated through a clear and concise business case.

Let's look at two examples.

Project Mercury

Project Mercury is about to start. In a previous project, the team had major problems with requirements creep and the architectural structure. The combination of these two problems was considered the main cause of a three-month slip. Project Mercury is

a very important project, and time is of the essence. A similar slip in this project would cost the company roughly $200K, and if the performance continues at current levels, the estimated cost to the department is expected to be roughly $300K per year. After analyzing the RUP, the project manager decides that the project would greatly benefit from deploying the Requirements, Analysis & Design, and Project Management disciplines. To support the new process, the team decides to invest in requirements management tools and visual modeling tools. It is decided that it would be too risky to introduce too much change at once, so no changes are made to areas such as testing and Change Management.

Project Genesis

Project Genesis is about to start, and a new project team is recruited with project members from a variety of backgrounds. Different team members have experience from different processes (including ad hoc) and tools. The development manager wants to ensure that the team shares the same view of how to develop software and that they use modern best practices and tools. The development manager expects these improvements to lead to roughly 5 percent productivity increase and 15 percent lower defect count on released products (based on experiences from past process improvement initiatives), which in turn would lead to bottom-line improvement of $170K per year. They decide to standardize on the RUP and one uniform set of tools. It is decided that all team members would use the RUP throughout the project.

In each of the two examples, the objectives in introducing the RUP were made clear, with quantifiable benefits, and based on those objectives, it was decided which parts of the RUP should be used.

Plan

The second step is to plan the rollout of the process and the tool environment. You need to plan when and how to do the configuration and customization of the process, tool environment, and training; you need to plan the delivery of JIT training and mentoring; and you need to plan the physical rollout of tools, including the purchase of tools and potential conversion of existing data to new tools. Performing JIT training is just one example of how you should drive all process improvement activities to maximize business benefits. Why train people today on something they will not use for another three months? Students will be less motivated, they may forget what has been taught, and some people may even leave the team before they can apply the knowledge. Let's again take a look at our two example projects.

Project Mercury

Project Mercury budgets for acquiring the Rational Unified Process, as well as tools for requirements management and visual modeling. Using the RUP Builder, the Project Mercury team produces a suitable RUP configuration (see Chapter 10 for more details on configuring the RUP). They assign a mentor to write the development case and roll out the tools according to Figure 11.1. Since they are inexperienced with iterative development and their Configuration Management and test automation solution is also rather poor, they decide that they can handle at best four iterations in the project. Their training budget is fairly tight, so they send only one person to each course of RUP Fundamentals, Principles of Managing Iterative Development, and Object-Oriented Analysis and Design. Down the road, they all get access to Web-based training for the RUP. They decide to budget for a part-time mentor to assist them in effectively using the tools and the process for the Requirements, Analysis & Design, and Project Management disciplines.

Project Genesis

Project Genesis budgets for acquiring the Rational Unified Process and tools. Using the RUP Builder, the Project Genesis team produces a suitable RUP configuration (see Chapter 10 for more details on configuring the RUP). They assign a mentor to write the

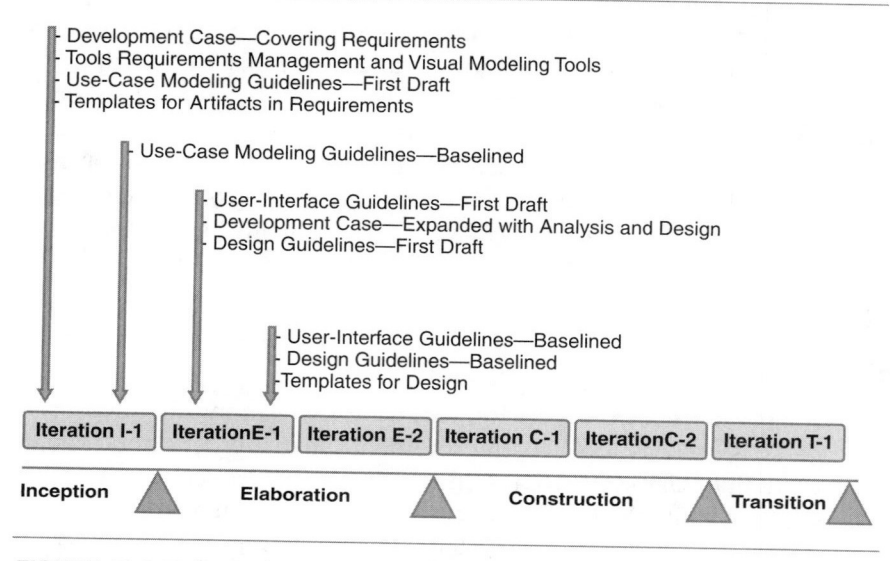

FIGURE 11.1 Rollout of the Requirements, Analysis & Design, and Project Management Disciplines. *The evolution of the development case, associated guidelines, and the rollout of tools to support the Requirements, Analysis & Design, and Project Management disciplines.*

development case and roll out the tools and the development case according to Figure 11.2. They feel comfortable using a highly iterative approach because several team members have past experience with it and they will have a skilled mentor on the project. Project Genesis has a substantial training budget, and they complete a combination of in-house training and open-enrollment training. Down the road, they all get access to Web-based training for the RUP. They decide to budget for a full-time mentor to assist them in effectively using the tools and the process.

As we can see, the way the rollout is planned varies a lot from project to project. The experience of the team, project funding, and the team's willingness to change are key factors that impact planning. We notice, however, that both projects use a mentor, that is, an expert project

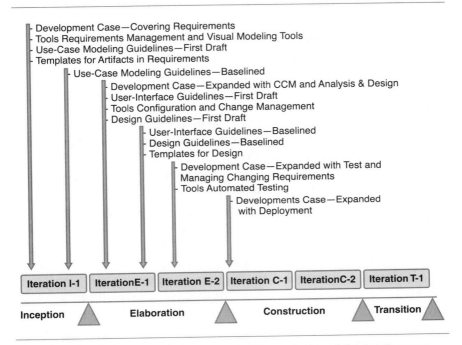

Development Case—Covering Requirements
Tools Requirements Management and Visual Modeling Tools
Use-Case Modeling Guidelines—First Draft
Templates for Artifacts in Requirements

Use-Case Modeling Guidelines—Baselined

Development Case—Expanded with CCM and Analysis & Design
User-Interface Guidelines—First Draft
Tools Configuration and Change Management
Design Guidelines—First Draft

User-Interface Guidelines—Baselined
Design Guidelines—Baselined
Templates for Design

Development Case—Expanded with Test and
Managing Changing Requirements
Tools Automated Testing

Developments Case—Expanded
with Deployment

| Iteration I-1 | IterationE-1 | Iteration E-2 | Iteration C-1 | IterationC-2 | Iteration T-1 |

Inception   Elaboration   Construction   Transition

FIGURE 11.2 Rollout of the RUP and Tools. *The evolution of the development case, associated guidelines, and the rollout of the RUP and supporting tools.*

member, to accelerate knowledge transfer. Our experience shows that the use of mentors (internal or external) is critical for the success of process improvement initiatives.

Configure and Customize

Configuration and customization requires tailoring the RUP to include only the parts you need for your project, developing additional guidelines you may need, customizing associated training material, and tailoring and integrating tools, as well as templates.

In Chapter 10, we discussed how to configure, instantiate, and customize the Rational Unified Process. In almost all cases where you adopt the RUP for only one project, you should focus on producing a RUP Configuration and Process View using RUP Builder and producing a development case. Both of these things can be done with a small investment in time. If you are using RUP on your second or third project, you should consider building Thin RUP Plug-Ins, but only very large projects (more than 80 people) or organizations should normally consider building Structured RUP Plug-Ins (see Chapter 10). Customizing the RUP also includes customizing templates that ship with the RUP, such as templates for describing use cases, software architecture documents, and so on.

Whenever possible, seek to minimize the number of artifacts to be produced, without compromising on quality.

You should perform only customizations that are necessary and lead directly to improved project results. It is a common mistake to roll out too "heavyweight" a version of the RUP, with too many artifacts that, in turn, require needless production by the project team. Whenever possible, seek to minimize the number of artifacts to be produced, without compromising on quality. When you are in doubt whether you need an artifact, you should normally not include it (you can always add it later if you realize you were wrong). You should, however, consider the benefit an artifact gives not only when developing the first version of the system, but also when maintaining and improving the system.

In many cases, you may be able to reduce the need for large customizations by having mentors assist you. A skilled RUP mentor can dynamically guide you by indicating which parts of the process to apply in what way, allowing for greater flexibility of the process implementation along the way. Once you have validated what works for your team, you can take the time to document it.

It is important that your training is adapted to your customized process. In most cases, you do not need to change the training material physically. Rather, the instructor must understand your development case to decide to either skip sections, quickly browse through, or spend extra time on them.

Customizing the tool environment may include building integration between tools, customizing templates, or setting up tools.

Execute

It is now time to deploy the process and tools in your project. Following the plan, you will train people, publish your development case and RUP Configuration, deploy your tools, and initiate the project. One of the benefits of iterative development is that it allows you to improve the process and tools throughout the project as you find out what works and what does not. Iterative development means that early in the project you do some requirements, some design, some implementation, and some testing. Introducing all tools on day one, however, will be overwhelming to the team, so you need to consider "lightweight" implementations of the tools up-front. For example, maybe you need to use only some very limited aspects of your visual modeling tool in Inception or even do the design on a whiteboard. Maybe you automate testing first in the second iteration of Elaboration.

Iterative development allows you to improve the process and tools throughout the entire project.

Following is a brief outline of what is done during a project:

- **Before the project starts.** Before the project actually starts, key people need to be trained—usually process engineers, architects, team leads, and project managers. These people need to set up the project, recruit the right people, and set forth the right plans for Inception and beyond. You typically also need to set up a basic tool infrastructure for Inception, such as tooling for requirements management and change and defect tracking. A mentor can help you with producing a development case, training, and planning the project and process implementation.

- **Inception phase.** During this phase, you typically focus on understanding how to improve the way you manage requirements (Requirements discipline) and how you manage the project (Project Management discipline). You want to set up a Configuration Management (CM) infrastructure for Elaboration, and you want to do JIT training in these areas. A mentor can perform the JIT training, as well as work side-by-side with team members to show them how to work with Requirements and Project Management disciplines. A toolsmith or mentor can help you with setting up a sound CM environment.

- **Elaboration phase.** By the end of the Elaboration phase, all processes and tools are in place. The most critical part of this phase is

often Analysis & Design and Configuration Management because you need to baseline your requirements and architecture, and you need to have a well-functioning Configuration Management infrastructure that enables your development teams to work in parallel. Inception and Elaboration are the two phases in which having a mentor is the most critical. A mentor guides people in what are the most essential tasks and what are the most essential best practices to adopt. The mentor performs JIT training to accelerate learning and avoid information overload. During the Elaboration phase you will test the architecture and key functionality; therefore you need to make sure that the test environment is up and running. You also need to pay special attention to the effective management of iterative development, since typically it is not obvious how to develop the architecture incrementally.

- **Construction phase.** No new processes or tools are introduced in this phase. The focus here is to produce the product; therefore, the development environment must be stable. In the Construction phase, the motivation is to get new team members on the project up to speed. A mentor helps fine-tune the process, introduce new team members to the process, and keep the project team focused on project results.

- **Transition phase:** No new processes or tools are introduced. In the Transition phase, the focus shifts from project-specific process improvement to project post-mortems, enabling you to improve the process and tools for future projects. Experiences from the current project are gathered, summarized, and packaged in a form that future projects can use.

Evaluate

Evaluating the performance of the team and the effectiveness of the implementation of the RUP and supporting tools should be a continuous activity so you can improve the process during your project. However, at the end of the project, you should spend time on assessing the overall effort and validate the business case for adopting the RUP and supporting tools. Did you achieve your established goals? Evaluate the people, the process, and the tools to understand the areas to focus on for any future process implementation effort. Document your findings in a post-mortem report.

Adopting the RUP in Small Projects

When adopting the RUP product on a small project with perhaps a handful of people, you use the same approach as for larger projects. The difference is not in the thought process or in what you do, but rather in the formality in which you document decisions and the rigor of the approach used when transferring knowledge. Let's walk through the five steps and point out some of the differences:

- **Assess.** Just as for larger projects, you need to understand what you want to achieve by introducing the RUP, and you need to decide the highest priority items to focus on. You will, however, probably not document this in a business case, but rather come to a verbal agreement within the project team or write up a memo used as a basis for investment decisions.
- **Plan.** You still need to plan how to introduce the process improvement. Since the effort is smaller, you do not need to document the plan as rigorously as for a larger project.
- **Configure and customize.** Configure the RUP, but avoid building Structured RUP Plug-Ins since they are most likely not worth the effort. Do minimal customizations to tool environments. Rather than customizing training material, use a mentor to guide you in applying the process and tools for your project and to provide you with an understanding of how your approach should differ from what was taught in any formal training classes.
- **Execute.** Deploy the process and tools in your project, train and mentor project members, and run your project. The main difference between large and small projects is that in larger projects you can rely more heavily on mentors to transfer knowledge (instead of having to depend exclusively on formal training), but you may still need to send a couple of people to attend training.
- **Evaluate.** Have a team meeting to evaluate project performance, and compare it to expectations going into the project. Identify opportunities for future improvements.

Achieve Effective Return on Investment Through Tool Automation

Iterative development itself creates a profound need for automated tools.

As you encounter problems with your software development, you need to analyze the problem, the impact it has on your business, and how it can best be addressed. Quite often you will find that to achieve bottom-line improvements, you need to improve best practices, tool automation, or both. Iterative development itself creates a profound need for automated tools. Because each iteration is a complete software development cycle executed in a very short amount of time, it thus requires tools that support short cycle times and allow for a high degree of change. Not having the right tool support may mean that you lose out on some of the potential benefits of iterative development.

This explains why the Rational Unified Process is tightly integrated with tools for the various parts of the lifecycle. The RUP, however, does not force you to adopt tools, but when you choose to do so, you find guidance within the RUP on how to use tools from IBM Software or other vendors.

In Table 11.1, we provide some examples of how you can map problems to business impact and what kind of automation can address the problem and hence improve business results.

This does not mean that you have to adopt all the described automation solutions. But when you encounter the problems described earlier or elsewhere, you need to understand their business impact and to what extent they can be addressed by improving best practices, tool automation, or both.

Adopting the RUP in a Large Organization

Implementing a software development process in a large organization with a hundred or more people is a complex task and needs to be done in a controlled manner. We recommend treating it as a program with clear business objectives, well-defined milestones, and dedicated staffing resources, and the program should be managed according to defined objectives and milestones.

TABLE 11.1 Tool Automation Can Address Core Development Problems. *To maximize return on investment (ROI) when using the RUP, you should consider adopting tools that fully support iterative development, such as tools for private workspaces, automated build, automated testing, requirements management, and defect tracking.*

Problems Encountered	Business Impact	Possible Solutions
• Product builds have missing files or old versions of files. • Development is based on old files.	• Quality is reduced. • Time is spent on rediscovering old defects.	• Introduce a Configuration and Change Management system. • Example: Rational ClearCase and Rational ClearQuest.
• Developers in each other's way, preventing parallel development.	• Longer lead-time, resulting in longer time-to-market.	• Introduce a Configuration and Change Management system providing private workspaces and diff & merge capabilities. • Example: Rational ClearCase and Rational ClearQuest.
• Iterative development introduces increased testing burden on regression testing.	• Test costs increase or defects are found late, making them more costly to fix.	• Automate testing. • Example: Rational Suite TestStudio.
• Unclear which requirements are current, and when they were changed.	• Investments in development are done toward obsolete requirements, increasing development costs and decreasing customer satisfaction.	• Manage requirements using a requirements management tool. • Example: Rational RequisitePro.
• Unclear which change requests should be implemented, and which should not. • Changes that should be implemented are not implemented, and vice versa.	• Reduced quality and increased development costs.	• Introduce a change and defect tracking system. • Example: Rational ClearQuest.

Organizations, just like individuals, can accommodate only a limited amount of change.

When looking at your organization's problems, you may feel the strong desire to fix everything at once, especially since many of these problems occur simultaneously. Organizations, just like individuals, can accommodate only a limited amount of change, and different organizations are better prepared for change than others. To understand the organizational capacity for change, we recommend that you interview people in the organization to understand their attitudes and willingness to change.

The process improvement program consists of a combination of the following types of projects:

- **Process and tool enhancement projects (PTEPs),** which aim to produce new baselined versions of processes and supporting tool environments used for internal deployments. They provide the right infrastructure to facilitate the introduction of the process and tools.
- **Pilot projects,** which are software development projects with the added objective to investigate the organization's ability to adopt a certain process and tool environment and verify that the process and tool environment is sound.
- **Software development projects,** which use the processes and supporting tool environments.

Following, we walk through each of the project types; and in the sections A Typical Program for Moderate Change, A Typical Program for Major Change, and An Aggressive Program for Major Change, we discuss different outlines of RUP adoption programs based on your ability to accommodate change, time constraints, willingness to take risks, and many other factors.

Process and Tool Enhancement Projects (PTEP)

A process and tool enhancement project aims to produce the next generation of the process and supporting tool environments (ideally accompanied with some reusable assets), tailored for the specific needs of the adopting organization.

Just as a RUP project is divided, we divide the PTEP into four phases, in which each phase has the same name and business objectives as a software development project using the RUP (see Table 11.2).

TABLE 11.2 Four Phases of a Process and Tool Enhancement Project. *A PTEP consists of four phases, with very similar objectives to a normal software development project using the RUP.*

Phases	Objectives	Description and Outcome of Each Phase
Inception	Understand the scope and objectives of the next generation of the process and tool environment.	• Assess the organization and decide what areas of improvements will provide the biggest return on investment. Should you, for example, focus on Requirements Management, Analysis & Design, or Configuration Management? • Develop the business case. Get buy-in on the business case from all stakeholders, and get a go or no-go decision from the sponsors. • Produce a high-level plan and budget for your project. Produce a detailed plan for the next phase and identify resources.
Elaboration	Prove the feasibility of the next generation of the process and tool environment within the context of your organization.	• Produce a detailed plan and prioritize the implementation of the customized process content, training material, and tool environment. Provide skeletal content for the most important/controversial customizations. • If you will develop RUP Plug-Ins, develop the plug-in *without* the content (see the section Develop RUP Plug-Ins, in Chapter 10). • Define and execute pilot projects to verify the ability of your organization to successfully adopt the outlined process and tool environment. • For major customizations, the Elaboration phase may need to be divided into several iterations, in which major risks associated with the customization are addressed in the first iteration. • Plan next phase.
Construction	Create project-consumable "beta" version of the next generation of the process and tool environment.	• Produce a complete version of the customized process (including any RUP Plug-Ins you may develop), supporting tool environment, and training material. The material should be of "beta" quality, meaning that you may still have to do some fine-tuning before it is released for organizationwide adoption.

(continues)

TABLE 11.2 Four Phases of a Process and Tool Enhancement Project. *(continued)*

Phases	Objectives	Description and Outcome of Each Phase
		• If the customizations have been extensive, try them out in practice through one or several pilot projects, or parts of pilot projects. This will provide you with the feedback necessary to improve customizations as necessary. • Identify risks and issues with the process, training material, and supporting tools. • Produce a training plan for the organization. Most training should be done just before the knowledge is needed, but some key people, such as mentors, trainers, project managers, and team leads, may need training outside the context of a project. • For major customizations, the Construction phase may need to be divided into several iterations, in which top risks are mitigated first. • Plan next phase.
Transition	Fine-tune the next generation of the process and tool environment, prepare for organizationwide deployment, and plan future improvement projects as necessary.	• Assess potential issues associated with the process and tool environment by deploying changes done to the process, the training material, and the tool environment during Construction in one or several pilot projects, or parts of pilot projects. Note that you do not necessarily need to start new pilot projects; you may instead deploy changes in a pilot project that was initiated during the Elaboration or Construction phases. • Prepare the organization for deployment of the new process and tool environment by training mentors, trainers, project managers, and team leads. Document how projects are supposed to deploy the new process and tool environment, including how to acquire and deploy the process and tool environment, how to get mentoring and training assistance, and how to provide feedback on the environment. • Identify the need for additional projects to improve the process and tool environment.

Pilot Projects

Pilot projects are software development projects with the added objective to examine and provide feedback on the new process and tool environment, including supporting material such as training material. Here are the things to consider when setting up a pilot project:

- **Purpose and timing.** A pilot project should mitigate your highest risk items in your process and tool enhancement project. For most organizations, the biggest challenges are related to adopting core RUP best practices such as iterative development, requirements management, Configuration Management, and Change Management, and the tools supporting these best practices. These risks need to be mitigated during the Elaboration phase of PTEP, which means that you need to run pilot projects in this phase. If you are doing major customizations to the RUP, you typically want to try these out. This is done by pilot projects during the Construction and Transition phases of PTEP.

- **Team size.** Most pilot projects work best if you have six to eight people on the project team. This is enough people to introduce some elements of complexity, but not enough to risk failure. Sometimes you may want to have more people, maybe because the main risk you are trying to mitigate—the main uncertainty—is whether the process or tool environment works for larger projects.

- **Length and time constraints.** You want fast feedback on the process and tool environment. Often, you do not have to run a complete pilot project to obtain the feedback you are looking for. In most cases, you want to go through at least one Construction iteration of the pilot project to obtain the feedback you are looking for, because by that time you will have deployed all tools and tried out most aspects of the process. In other cases, it may be sufficient to go through only one iteration of a project as a pilot project. The ideal length of a pilot project is typically two to six months, which is long enough to allow for some complexity and short enough to allow you to move on and put your experience to work on other projects. Furthermore, you don't want the time constraints to be too tight. You need to be able to take enough time for the project to learn to apply the process and tools appropriately.

- **Staffing profile.** Choose for your pilot those people who have an interest in learning something new and who have the ability and the opportunity to act as mentors on future projects. Having pilot team members act as internal mentors on other projects is the fastest way of transferring knowledge. Also, make sure that the project manager and the architect are qualified and work together as a team because these are the two most important roles.

- **Importance and complexity.** A pilot project should build real software that has a reasonably important business purpose. If the application isn't important or complex enough, people will say, "Well, building that application doesn't prove anything. Over here, we're building *real* software, and we still don't think you can do that with the RUP." In most cases you don't want your project to be so critical and complex that you run a risk of compromising your business in the face of failure. That won't prove anything, and you won't be any better off after the pilot than you were before. You will know only that the first time you used the RUP, under suboptimal conditions, it did not save a doomed project. There are, however, a number of cases in which you actually want to choose a very high-profile, critical project. This is typically the case when you have nothing to lose, or you must force a rapid improvement of the process and tool environment to ensure business success. The advantage in choosing a critical project is that these projects will likely employ the most talented people, the strongest management support, and the deepest pockets to pay for necessary training, mentoring, and tool support.

Software Development Projects

Deploying the RUP in software development projects was described in the earlier section Adopting the RUP in a Project. Here again are the five steps discussed in that section:

1. **Assess.** Assess what issues your team has been facing in the past and what issues are of the highest priority to address for the future.

2. **Plan.** Plan the rollout activities, such as customization of the process, training and mentoring, and purchase of required tools.

3. **Configure and customize.** Do necessary configuration and customization of the process, tool environments, and training material.

4. **Execute.** Deploy the process and tools in your project, train and mentor project members, and run your project.

5. **Evaluate.** Evaluate how the project went, and compare it to your expectations. Identify opportunities for future improvements.

Note that when you deploy the RUP in a project within an organizationwide RUP adoption program, a lot of the work within the three first steps (Assess, Plan, and Configure and Customize) may already be done for the individual project by the overall program. For example, the program may have already identified that the organization needs to enhance the RUP by providing increased guidance on building safety-critical systems. It may have facilitated a lot of the planning by describing how to roll out the process and the tools, and the program may have done the necessary configuration and customization. A supporting infrastructure in terms of mentoring and training services may also have been put in place, facilitating the Execution stage within the individual project. The fact that the process and tool enhancement project typically reduces the amount of work associated with assessing, planning, and configuring and customizing the RUP articulates one important aspect of the program: to increase the likelihood of success while reducing overall costs associated with individual projects, improving their process and tool environment.

A Typical Program for Moderate Change

In our first scenario for a RUP adoption program, we assume that the adopting organization has roughly 10 project teams with an average of 10 project members, and it plans to adopt all of the RUP disciplines and introduce new tools to support requirements management and visual modeling. They already have good tools in place for automated testing and for Configuration and Change Management. Even though some people in their organization have experience with the RUP, most do not. Many are new to iterative development, but quite a few have used other structured approaches. Based on the size, objectives, and experience level described earlier, they choose the program profile shown in Figure 11.3.

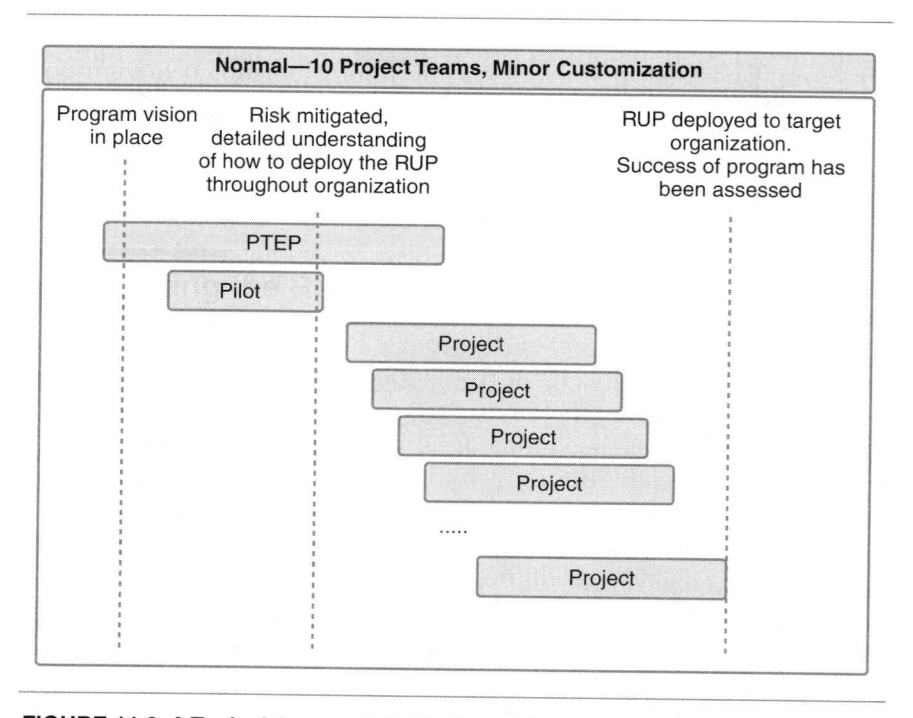

FIGURE 11.3 A Typical Approach to Implementing Moderate Change. *When implementing the RUP and supporting tools presents moderate change to your organization, it is normally sufficient to run one pilot project during your PTEP, and roll out the new process and tool environment to all projects at the end of the PTEP.*

- **PTEP.** They expect to be able to adopt the RUP and supporting tools with only minor customizations. They will produce three RUP configurations for stereotypical projects, customize some templates, produce stereotypical development cases, and set up a recommended mentoring and training program for projects. They do not plan to produce any RUP Plug-Ins or do any other major customizations to training material. They will use tools with a minimum of customization, so they need only one PTEP. (Of course, we still would recommend that the organization perform continuous process improvement—see the section Continuous Process Improvement.)

- **Pilots.** They need to verify that project can successfully adopt both the RUP and the tools that are new to the organization, so they need to run a pilot project. Because they do not need to verify any major customizations, they initiate the pilot during early Elaboration of the PTEP. If they feel that the three configurations of the RUP are radically different from each other and that their adoption is associated with a lot of risk, they may instead want to run three pilot projects, allowing them to test and gain experience with each of the three configurations.

- **Software development project.** As soon as the PTEP is done, the RUP and associated tools are rolled out, project-by-project.

A Typical Program for Major Change

In our second scenario for a RUP adoption program, we assume that the adopting organization has roughly 10 project teams with an average of 10 project members and it plans to adopt all of the RUP and tools for the full lifecycle. The organization has no previous experience with the RUP, and they have very specific needs forcing them to make a fair amount of customization to the RUP before it fits their needs. Many are new to iterative development, but quite a few have used other structured approaches. They have limited experience with the tools they plan to roll out, and they also need to build RUP Plug-Ins to address specific process needs.

They decide to roll out the RUP and associated tools in two increments, where iterative development, the internally built RUP Plug-Ins, requirements management, and Configuration and Change Management disciplines with associated tools are rolled out in the first increment, and all of the RUP and associated tools are rolled out in the second increment. Based on this, they choose the program profile shown in Figure 11.4.

- **PTEPs.** They need one PTEP project for each increment. In the first PTEP, they develop the RUP Plug-Ins and tailor the RUP to make

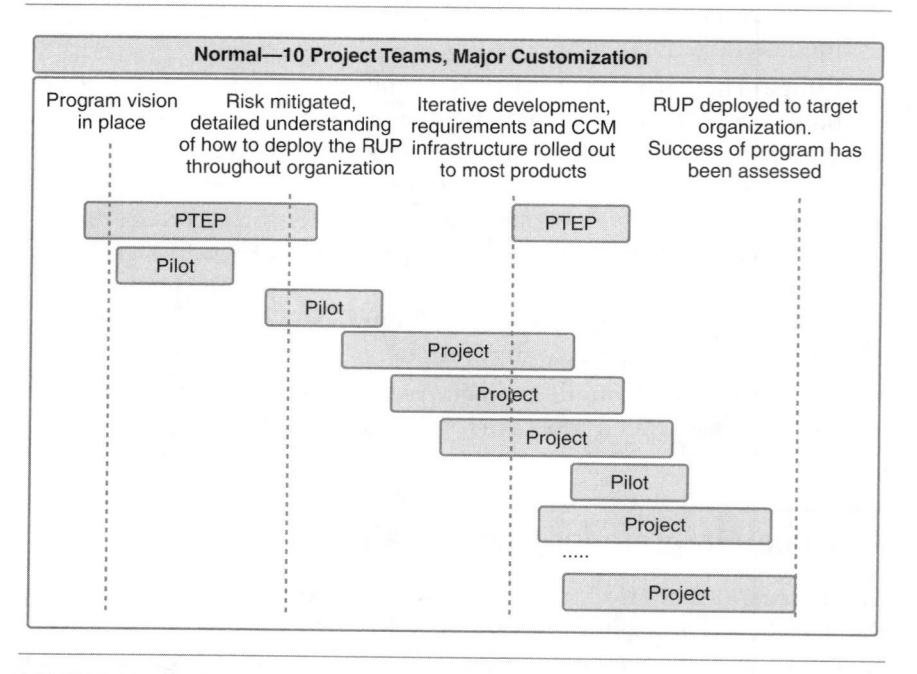

FIGURE 11.4 A Typical Approach to Implementing Major Change. *When supporting tools present a major change to your organization as you implement the RUP, you often need to do an incremental adoption of the RUP and supporting tools. This can be done by having two PTEPs, each supported by one or several pilot projects. At the end of each PTEP, you roll out the current process and tool environment.*

it fit with their existing process for Analysis & Design, Implementation, Testing, and Configuration and Change Management. In the second PTEP, they add RUP disciplines for Analysis & Design, Implementation, and Testing, as well as supporting tools. (Of course, we still would recommend that the organization perform continuous process improvement—see the section Continuous Process Improvement.)

- **Pilots.** They need to verify that projects can successfully adopt the RUP, tools for requirements management and Configuration and

Change Management, and associated process guidance. Therefore they need to run a pilot project early in Elaboration of PTEP. We highly recommend that the same people who do the customizations in the pilot projects act as mentors; in this way, the team not only learns what customizations are needed, but also sees the ideas behind the customizations tried out in the process. As the customizations have been formalized and draft RUP Plug-Ins have been produced, they initiate a second pilot project toward the end of the Construction phase of the PTEP. A third pilot is launched as they wind up the customizations of the second PTEP toward the end of the Construction phase to get feedback on the customizations.

- **Software development projects.** As soon as the first PTEP is done, the target process and tools are rolled out to a series of projects. As soon as the second PTEP is completed, the full (customized) RUP and associated tools are rolled out to all projects.

An Aggressive Program for Major Change

Our third scenario assumes that, as is sometimes the case, you do not have the time that the recommended approach described earlier requires. For example, when an organization suffers from such severe problems that any change is perceived as an improvement, a more radical program may be in order, in other words, the potential for improvement is greater than the problems the organization will inevitably encounter. The aggressive approach (see Figure 11.5) uses the process and tools directly in critical projects. These project(s) may still be referred to as pilot project(s), since their objective is to investigate the organization's ability to adopt a certain process and tool environment.

- **PTEPs.** They do all changes in one PTEP project, likely with several iterations in Elaboration and Construction. They use people, potentially contractors, who have previously done PTEPs to minimize risk and to save time. (Of course, we still would recommend that the organization perform continuous process improvement— see the section Continuous Process Improvement.)

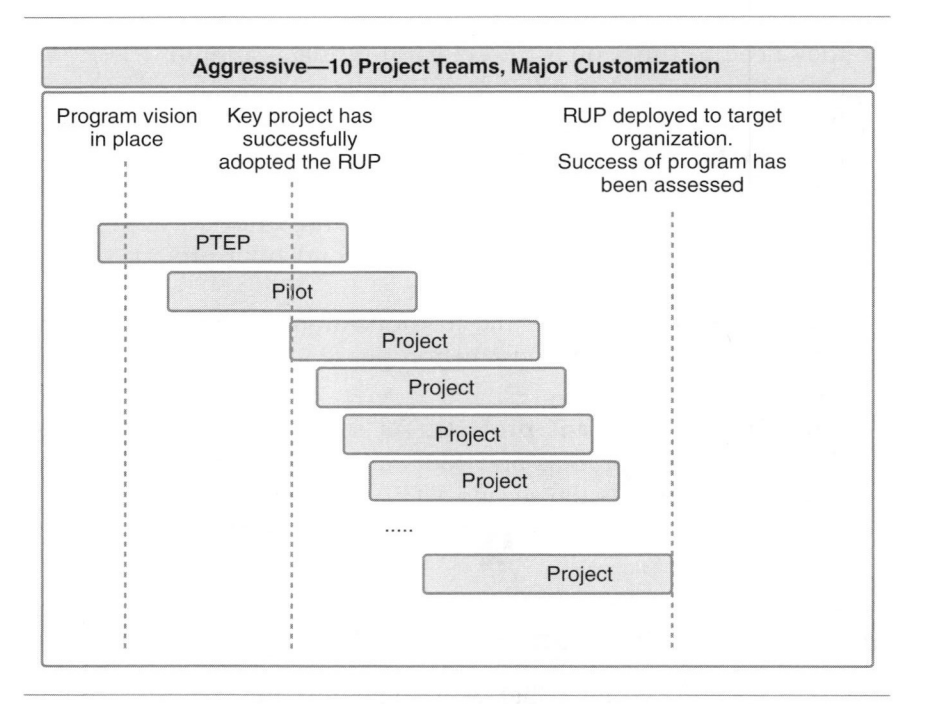

FIGURE 11.5 An Aggressive Approach to Implementing the RUP and Supporting Tools. *When your organization is facing major issues and time is of the essence, you may use an aggressive implementation approach where you have a PTEP that is closely linked to a pilot project. By choosing a pilot project that is critical and high profile, you guarantee that you get the most talented people. Once the pilot project can be considered a success, you roll out the new process and tool environment to the entire organization.*

- **Pilot.** They choose a critical project as a pilot project, which guarantees that they will have the most talented people, the strongest management support, and the deepest pockets to pay for necessary training, mentoring, and tool support. The pilot project is interacting with the PTEP on a daily basis. PTEP will steer their activities to address the needs of the pilot project, and will in return get immediate feedback on what works and what does not work.

- **Software development projects.** As soon as the pilot project can be considered a success, the RUP and associated tools are rolled out project-by-project, using the not-yet-finalized version of the process and tool environment produced by the PTEP.

Continuous Process Improvement

Improving projects results—a bottom-line benefit behind any RUP implementation—should be an ongoing effort, which means that you should continuously improve the process you follow, the tools you use, and your ability to get new teams and new team members up to speed with the process and tools. Once you are done with your initial RUP adoption program, you should put in place procedures for continually enhancing your process and tool environment. This may include the following:

You should put in place procedures for continually enhancing your process and tool environment.

- Creating a team responsible for process and tool enhancements. This team continuously performs minor fixes and initiates additional PTEPs when necessary.
- Setting up procedures for feedback from each project. This can be done by making project post-mortems a standard project feature, or by frequently interviewing team members. You can also take advantage of the feedback feature *within* the RUP product. It allows project members to suggest enhancements or report issues and send these suggestions and comments to IBM Software's RUP development team. Optionally, you can easily redirect these messages to go to your internal process enhancement team.

The availability of reusable assets can radically enhance your ability to develop software. You should consider putting procedures in place that allow you to reuse assets across projects. You may document and package your assets according to a Reuse Asset Specification (RAS),[1] which is a standard for documenting and packaging reusable assets. You should also continually survey what reusable assets are available from other companies.

---

1. See http://www.rational.com/rda/index.jsp.

Conclusion

The reasons for adopting the RUP product and supporting tools should be to obtain business benefits measured in improved project results.

The reasons for adopting the RUP product and supporting tools should be to obtain business benefits measured in improved project results in terms of higher quality systems, lower cost, or shorter time-to-market. Time spent on process improvement easily becomes overhead unless these objectives are clear in everyone's mind.

When adopting the RUP in a project, you walk through five basic steps: **Assess** whether you should adopt all or only some parts of RUP; **plan** the implementation; **configure and customize** the RUP, the tool environment, and the training material; **execute** the project; and **evaluate** the results of your RUP introduction.

Implementing the RUP for a larger organization is a complex task, and is best driven as a program consisting of three types of projects: process and tool enhancement projects (PTEPs), pilot projects, and normal software development projects. The amount of organizational change, your willingness for risk exposure, and the amount of customization of the RUP and supporting tools you plan to make greatly impact your RUP implementation program.

To accomplish major improvement in project results, you need to automate the process. Iterative development requires, among other factors, support for Configuration and Change Management, automated testing, and requirements management to be completed in a cost-effective manner. Other aspects of the RUP require other types of automation. Failure to consider automation as a part of a process improvement effort will likely lead to disappointing results.

Improving the process and tools should be an ongoing effort, giving you the capacity to tune your process continuously to fit your evolving needs.

CHAPTER 12

Planning an Iterative Project

Motivation

Planning an iterative project is both harder and easier than planning a waterfall project:

- It is harder and much more work, since the planning is more dynamic and ongoing.
- It is easier because it is much more in tune with the goals of the project. There is a short-term planning horizon and plenty of opportunities to adjust the plans.

Traditional planning of engineering projects is far too often organized from the top down and around a **product breakdown,** that is, the decomposition of the system into components and the various artifact products (specifications, blueprints, subassemblies, and so on), a style of planning that was inherited from the manufacturing and construction industries. Although at some point the plan needs to acknowledge the artifacts and the product structure, this is often done too early in the software development, at a point when little is known about the product.

Planning in the RUP is more focused on a **process breakdown,** that is, what needs to be done to achieve certain objectives over time. This is where you will see in action the concepts of **phases** and **iterations,** as well as the major and minor **milestones** that accompany them. You will use activities and workflow details. Planning in the RUP will use

Planning in the RUP is focused on a process breakdown, *that is, what needs to be done to achieve certain objectives over time.*

223

both a top-down approach and a bottom-up approach—top-down only in the early stages (Inception and Elaboration phases), complemented by bottom-up in later stages (Construction and Transition phases).[1] The bottom-up approach will use the defined artifacts and the architectural baseline. In practice, however, the planning approach is not quite that black-and-white, and there is a continuum across the development lifecycle.

This dynamic and iterative approach to planning allows you to achieve a better balance between **targets** (where you want to be at the end of the project) and **commitments** (what the team needs to do to get there). It is adaptive and driven by risks, as well as by what has been learned so far about both the product and the process used to develop it.

Key Concepts

Let's start by revisiting a few key concepts.

Cycle

A **development cycle** is the period of time that elapses from the very start of the project until product release (or project cancellation); it includes all the activities that are executed during that time.

We distinguish initial development cycles from evolution cycles or maintenance cycles.

Not all cycles have the same development profile. The importance of the phases, and the number of iterations required to fulfill the phase objectives, can vary greatly. We often distinguish **initial development cycles** from **evolution cycles** or **maintenance cycles.** An initial development cycle, leading to the very first release of a system, is often referred to as a "green-field" development. Figure 12.1 shows a typical time line for an initial development cycle.

Phases

Each cycle in the RUP is broken down into a sequence of four **phases,** called Inception, Elaboration, Construction, and Transition. Remem-

---

1. See Royce 1998, Chapter 10.

Time

FIGURE 12.1 Typical Time Line for an Initial Development Cycle. *The lead time for each phase varies greatly from project to project. This figure indicates an average breakdown for an initial development cycle.*

ber that the phases always exist and are important, not because of what is executed or because of their length, but because of what is achieved at the major milestone that concludes them.

Iteration

Inside each phase there may be one or more iterations. Software is developed in each iteration, which is concluded by a minor milestone, including a release (internal or external) that is a point for assessing the project progress. The software product grows incrementally as you iterate over the activities.

Build

Inside each iteration, the various developers or teams may produce software **builds** (sometimes at a high rate: daily or even more frequently), which allows continual integration, testing, regression testing, and general indication of progress. Often the last build of the iteration is part of the iteration's release.

Time-Boxing

Time-boxing is used to limit analysis-paralysis and gold plating.

Time-boxing is a top-down technique that tries to confine the achievement of a specific goal within a small time interval. This provides a structure for focusing on the most important mission goals and forcing engineering tradeoffs.[2] It is not about setting impossible or irrational

---

2. See Highsmith 2000, p. 303.

goals and delivering anything of poor quality within the time-box. It is a tool used to balance scope and schedule but also to force convergence and to limit analysis-paralysis or gold plating.

Coarse-Grain and Fine-Grain Plans: Project Plans and Iteration Plans

Because the iterative process is highly dynamic and adaptive and is meant to accommodate changes to goals and tactics, there is no purpose in spending an inordinate amount of time producing detailed plans that extend beyond the current project horizon. Such plans are difficult to maintain, rapidly become obsolete, and are typically ignored by the performing organization after a few weeks. These plans try to be very predictive and may use "inch pebbles" rather than milestones. Moreover, software development is a creative activity, not just a production activity or an administrative process with a more or less fixed workflow. So it is hard to commit to a plan before you actually know what it is that you are planning.

In an iterative process, two kinds of plans are recommended:

- **A coarse-grained plan.** The **project plan,** which focuses on phases and iterations, their objectives, and the overall staffing level
- **A series of fine-grained plans.** The **iteration plans,** one per iteration, which bring RUP activities and individual resources into perspective

The Project Plan

The project plan is a coarse-grained plan, and there is only one per development project.

Top management and external stakeholders are rarely interested in the details of who is doing what and when. They are interested in the final product. Therefore, they are primarily concerned with the release date, any milestones along the way, when major decisions must be made, and where they can get visibility over the progress, scope, difficulties, and resources of the project.

The **project plan** is a coarse-grained plan, and there is only one per development project. It acts as the overall "envelope" of the project for one cycle (and maybe the following cycles, if appropriate). The project plan includes the following:

- Dates of the major milestones:
  - **Lifecycle Objective (LCO) Milestone.** End of Inception, project well scoped and funded
  - **Lifecycle Architecture (LCA) Milestone.** End of Elaboration, architecture complete, requirements baseline set
  - **Initial Operational Capability (IOC) Milestone.** End of Construction, first beta release
  - **Product Release (PR) Milestone.** End of Transition and of the development cycle
- **Staffing profile.** What resources are required over time.
- **Dates of minor milestones.** End of iterations; include primary objectives, if known.

The project plan (usually one to two pages) is produced very early in the Inception phase and updated as often as necessary. The plan refers to the Vision Document to define the scope and assumptions of the project. This project plan is a section of the more encompassing Software Development Plan (see Section 4.2 in the RUP template).

The Iteration Plan

An **iteration plan** is a fine-grained, time-boxed plan; there is one plan per iteration. As the iteration plan focuses on only one iteration, it has a time span small enough that it provides team members with the insight to do the kind of detailed planning that they are familiar with: a plan that includes the right level of granularity on tasks and successful allocation to various team members.

An iteration plan is a fine-grained, time-boxed plan; there is one plan per iteration.

A project usually has two iteration plans "active" at any time:

- The **current iteration** plan (for the current iteration), which is used to track progress
- The **next iteration** plan (for the upcoming iteration), which is built toward the second half of the current iteration and is ready at the end of the current iteration

While the team is executing the current iteration plan, the project manager is writing the plan for the next iteration. The project manager needs to be far-sighted and able to quickly modify this second plan late in the current cycle so that the team can have a viable plan for the subsequent iteration, even if there are some changes brought about by late-breaking news. If some new discovery arrives late, the project manager needs to react in such a way that the team is not left at the starting gate because there is a "planning gap."

The iteration plan is built using traditional planning techniques and tools (Gantt charts and so on) to define the tasks and help allocate them to individuals and teams. The plan contains some important dates, such as major builds, arrival of components from other organizations, and major reviews. It defines objective success criteria for the iteration. It is made up of RUP activities, or sometimes aggregates of activities such as the workflow details. Since the activities are uniquely associated to a role—and the individuals in the team may be competent to play specific roles—the plan will tie to the resources. Simple projects may just use a list of "things to do."

You can picture the iteration plan as a **window** moving through the project plan (or phase plan), acting as a magnifier (as shown in Figure 12.2).

The iteration plan is a separate artifact in the RUP and is not maintained beyond the duration of the iteration.

Building a Project Plan

To build a **project plan** you will need an initial estimate of the overall size of the project (see Figure 12.3). We will visit the estimation part in the section Estimating later in the chapter. Once you have an initial guess at the overall size, there are well-known recipes (such as the COCOMO model) to estimate the right level of staffing.

Most projects will not function efficiently if staffed with a constant number of people. There is usually a staffing profile that increases from Inception to Construction, plateaus for a while, and then drops a bit toward the end of Transition.

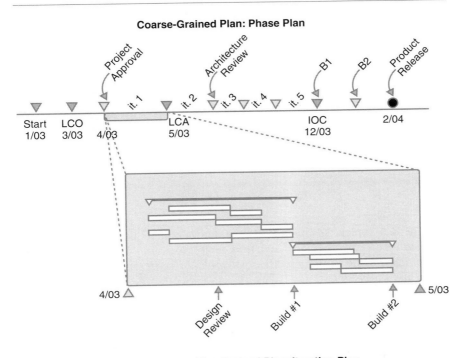

Coarse-Grained Plan: Phase Plan

Fine-Grained Plan: Iteration Plan

FIGURE 12.2 Project Plan and Iteration Plan. *The project plan is a coarse-grained plan that acts as the overall "envelope" of the project for one cycle. The iteration plan is a fine-grained, time-boxed plan, one for each iteration (from Kruchten 2000a).*

As with many other aspects in the RUP approach, consider this profile only as an example. It must be adjusted to suit your own experience and your own context. For example:

- With many unknown factors and risks, and the added element of new people or tools and technologies, the Elaboration phase may last longer.
- For evolution cycles, Inception and Elaboration may be shortened.

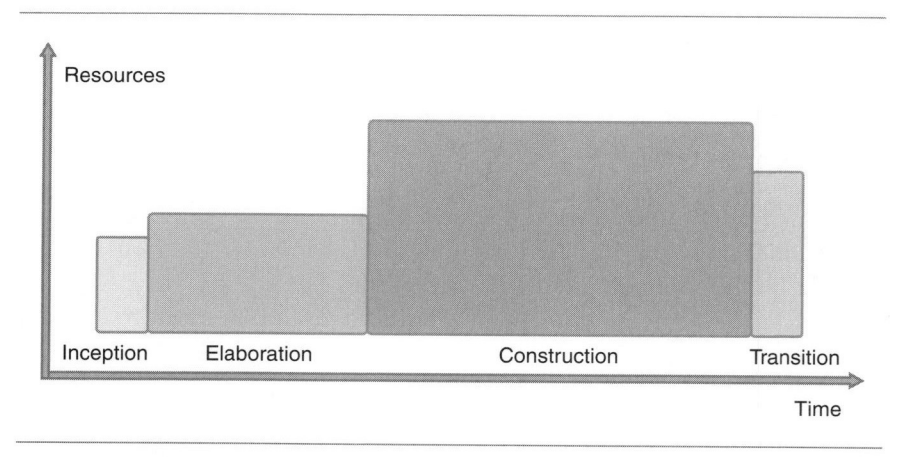

FIGURE 12.3 Typical Resource Profile for a Development Cycle. *The resources used within each phase vary greatly from project to project. This graph provides you with a starting point for a discussion around resource needs (from Kruchten 2000a and Royce 1998).*

Once you have planted the dates of the major milestones on the calendar, the next questions to address are how many iterations and how long. Opinion varies greatly among iterative development practitioners. First, remember to not confuse a build, like a weekly build, with an iteration. Many avid fans of iterative development think of an iteration as lasting around two to five weeks. This may be fine for most small- to medium-sized projects, but not for large and very large projects where hundreds of people, often distributed over several sites, may have to be coordinated.

How quickly you can iterate depends mostly on the size of the development organization.

For example:

- **5 people, 1 week.** A team of five people can do some planning on a Monday morning, have lunch together every day to monitor progress, reallocate tasks, start doing a build on Thursday, and complete the iteration by Friday evening. The iteration takes 1 week.

- **20 people, 3 to 4 weeks.** The 1-week scenario will be very hard to achieve with 20 people. It will take more time to distribute the work, synchronize between subgroups, integrate, and so on. An iteration could instead take 3 to 4 weeks.

- **40 people, 8 weeks.** With 40 people, it already takes a week for all the "synapses" to fire from the "brain" to the "extremities" of the development organization. You have intermediate levels of management; the common understanding of the objective will require more formal documentation, more ceremony. Eight weeks is a more realistic iteration length.

How quickly you can iterate depends mostly on the size of the development organization.

Other factors come into play: the degree of familiarity of the organization with the iterative approach, including having a stable and mature organization, and the level of automation the team is using to manage code (for example, distributed CM), distribute information (for example, internal Web), automate testing, and so on.

- Rational products are all produced through synchronized releases with 700 people/team members involved, and iterations that are 5 to 8 weeks long.

- Craig Larman from Valtech reports projects having 10 iterations or more in a little more than a year.

Be aware also that there is some fixed overhead attached to an iteration: in planning, synchronizing, analyzing the results, and so on.

So, while convinced by the tremendous benefits of the iterative approach, you might be tempted to iterate furiously, the human limits of your organization are going to slow your fervor.

- Iterations of **less than 1 month need to be scoped carefully.** Typically, short iterations are more suitable for the Construction phase, where the degree of new functionality to be included and the degree of novelty are low. Short iterations may include little or no formal analysis or design, and may simply be incrementally improving on an existing and well-understood functionality.

- Iterations of **more than 3 months probably need intermediate milestones** built in to keep the project on track. Consider reducing the scope of the iteration to reduce its length and ensure a clear focus.

- Iterations of **more than 12 months** in multiyear projects **create additional business risks** because the iteration spans the annual funding cycle. A project that has not produced anything visible in 12 months is at risk of losing its funding. You would not reap much benefit from iterative development. Rethink your strategy.

Iterations need not all be the same length: Their length will vary according to their objectives. Typically, Elaboration iterations will be longer than Construction iterations. Within a phase, iterations are generally the same length (it makes planning easier). But having a good, regular tempo for a project with many iterations provides an environment that favors balanced iteration lifecycles.

Determining the Number of Iterations

Related to the length of an iteration is the delicate issue of the **number** of iterations.

A **very simple project** may have only 1 iteration per phase:

- **Inception: 1 iteration,** perhaps to produce a proof-of-concept prototype or user-interface mock-up **or no iteration** at all, for example, in an evolution cycle.
- **Elaboration: 1 iteration** to produce an architectural prototype.
- **Construction: 1 iteration** to build the product (to a beta release).
- **Transition: 1 iteration** to finish the product (full product release).

For a **more substantial project, in its initial development cycle,** the norm would be

- **Inception: 1 iteration,** possibly producing a prototype.
- **Elaboration: 2 iterations,** one to develop an initial architectural prototype and one to finalize the architectural baseline.
- **Construction: 2 iterations,** one to expose a partial system and one to mature it for beta testing.
- **Transition: 1 iteration,** to go from beta to full product release.

For a **large project, with many unknown factors, new technologies, and the like,** there may be a case for additional iterations:

- **Inception: An additional iteration** to allow for more prototyping (so 2 iterations in all).
- **Elaboration: An additional iteration** to allow different technologies to be explored, or to phase in the introduction of architectural solutions, bringing this phase to 3 iterations.
- **Construction: An additional iteration** because of the sheer size of the product, also 3 iterations.
- **Transition: An additional iteration** to allow for operational feedback halfway through.

Therefore, over a development cycle, we have several possible degrees of iteration (see Table 12.1).

In general, plan to have 3 to 10 iterations. Observe, though, that the upper and lower bounds connote unusual circumstances: **Most developments will use 6 to 8 iterations.**

Many variations are possible depending on project risks, size, and complexity:

- If the **product is intended for a totally new domain,** you may need to add some iterations in Inception to consolidate the concepts, show various mock-ups to a cross-section of customers or users, or build a solid response to a request for proposal.

TABLE 12.1 Degrees of Iteration in Different Projects. *This table can be used as a starting point when deciding how many iterations to have. The number of iterations and iteration length depend on a lot of different factors.*

Project Size (People)	Project Length (Months)	Iteration Length (Weeks)	Number of Iterations Per Phase			
			Inception	Elaboration	Construction	Transition
3	4	2–3	1	1	3	1
10	8	4	1	2	3	2
80	20	7–8	2	3	4	2

- If a **new architecture must be developed or there is a large amount of use-case modeling to be done, or there are very challenging risks,** you should plan to have 2 or 3 iterations in Elaboration.
- If the **product is large and complex** and to be developed over a long period of time, you should plan to have 3 or more iterations in Construction.
- If you feel **you may need a lot of small adaptations to the user base after a period of use,** you should plan to have several iterations in Transition.
- **A simple evolution cycle or a maintenance cycle** can be done with few iterations: none in Inception and Elaboration, 1 in Construction, and 1 in Transition.
- Or an **organization that has never done iterative development** may choose a modest start with a low number, such as 3 iterations.

Alternatively, you might settle on an iteration length that your organization is comfortable with, and just proceed by fitting as many iterations of that length as you can in each phase. It is obviously easier, but you need to have done this before with your current organization, or with an organization comparable in size and experience, to be certain about iteration duration. Again, there is no "one-size-fits-all" approach. Do not try to optimize too much. Take a first shot at it, and modify it as you learn.

Iteration Length

As a first approximation, obtain the iteration length by dividing the length of the phase by the number of iterations. If the duration obtained is not quite right, according to the rules of thumb given earlier, revisit the process. Now is the time to make some adjustments, either to the length of a phase or to the number of iterations. Then also take into account major holidays, planned vacations, or plant closures to adjust the project plan to a realistic time frame. For example, it is never a good idea to plan a major milestone between Christmas and New Year's Eve (in some countries, at least).

It's not necessary get your plan 100 percent right on day one, because you will revisit this plan several times during the development cycle.

Start with something realistic, create a baseline of your project plan, and revisit it as you grow wiser at the end of each iteration.

Iteration Objectives

Once you have an idea of the number of iterations in your coarse-grained plan, you need to define the **contents** of each iteration. It is even a good idea to find a name or title to qualify the release you have at the end of each iteration, and to help people gain a better focus on the next target.

> *Example: Names of Iterations for a Private Telephone Switch*
>
> Iteration 1: Local station-to-station call
> Iteration 2: Add external calls and subscriber management
> Iteration 3: Add voice mail and conference calls
> ...And so on

Again, do not put too much effort into this. You will revise these several times throughout the cycle. Planning is iterative and adaptive.

Staffing the Project

The next step is to allocate the right level of resources to the project alongside the lifecycle. Figure 12.4 shows a typical staffing profile.

Your actual staffing profile will vary depending on your project.

- For an **initial development cycle, a green-field development,** it is not a good idea to start with too many people during Inception and Elaboration. Since there is nothing in place, you will struggle just to keep everyone fully employed. Fifty people will not shape the vision document together. Staffing can peak during Construction.
- In an **evolution cycle or a maintenance cycle,** the staffing profile may be more flat. The same five people may be permanently allocated to it, and the work done looks like Transition, or Construction and Transition.

Models such as COCOMO will help you determine the optimal number of people versus duration of the phase for the various phases, taking into account various parameters (cost drivers).

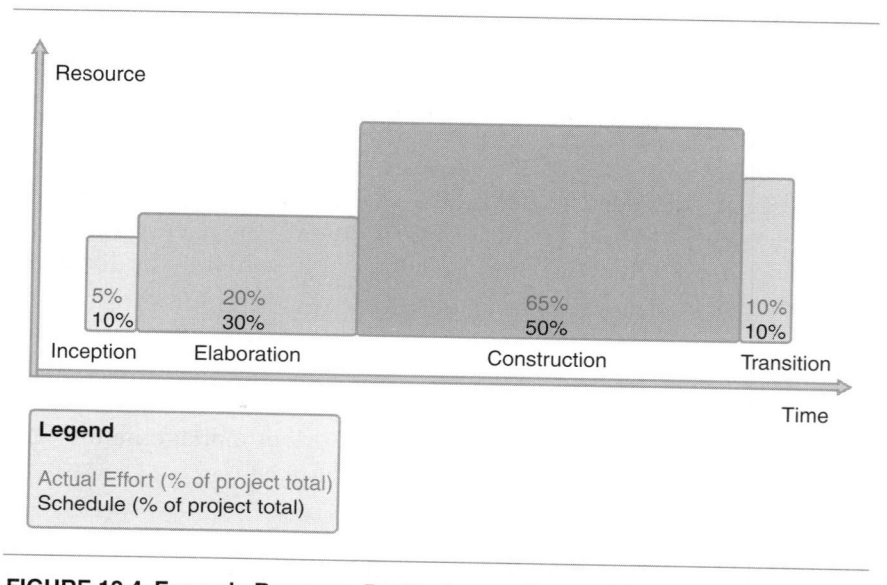

FIGURE 12.4 Example Resource Profile Across Project Lifecycle Phases. *The effort spent on each phase varies greatly from project to project. This graph shows an example staffing profile for a project.*

You will need the right mix of competence to allocate the activities to individual resources; this can be done by tabulating for each team member the RUP roles that he or she is likely to play.

Iteration Planning

The development of an **iteration plan** has four steps:

1. **Determine the iteration scope.** Determine the intent—what you want to accomplish in the iteration.

2. **Define iteration evaluation criteria.** Define how to objectively evaluate the accomplishments at the end of the iteration; specify which artifacts will be worked on.

3. **Define iteration activities.** Establish what needs to be done and on which artifacts.
4. **Assign responsibilities.** Allocate resources to execute the activities.

How to proceed with the first three steps will vary greatly across the lifecycle.

Inception and Elaboration

At the beginning of a project, especially a **green-field project,** you have no design elements identified and no elements specific to this new system on which to base your reasoning for planning the iteration. Use a top-down approach, with rough estimates derived from other projects, as a basis for your planning assumptions—you probably did this for the project plan.

If, however, you are dealing with an **evolution cycle** of an existing software product (a "brown-field" project), Inception and Elaboration are likely to be shorter, you may have fewer risks to mitigate, and planning iterations will look more like what is described in the next section, Construction and Transition.

The objectives of the iteration will be determined primarily by risks. Risks will in turn determine which use cases, scenarios, algorithms, and so on will be developed during the iteration, together with the means to assess that the risks have been mitigated.

Risks will determine which use cases, scenarios, algorithms, and so on will be developed during the iteration.

Construction and Transition

Now you have an overall architecture in place and some measurements from previous iterations both on the artifacts (lines of code, defects, and so on) and on the process (time to complete certain tasks). Hopefully, you have mitigated most of your risks. You can use this information to progressively modify the way you plan iterations.

You can proceed with a bottom-up, artifact-based planning, using the elements of the design, such as class, component, subsystem, use case, test case, and so on, as well as any measures from previous iterations to estimate the effort. A word of warning: **A bottom-up approach tends to be pessimistic** relative to the schedule, especially when

summing up the individual estimates of dozens of people. And it is known that novice developers have a tendency to be overly optimistic about their performance.

The iteration objectives will be determined primarily by completion objectives and the achievement of a set level of quality.

The iteration objectives will be determined primarily by completion objectives and the achievement of a set level of quality. This also includes specific defects to correct, primarily the ones that prevent the use of major functionality, or make the system crash, deferring "nice to haves" for a future release.

Identifying Activities

Use your RUP development case as the reference list for activities required within an iteration. If you find the activities are too granular, you may replace them by workflow details, especially in the early stages.

There are some activities that need to be run only once per iteration (or per phase or even per cycle); for example, the RUP activities named Plan an Iteration or Lifecycle Milestone Review.

But there are other activities that must be instantiated (replicated) for each element, and this element is usually the major output of this activity. For example, the activity Code a Class must be done for each class, Integrate Subsystem for each subsystem, and Describe Use Case for each use case.

Consequently, in the very early iterations of a new project, since the design elements have not been identified, you will only be able to give that activity a sort of global "ballpark" figure, for example:

>   Code (all) classes: 10 person-days

Or simply picking a higher-level artifact:

>   Develop proof-of-concept prototype: 42 person-days

In later iterations, when the design elements are identified, the activity can be associated with these elements with a finer estimate; for example:

Code Customer class: 2 person-days
Code Invoice class: 1 person-day

Estimating

One key ingredient that we conveniently skipped so far is the thorny issue of estimation. How big is this project? How many people are needed?

By far the best tool a project manager can use to estimate a project, a phase, an iteration, or a simple activity is historical data. The most basic approach is to record effort, duration, or size estimates as well as estimate processes and assumptions, and then record the actual results from each estimated activity. Comparing actual outcomes to the estimates helps generate more accurate estimates in the future. Estimating procedures and templates that itemize tasks help avoid the common problem of overlooking necessary work. The RUP constitutes such an inventory of activities.

By far the best tool a project manager can use to estimate a project, a phase, an iteration, or a simple activity is historical data.

There are estimation tools, such as COCOMO, but they will not tell you how much effort is required for your *new* project; they will only help you estimate how long and how many people, by adjusting the numbers for various cost drivers, integrating the performance of your team, and assessing the difficulty of the project. For the project plan, early in Inception, it is best to calibrate the new project relative to another one for which you already know the total effort. Then a model such as COCOMO will derive an estimation of duration and level of staffing. Remember that software developers are notoriously nonfungible; this is what makes planning software projects a bit more tricky.

Once the project is started, you might want to combine top-down and bottom-up approaches and exploit not only your growing knowledge of what you want to accomplish, but also that of your development staff. Most likely they have started doing some early prototyping and using their understanding of the tools, from which they can draw better estimates. See the next section for a simple but effective approach: using the best of your people and whatever known input you have.

More sophisticated methods include using the function-points method and its various derivatives. Use cases can be used as a starting point for function-point-like techniques to estimate the "size of the mountain."[3]

An Iterative Estimation Technique: Wideband Modified Delphi

This method was introduced by Barry Boehm in the 1970s,[4] and it has spawned several variants. It is often referred to as the **Wideband Modified Delphi**. The principle is to bring several heads together on an issue and try to reach a consensus. When these "heads" used are the actual development team, this approach is more likely to get their commitment than would random numbers raining from above. This is roughly how it works:

1. The project manager defines what is to be estimated, the units of measure, and the assumptions. The manager then gathers data for similar tasks or projects if available (for example, data from previous iterations or a previous project). Participants are selected.

2. All the participants are briefed on the procedure and the goals, and given any available data.

3. The participants develop their own estimate (each one on his or her own), preferably not interacting with each other.

4. The project manager gathers all the data, tabulates it in a spreadsheet, and compares it.

5. All participants meet again. Where the numbers match, they have a likely estimate. If the numbers are widely scattered, it is interesting to discuss with participants what motivated higher and lower numbers. What was the reasoning behind their estimate? When they explain their assumptions, other team members may react in one way or another: Some important parameter was forgotten, some new risk has arisen, and so on.

---

3. See Albrecht 1979.
4. See Boehm 1981.

6. The participants are then given a chance to adjust their estimate based on the discussion.

7. The new numbers become the working estimate.

As the phase or iteration unrolls, actual data is then collected for these tasks and is used in the next estimate. At the next round (the next iteration, for example), when it is time to do another estimation, the previous estimates and the actual numbers are given to the participants, to help them adjust their natural optimism or pessimism.

There are plenty of variants and refinements, as you can imagine. You could iterate on steps 5 and 6 (although it is often not necessary). You can choose an informal route, using e-mail or simply walking from cubicle to cubicle with a notepad to discuss planning hypotheses with the people who had given great variance. You can do it very formally, using templates and tools to compute ranges and uncertainties, even using Monte Carlo simulations to generate a probability distribution of possible estimate outcomes based on the final estimate values. See Wiegers 2000 for another, more detailed description of this Wideband Delphi estimation technique.

Optimizing the Project Plan

Beyond the basic recipe just described for planning an iterative project, the bold project manager can attempt to optimize the project plan.

Overlapping Iterations

A certain amount of overlap can occur between one iteration and the next, and this is probably healthy to keep everyone busy. The planning of the next iteration should not wait until you come to a complete stop. Don't lose sight of the fact that to reap the benefits from iterative development, you need the lessons learned from iteration N to do a better job in iteration N+1—too much overlap will defeat this built-in mechanism for refining requirements, goals, and process.

Parallel Iterations

When a product has many parts or is developed by a distributed team, it may be tempting to have each team or subcontractor do its own planning. This is fine, providing the work packages are fairly independent. If they are not, then it is better to have everyone work according to the same global clock and to integrate the various subsystems together at the end of an iteration. In some cases, a team may not deliver anything new at the end of an iteration if what they delivered at the previous iteration is sufficient for the other group(s) to proceed.

For example, a group may be responsible for infrastructure code, where the infrastructure is rather mature and its interface stable, and the development may not need to release a new infrastructure at each iteration.

Remember that the slowest team or group is the limiting factor: It will slow down everyone else and force the other teams to synchronize with its schedule.

Conclusion

To conclude this chapter, a word of advice from our colleague Walker Royce:[5]

> *Plans are not just for managers. The more open and visible the planning process, the more ownership there is among the team members who need to execute it. Bad, closely held plans cause attrition. Good, open plans can shape cultures and encourage teamwork.*

---

5.   See Royce 1998.

CHAPTER 13

Common Mistakes When Adopting and Using the RUP ...and How to Avoid Them

In this chapter, we will walk through some of the more common mistakes, or what you might call anti-patterns, that project teams make when adopting and using the RUP and how to avoid them. The list of mistakes is based on the observations that we and the Rational field organization have made in working with thousands of customers over the years. We divide the mistakes into three areas:

- Mistakes when adopting the RUP
- Mistakes when managing iterative development
- Mistakes when doing analysis, architecture, design, implementation, and testing

Mistakes When Adopting the RUP

The objective of implementing the RUP approach is to help you deliver working software, with fewer defects, in as short a time as possible. Implementing the RUP can potentially have far-reaching implications to the adopting organization. Those implications are both technical (with new tools being adopted to automate certain

aspects of the process) and social (with the introduction of new working practices and culture). The implementation should therefore be treated as a project or a program. These are some of the common mistakes we have found when organizations adopt the RUP:

- **Adopting too much of what is in the RUP** may slow down your development effort, reduce your flexibility, and increase development costs.

- **Adopting everything at once, rather than incrementally,** may overwhelm project members, likely leading to a failed RUP implementation.

- **Not planning the implementation of the RUP** may, among other things, lead to a lack of stakeholder buy-in, insufficient funds, or a lack of resources for mentoring and training.

- **Not coupling process improvement with business results** makes it harder to get stakeholder buy-in and may derail the RUP implementation so it does not provide expected returns.

- **Customizing too much of the RUP too early** leads to an overengineered process, or time spent on needless customization due to lack of understanding of what process is really needed.

- **Playing lip service to the RUP** makes stakeholders think that you have adopted the RUP, while you have done so only on the surface. You may lose your credibility, and the RUP may be blamed for failure, when it really is the process predating the RUP that is to blame.

- **Not managing the RUP rollout as a project or a program, consisting of a series of projects,** thus adopting the RUP but not measuring and assessing its success, making changes, or fine-tuning its usage over time (see Chapter 11).

The most common mistake people make when adopting the RUP is to use too many of the artifacts or to do too many of the activities found in the RUP.

Let's look at some ways to avoid these mistakes.

Adopting Too Much of What Is in the RUP

Possibly the most common mistake people make when adopting the RUP is to use too many of the artifacts or to do too many of the activities found in the RUP. Adopting too much of the RUP will slow down your development effort, and rather than providing you with increased flexibility, shorter delivery times, and reduced cost, it is likely to lead to the opposite and, ultimately, major failure. The RUP process framework is like a smorgasbord, and you're much better off not eating all the dishes if you want to stay healthy and happy. Adopt only the aspects of the RUP that add value to your project. See Chapter 11 for a discussion on adopting the RUP and Chapter 10 to understand how to streamline the RUP for your project.

The entire RUP knowledge base contains a lot of artifacts, and most projects should not try to use more than a fraction of them. What you *should* do is decide which of these artifacts makes sense for your organization and your particular project. For example, you may choose not to use any of the 8 artifacts for business modeling, to use only 4 of the 14 artifacts for identifying requirements (say, Vision, Actor, Use Case, and User-Interface Prototype), and so on. In total, you may find that 15 or 20 of the total RUP artifacts are the most useful for your organization. This may still sound like a lot, but remember that the RUP treats as artifacts many project elements that you may not normally think of as artifacts, such as Component, Build, Change Request, Design Class, and Subsystem. In the RUP, these are considered artifacts, even if you draw them on only a whiteboard—or even a napkin. Note that the formality with which you document and review the artifacts is often more important than the number of artifacts you produce.

Using too many artifacts will slow you down. People may pay more attention to perfecting various artifacts than on building the right system. On the other hand, if you do not have enough artifacts, you may find that you repeatedly solve the same problems, increasing rework due to miscommunication. The same may be true if you document the artifacts in too informal a way. For example, you may have created a great implementation for storing persistent data, but if your solution is documented on a whiteboard, it cannot be used by team members at other sites. You need to formalize the documentation, perhaps using a visual modeling tool. So it is important not only to choose the right artifacts, but also to make them accessible to all project members. As discussed in Chapter 3, you need to choose the right balance between low and high ceremony for your project.

Choose the right balance between low and high ceremony for your project.

When faced with a decision on whether to include a particular artifact, ask the questions, "What would be the implication of not having this artifact present now or in the future?" and "What risk is this artifact mitigating?" Even though you want to use a minimum set of artifacts, the RUP uses artifacts for a reason. It is important that you consider the value of the artifact and its level of ceremony in this as well as future maintainence projects.

Adopting Everything at Once, Rather Than Incrementally

Focus on adopting the parts of the RUP that give the highest return first.

We highly recommend that you adopt the RUP incrementally. If you are not already using a very similar approach, trying to adopt a complete process all at once will prove overwhelming, potentially leading to decreased productivity and ultimately a rejection of the RUP. Hence, we recommend that you focus on adopting the parts of the RUP that give the highest return first.

Assume that you have set a goal of 18 months in which you would like to have guidelines for and consistency around producing the 15 or 20 artifacts that make the most sense for your organization. How do you get there? Let's look at an example.

Your team is working on three 6-month projects in these next 18 months. You choose which artifacts to produce for the first project, which ones you should add for the next project, and so on. Your plan might look as follows (italics indicate artifacts):

Project 1. Focus on Requirements Management and Iterative Development

Goal: To get a grip on requirements and start using an iterative and risk-driven approach. These areas are critical for the success of many projects.

To achieve the goal, the project introduces seven artifacts:

- Identify *actors* and *use cases*, and produce *user-interface prototypes*.
- Adopt an iterative and component-based process.
- Identify *risks*, and make sure to mitigate major risks in early iterations.

- Do not create a formal design, but produce well-defined *components* organized into *implementation subsystems,* and have these peer-reviewed.
- Do *builds* every week of the project.

Project 2. Focus on Configuration and Change Management, and Testing

Goal: To increase quality by addressing Configuration and Change Management as well as testing. Measure progress primarily by assessing what code works as expected, rather than what supporting artifacts have been completed.

To achieve the goal, the project introduces seven artifacts:

- Introduce a *test plan* and a *test case,* and produce *test scripts* to improve the testing process. These test artifacts should be derived from the requirements.
- File *change requests* (such as defects) when appropriate, and monitor these requests to assess how you are doing.
- Introduce Configuration Management tools supporting a *project repository* and developer and integration *workspaces.*
- Do *builds* every day during the last two months of the project, using an automated build process.

Project 3. Focus on Design and Architecture

Goal: To focus on design and component-based architectures in order to ensure that you actually implement the requirements and that the system is easy to maintain.

To achieve the goal, the project introduces four artifacts:

- Introduce *design classes* and *design subsystems* in order to build component-based architectures. Ensure that a baseline of the architecture is created by the end of Elaboration.
- Introduce *use-case realizations*—that is, produce sequence or collaboration diagrams for each use case—to ensure that your design incorporates your requirements.
- Enhance your requirement management process by producing a *vision* document.

TABLE 13.1 Incremental Improvements Across All Fundamental Principles. *In each of the three projects, we made incremental improvements by using several of the fundamental principles representing "the Spirit of the RUP." Each organization needs to determine what principles would provide the greatest gain and prioritize process improvements accordingly.*

Principle	Project 1	Project 2	Project 3
Attack major risks early and continuously, or they will attack you.	Risks were introduced as a way of determining what to do in each iteration.		
Ensure that you deliver value to your customer.	Requirements were documented.	Requirements were tested.	Requirements in the form of use cases have a design, a so-called use-case realization.
Stay focused on executable software.	Weekly builds and iterative development.	Daily builds toward the end of project. Strong focus on testing.	
Accommodate change early in the project.	Started with iterative development.	Formalized a Change Management process.	
Baseline an executable architecture early on.			Created a baseline of the architecture at the end of Elaboration.
Build your system with components.	Defined components in an informal way.		Formalized the development using components.
Work together as one team.	Iterative development forced closer team collaboration. Changed requirements practices enabled closer collaboration with customer.	Increased focus on face-to-face meetings to resolve issues quickly.	
Make quality a way of life, not an afterthought.		Quality assurance established throughout the project.	

Earlier we saw a concrete example of how you can make an incremental adoption. As you do an incremental adoption, you often need to modify the original plan because you may not make progress as expected or your priorities may change. But how do you decide where to start?

In Chapter 2, we discussed eight fundamental principles of the RUP. In Table 13.1, we outline how we made incremental improvements by using many of these principles in each of our three projects.

Assess your organization to see where you experience the biggest challenges and where your needs are the greatest, as we discussed in Chapter 11. Which of the eight principles in Chapter 2 should you adopt to get the biggest return? The organization in the earlier example adopted the principles in a certain order; the priorities may look very different in your organization.

Not Planning the Implementation of the RUP

Trying to implement the Rational Unified Process without proper planning is likely to lead to failure. Implementing the Rational Unified Process should be treated as a project or program by itself, supported by a business case and rooted in clear objectives such as reduced cost for software development, increased quality, and reduced project lengths. You need to figure out what is the best way for your organization to adopt the RUP, such as the incremental adoption we described earlier. This type of adoption does not "just happen"; it requires continuous planning and support to ensure successful project execution. You should also consider starting the adoption of the RUP in a pilot project, where you can use the RUP and supporting tools in a project set up to ensure successful adoption and to maximize the learning of the process and tools.

Trying to implement the RUP without proper planning is likely to lead to failure.

Soft issues, such as getting buy-in from executive management and middle management and making sure project members are motivated to change to a new process (and possibly a new tool environment), are crucial for the success of the RUP implementation. Many organizations are especially challenged with getting buy-in from middle management since they face not only the project risks, but

also the risk of managing a project in a new way. There are also financial considerations, and you need to budget for mentoring, training, and potential tool purchases. You also need to ensure that you have the competency, or can acquire the competency, to do necessary customizations of the RUP, including developing project- or organization-specific guidelines for use-case modeling, design, programming, and so on.

Having a person, or a group, responsible for the RUP implementation greatly enhances the likelihood of successful implementation, at least if this person or group is given sufficient mandate to take necessary actions, has the necessary funds, and is measured on the success of the implementation. This person or group drives the implementation project forward, ensures cross-fertilization between groups to ensure that mistakes are not repeated, and alerts management when appropriate. The person or group must, however, be an active participant adding value in project work, not seen as a process police force that adds no value. It should be noted that you might greatly benefit from having an experienced mentor assist you in the implementation of the RUP, helping you avoid falling into common pitfalls. Revisit Chapter 11 if you experience problems with implementing the RUP.

Not Coupling Process Improvement with Business Results

Decide what business results you are trying to achieve, and communicate expected achievements to all stakeholders.

Improving your process by adopting the Rational Unified Process takes a lot of effort and carries with it costs for training, mentoring, and tooling. It is important that you as an organization decide what business results you are trying to achieve, and that expected achievements are properly communicated to all stakeholders. Otherwise, the RUP implementation project is likely to derail, due to lack of stakeholder buy-in (among other things), and you may not see the expected returns.

By focusing on business results, it is easier to get buy-in from higher level management, as well as from project members. Without buy-in from all these groups, it is very difficult to succeed with a RUP implementation. It is therefore important that a solid business case is developed for the RUP adoption. This business case should define future achievements of the rollout of the RUP and should drive the measurement of the RUP implementation.

Customizing Too Much of the RUP Too Early

Just as we recommend that you use an iterative approach when developing software, we recommend that you use an iterative and incremental approach when customizing and adopting the RUP. Do not start with a six-month project in which you customize the RUP before you have tried it out on a few smaller projects. Before you have tried out the RUP in practice, you do not have enough information to truly say what benefits you will reap from changes to the RUP. Instead, make a minimum of customizations and configurations, try the RUP on a project, then customize and configure the RUP a little bit more to address missing key areas, and so on. For example, for your first project you may be satisfied with generating a RUP Configuration, producing a light development case (see Chapter 10), and making external references to process guidance you have elsewhere, before you take on the project of incorporating external process material into a RUP Plug-In.

Use an iterative and incremental approach when customizing and adopting the RUP.

Paying Lip Service to the RUP

The Rational Unified Process has become very popular, and many organizations find big business value in saying that they are using the RUP. The drawback of this is that some customers seem to be more interested in getting the stamp, "We are using the RUP," than in achieving real process improvements. They may adopt some of the artifacts of RUP and use some of the RUP terminology, but they do not adopt "the Spirit of the RUP" (see Chapter 2). This is likely to backfire on the adopting organization; as stakeholders realize that the adopting organization is not achieving expected benefits, they will lose confidence in the organization and its ability to effectively develop software.

Some of the symptoms of paying lip service include the following:

- You rename functions as use cases, allowing you to state incorrectly that you are doing use-case-driven development rather than producing use cases that are complete and provide one or several actors with a measurable value.

- You produce a risk list, but do not use it to impact the order in which you attack the many problems you always face in a project.

- You detail all requirements before you start with design rather than using an iterative approach with a balanced investment in requirements, analysis, design, implementation, and testing within each iteration.

- You plan a project in detail up-front, from start to finish, rather than producing detailed iteration plans just before you start each iteration.

- You use a waterfall approach, rather than iterative development, or have such long iterations that you lose almost all the benefits of iterative development.

- You measure progress primarily in terms of the number of produced use-case descriptions and a completed design document, rather than in terms of executable software and successfully completed test cases.

- You ignore architecture, including the testing of the architecture, until too late in the project, when architectural rework becomes extremely expensive and causes project delays and budget overruns.

Note that there is a big difference between paying lip service to the RUP and doing an incremental adoption of the RUP. When incrementally adopting the RUP, you should expect to experience some of these symptoms. But when incrementally adopting the RUP, you acknowledge that you have not addressed them, and either have a plan in place for when to address them, or decide that for your organization, you do not see that it is feasible or desirable to address the symptom(s).

Mistakes When Managing Iterative Development

Transitioning from a waterfall approach to an iterative approach requires changes in the working procedures of all team members, and it is sometimes especially difficult for project managers and architects. Organizations going through this transition often hold on to certain patterns and thought processes that lead to flawed project execution. Among these common mistakes, we find the following:

- **Having a functional, specialized organization,** as opposed to deploying cross-functional teams
- **Not setting the right stakeholder expectations or using an old-fashioned acquisition model,** making stakeholders expect the same deliverables and a project lifecycle as in a waterfall approach
- **Having too many developers at project start,** before understanding what to do
- **Solving the easy stuff first,** rather than first attacking high-risk items
- **Having an extended initial iteration;** trying to do too much at the beginning
- **Having overlapping iterations;** starting the next iteration before you can benefit from any feedback from the current one
- **Allowing too many changes late in the project,** leading to major delays, cost overruns, and potentially poor quality

Let's look at these mistakes in detail and examine some ways to avoid them.

Having a Functional, Specialized Organization

An iterative approach means that every iteration goes through a full lifecycle: analysis, design, implementation, integration, and test. If a project team is organized around these functional areas, then there needs to be a lot of knowledge transfer among these teams. This increases the risk of miscommunication (see Figure 13.1) and typically means that a lot more time is spent on unproductive activities such as documenting, managing, and reviewing everything. Sure, some

A functional organization typically means that a lot more time is spent on unproductive activities.

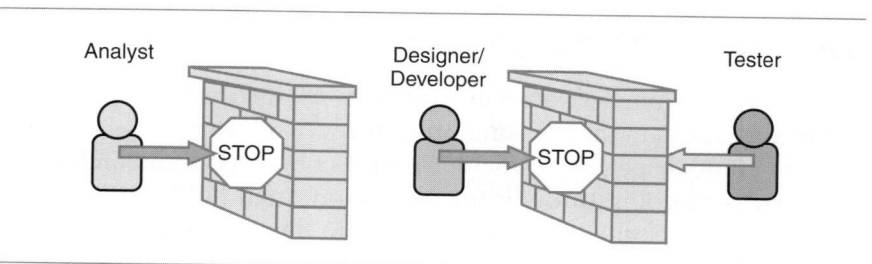

FIGURE 13.1 Functional Teams Have Inherent Communication Barriers. *An iterative approach requires high-bandwidth communication, which is very difficult to achieve if analysts, developers, and testers work in different teams. Assemble a cross-functional team, including some generalists, to address this issue.*

documentation is good, but functionally oriented teams tend to spend too much time on documentation, taking away valuable time from productive activities such as developing executable software.

Ideally, the team should be cross-functional, with at least some generalists who have more than one area of expertise. In Inception, you typically start with a small team—maybe 3 to 5 people for what may later become a 15-person project. For example, you might have

- A project manager who can help out with analysis.
- One or two analysts.
- An architect who can help to code the architecture.
- A lead developer to do design and implementation.
- A part-time tester for the whole system.

Each team member should also take responsibility for the quality of his or her own deliverables.

Not Setting the Right Stakeholder Expectations or Using an Old-Fashioned Acquisition Model

It is important to set the right stakeholder expectations. If executive management, customers, or other key stakeholders are used to another project lifecycle, you may experience a lot of problems. You may, for example, be required to

- Complete detailed planning of the entire project up-front, rather than creating an initial coarse project plan, complemented by detailed plans for the current and next iteration.
- Produce a complete requirements specification at the end of Inception, before funds are committed to the remainder of the project.
- Commit to a budget for the entire project by the end of Inception, before you have the necessary information. A majority of risks will be mitigated first during Elaboration, and any estimation of overall cost before major risks have been mitigated will by necessity contain a large degree of uncertainty.

These constraints may force you into following a waterfall approach —rather than an iterative one—with all the associated drawbacks. One common situation driving people toward a waterfall mentality is the use of an old-fashioned model for acquisition (contracting), where at the end of Inception you force a fixed bid on the remainder of the project, with fixed requirements, plans, and costs for the entire project. Rather, you should divide the project into two bids (see Figure 13.2), with one bid for the Elaboration phase and another (potentially fixed) bid on the Construction and Transition phases. This will drive the project toward a more economical and sound project lifecycle and avoid major risks such as late discovery of costs, schedule overruns, and failed implementations of requirements.

Too Many Developers at Project Start

A couple of years ago, one of our colleagues came to us and complained about a project on which he had just started work. Management had put 40 developers into the project from the start, together with a group of 7 or 8 analysts and architects to analyze the requirements and decide on the architecture. Our colleague, who was the lead analyst, continuously had developers in his office asking him for tasks, forcing our colleague to spend more time making up bogus tasks for the developers than analyzing requirements. There is no point adding large numbers of developers to a project before you have

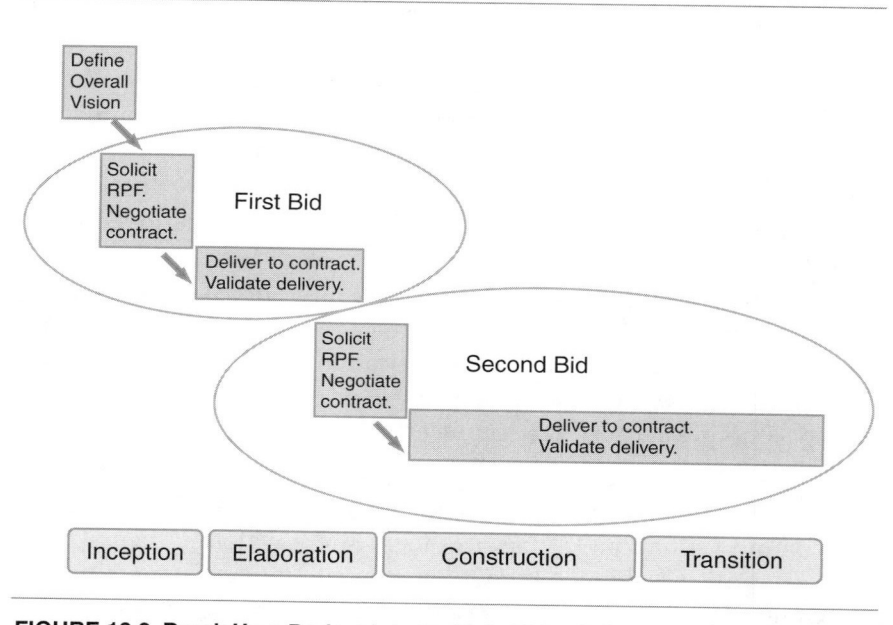

FIGURE 13.2 **Break Up a Project into Multiple Bids.** *Subcontracting of iterative projects should preferably be done through two or more bids. As an example, you can have one bid for the Elaboration phase and another bid for the Construction and Transition phases.*

a baselined architecture and before you know what problems you are trying to solve.[1] Everything that is built is being built on quicksand, you typically end up having to rewrite almost everything that is written, and the first delivered system becomes a patchwork.

---

1. There are naturally exceptions. In one project, we tasked a set of developers to independently develop a framework for later use, while we figured out what the application should do. This was somewhat successful since the developers happened to be very familiar with the domain and could make good assumptions of what components they would need later on. The risk with this approach, however, is that you may have to throw away a lot of your components that were not needed because they did not address the requirements.

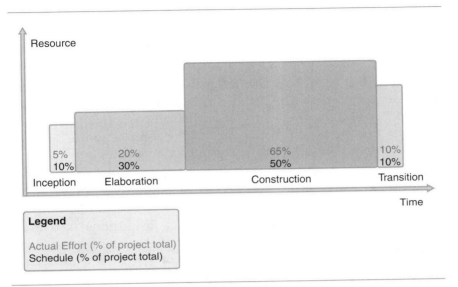

FIGURE 13.3 The Number of Developers Should Be Limited at Project Start. *You want to avoid having too many people in your project at the start. This figure shows that you typically start with a small team in Inception, increase a little in Elaboration, and then add more developers and testers to the team during Construction.*

Note that you need some development resources during Inception and especially in Elaboration. Since you need to design, implement, and test the architecture, you should typically have your most skilled developers involved during Elaboration, as they are building the skeleton structure upon which all future development is based. So have a small, highly skilled team through Elaboration, and scale up with additional developers as the architecture stabilizes (see Figure 13.3).

Solving the Easy Stuff First

It is often tempting to say, "This is a delicate issue, a problem on which we need a lot of time to think. Let us postpone its resolution until later, which will give us more time to think about it." The project

then embarks on all the easy tasks, never dedicating much attention to difficult problems. When it comes to the point at which a solution is needed, hasty solutions and decisions are made, or the project simply derails.

If at all possible, always attack the biggest risks first.

You want to do just the opposite: Tackle the hard stuff immediately. You should have a continuously updated risk list that should guide you in what to focus on in any given iteration. If at all possible, always attack the biggest risks first. If a project must fail for some reason, let it fail as soon as possible, before you have expended all your time and money.

Another related common mistake is not to continuously update the risk list. You performed a risk analysis at Inception and used it for planning, but then you forgot about risks that develop later in the project—and they come back to hurt you later. Risks should be re-evaluated constantly, on a monthly, if not weekly, basis. The original list of risks you developed was just tentative. It is only when the team starts doing concrete development that they will discover many other risks.

Having an Extended Initial Iteration

There is a risk in trying to do too much in the first iteration. Typically, there are one (maybe two) iteration(s) in Inception, and you want to make sure that those iterations are successful. This means that you need to deliver what you said you would deliver—on time. Sure, some minor delays might be acceptable, but massive delays are not. They set a bad precedent for the project team and make failure likely for the entire project. During Inception, **you want to establish an even rhythm for the project:** "We deliver a release every six weeks; we deliver a release every six weeks; we deliver...." Grady Booch refers to this as "developing a steady beat."[2]

If you do start running very late, do *not* just let the first iteration go on forever. Cut the scope, and if necessary add one more iteration, but make the team commit to a certain iteration length—two, four, or six weeks, for example. A steady rhythm will help you monitor whether the project is on track and distribute the stress in smaller increments

---

2. See Booch 1996.

FIGURE 13.4 Similar Iteration Lengths Help to Develop a Project Rhythm. *It is important not to have the first iteration be too long. Ideally, each iteration within the same phase should be the same length, so that the project will develop an even rhythm.*

every two, four, or six weeks, rather than subjecting the team to one big panic during the two months prior to delivery (see Figure 13.4). Note that the iteration length may vary based on objectives of the iteration and which phase you are in, but planning is, in general, simplified if iterations are of similar length (at least within the same phase). See Chapter 12 for more a detailed discussion on project planning.

Having Overlapping Iterations

Another very common trap is making iterations overlap too much (see Figure 13.5). Starting to plan the next iteration somewhere toward the last fifth of the current iteration, while attempting to have a significant overlap of activities (for example, starting detailed analysis, or designing and coding the next iteration before finishing the current one and learning from it), may look attractive when staring at a Gantt chart, but it will lead to problems. Some people will not be committed to following up and completing their own contribution to the current iteration. They may not be very responsive to fixing things, or they will just decide to take any and all feedback into consideration only in the next iteration. Some parts of the software will not be ready to support the work that has been pushed forward, and so on.

Although it is possible to divert some personnel to perform work unrelated to the current iteration, this should be kept to a minimum and only as an exception. This problem is often triggered by the

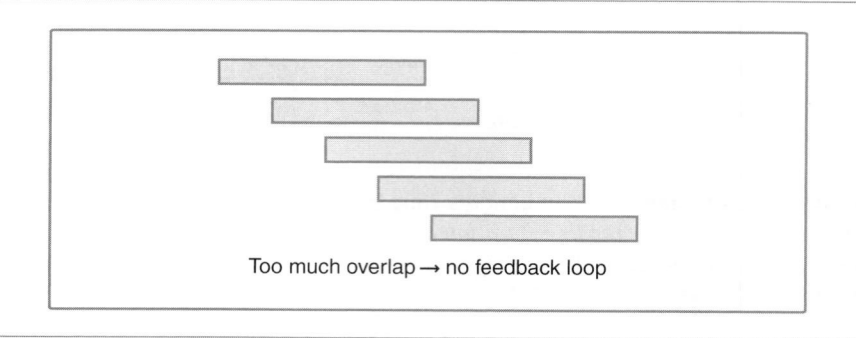

Too much overlap → no feedback loop

FIGURE 13.5 Large Iteration Overlap Defocuses Teams. *Having a large overlap between iterations may make team members less committed to completing current tasks and instead more apt to jumping to solve the latest problem. Overlapping iterations can also radically increase management overhead and prevent an effective feedback loop.*

narrow range of skills of some of the organization's members or a very rigid organization: Joe is an analyst, and this is the only thing he can or wants to do; he does not want to participate in design, implementation, or test. Another negative example: A large command and control project has its iterations so overlapped that they are basically all running in parallel at some point, requiring management to split the entire staff across iterations with no hope of sending back lessons learned from the earlier iterations.

Allowing Too Many Changes Late in the Project

Scrap and rework have to diminish from iteration to iteration.

In Chapter 2, we discussed that you should embrace change, especially early in the project. Change is good; it allows you to improve your solution. But iterative development does not mean scrapping everything at each iteration. Scrap and rework have to diminish from iteration to iteration, especially after you have a baselined architecture at the end of the Elaboration phase. If you allow too much change too late in the project, you are likely to run into delays, cost overruns, and potentially low or unsatisfactory quality. This means that you need to carefully consider what changes are worth making, especially toward the end of the project.

Developers often want to take advantage of iterative development to do gold plating: to introduce yet a better technique, to rework, and so on. The project manager has to be vigilant so as to avoid the rework of elements that are not broken—ones that are OK or good enough. Also, as the development team grows in size and as some people are moved around, new people are brought in. They might have their own ideas about how things should have been done.

Similarly, customers (or their representatives in the project: marketing or product management) may want to abuse the latitude offered by iterative development to accommodate changes or to change or add requirements with no end. This effect is sometimes called "requirements creep." Again, the project manager needs to be ruthless in making tradeoffs and in negotiating priorities. Roughly, by the end of the Elaboration phase, the requirements are baselined, and unless the schedule and budget are renegotiated, any change has a finite cost: Getting something in means pulling something out. Remember that "Perfect is the enemy of good."

Mistakes in Analysis, Architecture, Design, Implementation, and Testing

Transitioning from a waterfall approach to an iterative approach requires changes in the working procedures of all team members. It means that analysts, developers, architects, and testers need to change their working procedure and mindset. Among the common mistakes, we find the following:

- **Creating too many use cases** makes the requirements incomprehensible and is a sign of doing functional decomposition using the use-case symbol.
- **Analysis-paralysis** prevents effective iterative development and is caused by getting hung up on details.
- **Including design decisions in your requirements** forces design decisions to be made prematurely.

- **Not having stakeholder buy-in on requirements** leads you to implement a system that is likely to be rejected or radically changed later in the project.
- **"Not invented here" mentality** normally increases development and maintenance cost, as well as reduces the quality of the solution.
- **Ending Elaboration before the architecture is sufficiently stable** causes excessive rework, resulting in cost overruns and lower quality.
- **Focusing on inspections instead of executable software** causes an inefficient quality assurance process and creates a focus on byproducts of software development rather than on software itself.

Let's look at some of these mistakes and examine ways to avoid them.

Creating Too Many Use Cases

A common trap is breaking down use cases into snippets of functionality so small that you lose the benefits of the use-case paradigm. Typically, a 6-month project with 8 people would involve roughly 10 to 30 use cases. Decomposing the functions much further than this doesn't do you or anybody else any good.

Let's first look at what you should be trying to achieve with use cases. Each use case should do the following:

- Describe an interaction that's meaningful to users of the system and has a measurable value to them.
- Describe a complete interaction or flow of events between the system and the user. For instance, for an ATM system, making a withdrawal is a complete interaction; just entering your PIN, which is one of the steps in this flow, isn't.
- Drive the design effort by clarifying how elements collaborate to address a real user need. Component modeling alone often leaves glaring holes in a design; focusing instead on achieving desired user functionality ensures that the design works and is complete.
- Drive the testing effort by describing common ways that users want to interact with the system and ways that can be tested.

- Serve as a management tool by defining a set of functionality that management can assign to one or more team members to work on.

When you have too many use cases, here's what happens:

- It's hard for users to look at the use cases and state whether they provide value to them, since the approach to delivering functionality is so piecemeal.
- Since the use cases will describe a piecemeal functionality outside the context of useful user scenarios, the design effort becomes focused on delivering an operation or two, rather than on the necessary collaboration for addressing real user needs.
- The testing effort becomes bogged down in having to combine many test cases (derived from the use cases) to create meaningful tests.
- People assigned to work on different use cases continually run into each other and get in each other's way, since the use cases are so closely coupled.

To avoid this, look for the following signs indicating that your use cases are broken down too far:

- You can't measure the value that a use case provides to the user. This indicates that it represents too small a slice of a complete interaction.
- Use case A is always followed by use cases B and C. This indicates that they're probably one use case and should be merged.
- Two or more use cases have almost the same use-case description, only with smaller variations. Again, this indicates that they're probably one use case and should be merged.
- There are more "includes" and "generalizations"[3] than use cases. You should in principle never have more than one level of abstraction, and definitely never more than two levels.
- You can't come up with use-case descriptions (flows of events) that are more than a couple of paragraphs in length.

---

3. "Includes" and "generalizations" are relationships between use cases used to structure a use-case model. See Bittner 2003 for a discussion on when to use these relationships.

Having Analysis-Paralysis

The RUP is an iterative process. This means that you will have time later on to detail the requirements. **Do not spend too much time detailing the requirements in the Inception phase,** because you need to come up with an executable architecture quickly in order to eliminate key risks early on. And since you will baseline the executable architecture early in the next phase, Elaboration, your goal is to finish up the work in the Inception phase and move on.

The objectives of Inception are to define the scope and get an understanding of the most important requirements. You will be done with the requirements part of Inception once you have

- **Compiled a reasonably complete list of the expected actors and use cases.** It is fine to make smaller adjustments to the set of use cases later in the project, but typically not major changes. For example, if you have identified 20 use cases in Inception, in Elaboration you might add 1 and remove another.

- **Detailed the essential or critical use cases**—roughly 20 to 30 percent of all the use cases—so that you have a fairly solid idea of those use cases, ideally with accompanying screen prototypes or something similar. Continuing with the example, between 4 and 7 of the 20 use cases should have two-page descriptions; the rest need only a couple of paragraphs.

It should also be noted that small, co-located teams might choose to do less detailed documentation of use cases to save time.

Including Design Decisions in Your Requirements

Especially when writing requirements in the form of use cases, it is common that analysts include design decisions, such as the layout of the GUI or the implementation of various algorithms. This may cause bad design decisions to be locked in, as well as to defocus users and analysts from the objective of capturing and agreeing on requirements.

The following is an example of a requirement that includes design decisions:

> *The system searches through the database using start time and end time as search keys to verify which conference rooms are available at the indicated time. Available conference rooms are listed in green, and unavailable conference rooms are listed in red.*

Instead, you should remove design decisions such as how things are presented and what search algorithms will be used:

> *The system verifies which conference rooms are available during the indicated time. The system presents a list of all conference rooms and where available, conference rooms are graphically differentiated, making it easy to detect which rooms are available and which are not.*

Not Having Stakeholder Buy-In on Requirements

As you detail the vision, use cases, and nonfunctional requirements, you need to get buy-in and involvement from the whole project team, including customers, developers, and testers, to ensure that these are the right requirements. Failure to do so may mean that you are making investments toward requirements that will need to be radically changed, causing unnecessary rework. This does not mean that you should develop all requirements up-front or that all communication should be through requirements specifications, but you need to establish a common understanding of what system is being developed.

"Not Invented Here" Mentality

Architectures, or parts of architectures, are often reusable. Integrated Development Environments (IDEs) contain architectural mechanisms, patterns are available through the Web and through books,[4] you or other people in your company may have built similar types of systems before and know what works and what doesn't, and you may find Commercial Off-the-Shelf (COTS) components or package software that fits your needs. Whenever possible, you should strive to reuse solutions that work—whether they are components, patterns, processes, test plans, or other artifacts.

---

4. See Gamma 1995.

Unfortunately, some developers are extremely skeptical about using other, potentially suboptimal, solutions and prefer to develop a solution from scratch themselves. What is important to remember is that "Perfect is the enemy of good" (as we said earlier in the section Allowing Too Many Changes Late in the Project). You may be able to build a better solution yourself, but at what price?

Especially as an architect, you need to make sure that architectural patterns that have been developed during the Elaboration phase are not reinvented by various project members during later phases. This can be achieved by having training and design reviews. It is important that you properly communicate the availability of patterns and architectural mechanisms to all project members.

When considering the reuse of third-party components, these are a few considerations to make:

- You need to understand what requirements the components must meet. Then you need to see if the reusable component(s) fit those requirements or can be made to fit them. If not, you need to do a tradeoff: What is the cost saving versus how much you need to compromise on the requirements?

- You need to assess the quality of the reusable component. Is it properly documented and tested? If not, cost may become higher than writing something from scratch.

- Will a third party maintain the component, or do you need to maintain it?

- You need to look into legal rights and potential royalties. Is it economically feasible to use a third-party component? Do you still fully own the final product? What are your liabilities?

As you can see, it is not always obvious that you should reuse existing components, but the upside with reuse is in general much greater than the downside. Also be aware that projects often underestimate the complexity in doing something themselves, and feel they can do everything better and faster themselves. Many years ago, we attended a conference where the speaker asked one half of the room to write down how long they thought it would take them to solve a certain problem. The other half of the room was asked to write down how long they thought it would take the person next to them to solve that same problem. Amazingly enough, the average person thought he or she could solve the problem in almost half the time as the other person.

Ending Elaboration Before the Architecture Is Sufficiently Stable

There are several benefits for baselining the executable architecture by the end of Elaboration, including

- Allowing you to mitigate technical risks.
- Providing you with a stable foundation upon which to build the system.
- Enabling effective reuse of large-scale components.
- Facilitating the introduction of more developers and more junior developers, since many of the most difficult design issues have been resolved and developers can work within well-defined areas.
- Allowing you to accurately estimate how long it will take to complete the project.
- Allowing much more parallel work.

By rushing ahead and initiating Construction before you have a designed, implemented, and tested architecture, you will lose out on some or all of the benefits, ultimately causing excessive rework, resulting in cost overruns and lower quality. You need to decide whether to add another iteration in Elaboration, and hence accept a delay in the project, or whether to move into Construction and build your application on a brittle architecture. The following provides you some guidance on when to choose which approach:

- If you add an iteration to Elaboration, you are less likely to run into major rework due to architectural issues later in the project. The delay introduced by adding an iteration can be recuperated by, for example, cutting scope or quality levels. As an alternative, you can accept that the delay in getting the architecture right will cause a delay in the delivery of the final product. Large projects, architecturally complex systems, unprecedented systems, or

systems with a lot of new technology should consider choosing this alternative.

- If you choose to move into Construction in spite of the architecture being unstable, you risk having to rework the architecture at a later stage, causing delays to the project that could be substantial. You may also lose out on other of the mentioned benefits, which have a baselined architecture. Smaller projects, or projects with limited architecture, familiar technology, or familiar domains, should consider choosing this alternative.

It should be noted that the more unstable the architecture is, the more risky the second approach is. It should also be noted that the Extreme Programming (XP) process in general favors the latter approach, which also explains why XP is more suitable for smaller to medium-sized projects with limited architectural risks. XP assumes that refactoring will allow you to evolve to a good architecture without causing major or unnecessary rework. We believe these are risky assumptions to make. This issue is probably one of the larger points of disagreement between the RUP and XP.

But how do you know that you are sufficiently done with the architecture? There will still be a need for doing some rework of the architecture, but the rework should be in the ballpark of 5 to 15 percent of the architecture (measured, for example, in changes to defined interfaces of components and subsystems). The best indicator for whether you are done is to look at the rate of change of code and interfaces. Toward the end of Elaboration, the rate of change in interfaces (operations defined for key components and subsystems) should diminish. By extrapolating the curve in Figure 13.6, you can assess when you reached the stage where future changes will be less than 15 percent.

When doing iterative development, you will find the rate of change in code, requirements, designs, and so on to be an excellent measure of completion. Ask yourself: Are requirements and architecture stable toward the end of Elaboration? Is the code stable toward the end of Construction?

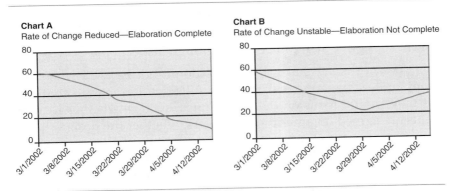

FIGURE 13.6 Rate of Change in Interfaces Indicates When Elaboration Can Be Ended. *In Chart A we see a clear diminishing and consistent trend in the rate of change of interfaces, making us comfortable that the architecture is stabilizing. In Chart B, we do not see such a clear trend, alerting us that we are not moving toward a stable architecture. Elaboration cannot be completed.*

Focusing on Inspections Instead of Assessing Executable Software

A strong focus on inspections is a sign of a waterfall mentality, where the majority of quality assessment activities focuses on byproducts of software development, such as plans, requirements, and designs, rather than on the primary products (software and its quality).

The old school of quality assurance compares a waterfall approach with no inspections to a waterfall approach using inspections and finds that the latter produces code of considerably higher quality. This is a correct observation but fails to recognize the fundamental problem: the usage of the waterfall development approach itself.

Rather, you should compare a waterfall approach using inspections with an iterative approach focusing on continuous integration and testing. By using automated testing, such as runtime analysis (memory leak testing and application performance testing), developers can

discover defects before they consider development to be complete. Automated testing technology and the use of continuous integration and testing typically allows you to identify and correct many defects at a cheaper price than can be done through inspections.

This does not mean that inspections should not be used when you adopt an iterative approach; they are still useful in many situations. But they should focus on the right things, such as whether requirements are agreed on among stakeholders, whether the design guidelines have been followed (are architectural mechanisms properly used?), or whether there are opportunities for reuse. But most classical design inspections can either be automated by tools or can find defects that could have been found by a less-expensive method by developers and testers using proper automation.

At the end of the day, what really counts is how good your code is, not how good your byproducts of software development are.

Conclusion

There are common mistakes project teams can make when adopting and using the RUP. Derived from our experiences and those the Rational field organization has made in working with thousands of customers over the years, we divided the mistakes into three areas:

- Mistakes when adopting the RUP
- Mistakes when managing iterative development
- Mistakes when doing analysis, architecture, design, implementation, and testing

Knowing how to detect these anti-patterns, and knowing how to avoid them, will help you adopt the RUP more effectively.

PART IV

A ROLE-BASED GUIDE TO THE RATIONAL UNIFIED PROCESS

CHAPTER 14

A Project Manager's Guide to the RUP

You are a project manager and are just about to use the RUP approach. This chapter is a guide to understanding your role in a software development project using the RUP. You will find a definition of the **role** of project manager and its interactions with other roles. We will introduce some of the key artifacts that project managers will develop and use. Finally we will review some of the key RUP **activities** project managers are involved in.

The Mission of a Project Manager

There are many reasons why a project may fail or result in poor quality. Many of them may be attributed to all kinds of technical reasons, and we are often pretty quick to do so; technology is a convenient and nameless scapegoat. But authors and consultants such as Roger Pressman who have witnessed many projects can testify: "If a post-mortem [assessment] were to be conducted for every project, it is very likely that a consistent theme would be encountered: *Project management was weak*."[1]

---

1. See Pressman 2001, p. 55.

A Complex Role

"People, product, process, project—in that order," is how the same Roger Pressman defines the scope of software development project management.

- **People.** Software development is very human-intensive and depends highly on the skills and the coordination of work among people. Many of the activities of a project manager will rotate around people and are focused mainly on the development team.

- **Product.** Nothing can be planned, studied, or produced if the objectives and scope of the software to be developed are not clearly established, and although the project manager does not define all the details of the requirements, your role is to make sure that the objectives are set and that progress is tracked relative to these objectives. This involves extensive communication with parties external to the development team, as well as with the development team.

If one person has to fully understand the process of developing software, it is the project manager.

- **Process.** If one person has to fully understand the process of developing software, it is the project manager. Project management is the embodiment of process. Having the RUP or not having it makes no difference if project management is not fully process-literate and does not drive the process. The process, supported by the right tools, is the common roadmap, understood and used by all team members.

- **Project.** And then, once on the road, the project manager manages the project itself, planning, controlling, monitoring, and correcting the trajectory as often as necessary. The project manager is dynamically steering and adapting.

Throughout the lifecycle, the project manager should keep focused on the results.

In the very end, though, the manager of a software project will not be judged on good efforts, good intentions, using the right process, or having done everything "by the book," but on *results*. So throughout the lifecycle, the project manager should keep focused on the results, or any partial results that are getting the project closer to success. A RUP project is a collaborative effort of several parties, including the project manager. And within the very dynamic context of iterative development, the role of the project manager is more to "steer and adapt" than to "plan and track" (as often is the case in other domains).

So the role of the project manager is complex and requires many different skills to be able to dynamically steer and adapt:

- **Technical skills** to understand the issues at hand—the technologies and the choices to be made. Far too often, we run into organizations that still believe that a project manager just manages resources (including people), and does not need to understand the product or the process. As a project manager, you do not need to be a technical expert in all aspects, and you should rely on the right people to help you on the technical side (see the Chapter 16 on architects and their relationship with the manager), but a good level of understanding of the technical issues will still be necessary to achieve the best results.

- **Communication skills** to deal with many different stakeholders and have an ability to jump from one style to another. For example, from personal communication (face-to-face, such as interviews and meetings) to impersonal (status reports), from formal (customer reviews and audits) to informal (small group brainstorming, or just walking around the project to test the mood).

A Person or a Team?

We tend to think of *the* project manager as one person. And in most small- to medium-sized projects (3 to 15 people), only one person will fulfill this role. But the RUP describes the project manager not as a person, but as a **role** that a person will play, and it is likely that on large projects, more than one person will play this role. There will still be reason to have one clear project leader, but that person should not feel the need to run *all* the RUP activities in the project management discipline.

It is likely that on large projects, more than one person will play the Project Manager role.

First, there can be a small team of people doing the project management. One can be focused on planning; another one can deal with some of the key communication interfaces, with product management or the customer; another one can follow internal progress. Note that some of this specialization is already acknowledged by the RUP,

which defines more than one manager role; there are managers' roles with specialized expertise, for example, configuration manager, deployment manager, test manager, and process engineer.

Also, for larger software development organizations, say 25 people or more, it is common to have the organization broken up into smaller teams, and each team lead will be delegated part of the project management role, relative to one team. In other words, the project manager has delegated some of the routine management and will get some "eyes and ears" all across the project.

Finally, in larger projects, some groups can be set up to handle some of the management activities in a more formal way and to support the project manager:

- To monitor the project's progress: a Project Review Authority (PRA) and a Change Control Board (CCB)
- To set up and improve the software process: a Software Engineering Process Authority (SEPA, sometimes also called SEPG)
- To drive the definition and adoption of tools, a Software Engineering Environment Authority (SEEA)

These groups are set up with people of the right expertise and authority, sometimes with full-time people, and they operate when necessary to support the management group or when dictated by the process.

Project Management

"Project management is the application of knowledge, skills, tools, and techniques to project activities in order to meet and exceed stakeholders' needs and expectations from a project."[2]

Meeting or exceeding stakeholders' expectations invariably involves balancing competing demands among

---

2.   See PMI 2000.

- Scope, time, cost, and quality.
- Stakeholders, internal and external, with different needs and expectations.
- Identified requirements (needs) and unidentified requirements (expectations).

Scope of the Project Management Discipline in the RUP

An important warning is now due. The RUP deliberately does *not* cover all aspects of project management, and it remains focused on the engineering aspects.

Despite what we wrote above about the first "P," **People,** the project management discipline in the RUP does not cover many of the aspects related to managing people—all the **human resources** management. So, in the RUP you will not find guidance on how to hire, train, compensate, evaluate, or discipline people.

Similarly, the RUP does not deal with **financial** issues, such as budget, allocation, accounting, or reporting. Nor does it deal with legal and contractual issues, acquisition and sales, licensing, or subcontracting. Additionally, the RUP does not deal with some of the administration issues associated with people, finances, and projects.

There is a wide range of practices around the world on these topics. And there is a wide body of knowledge accessible and not specifically linked to software development.

One great source of information is the *Guide to the Project Management Body of Knowledge (PMBOK),* developed under the auspices of the Project Management Institute (PMI) and endorsed by IEEE as Standard 1490-1998, *Adoption of the PMI Guide to PMBOK.*

The RUP does, however, concentrate on the software-specific aspects of project management, that is, the areas where the nature of software has an impact, making it different. The activities that are not covered by the RUP do take a significant amount of time and effort, and they require some skills. So they should not be overlooked when establishing the schedule of the people managing a project.

The RUP deliberately does not cover all aspects of project management, and it remains focused on the engineering aspects.

Software Development Plan (SDP)

It is hard to reduce software project management to a handful of recipes, but let us try to define the overall pattern—the good practice.

The best approaches we have found so far is for the project manager:

1. To express the project's **plans** (the expectations as seen from the project management) in the various areas: scope, time, cost, quality, process.

2. To understand what could adversely affect these plans over time; that is, what are the **risks** if the project does not follow these plans.

3. To monitor progress to see how the project stays aligned to the plan, using some objective metrics whenever possible.

4. To revise any of these plans if the project goes significantly off-course.

5. Finally, to learn from your mistakes, so that the organization will not repeat them in the next iteration or the next project.

Consequently, the key artifact a project manager will focus on is a **Software Development Plan**, which is an umbrella artifact containing many different plans, each one dealing with one management topic:

- Project plan and iteration plans (see Chapter 12)
- Test plan
- Configuration Management plan
- Measurement plan
- Risks
- Documentation plan
- The specific process the project will use—its development case

For better clarity, visibility, and accountability, the Software Development Plan may be one of the few formal artifacts of a project.

As the project unfolds over time, these plans are refined, corrected, and improved, as one may expect from iterative development; and to achieve this, other tactical artifacts are created. They are usually taking a snapshot view of the project to allow concerted reasoning about some tactical decision to be made:

- Review record (minutes)
- Issues lists
- Status assessment

One important aspect of the SDP is to define more precisely the process the project will use: This is the role of the **development case** described in Chapters 10 and 11. The project manager will set up and maintain the right degree of formality, the "level of ceremony" as Grady Booch calls it, that is adequate for this project. And this development case will also evolve as the project unfolds, based on the lessons learned at each iteration.

Iterative Development

This sounds like a leitmotiv in this book, but it is worth mentioning again. In an **iterative development,** you do not plan once and then monitor the project and try to coerce it to conform to the plan at any cost. You plan, and then replan, as necessary, again and again. You may therefore end up in a different spot from where you had intended to arrive in the very first plan, but you will find yourself at a better spot, or a more modest but more realistic spot, which is better than never arriving anywhere.

If you have never managed an iterative project, it can be daunting the first time.[3]

Risks

To effectively manage iterative development, the second concept the beginner RUP project manager must master and keep constantly in mind is that of **risk.** There are inherently many risks, of various magnitude and probability, that could affect a software project. Managing a software project is not a simple matter of blindly applying a set of recipes and templates to create wonderful plans engraved in stone and then bringing them back to the team for execution. Managing a project involves being constantly aware of new risks, new events,

Managing a project involves being constantly aware of new risks, new events, situations, and changes that may affect the project and reacting rapidly to them.

---

3. See Kruchten 2000b.

situations, and changes that may affect the project and reacting rapidly to them. The successful project manager is the one who is present, is curious, speaks to team members, inquires about technology, asks "why" and "how" and "why" again to identify new, unsuspected risks—and then applies the appropriate recipes to mitigate them.

Metrics

Another key word for the RUP project manager is **metrics.** To avoid being sidetracked by subjectivity or blinded by biases, experiences, or knowledge deficiencies, the project manager establishes some objective criteria to monitor (more or less automatically) some aspects of the project. A few measurements can be put in place to help you gather variables such as expenditure, completion (how much of the functionality is complete), testing coverage (how much have you tested), and defects (found and fixed), as well as the trends over time. Other useful metrics involve changes over time: amount of scrap and rework, or requirements churn, which can be tracked via a good Configuration Management system. The smart project manager would want to automate as much as possible the collection of these metrics to free more time for activities that might require more human interaction.

Metrics, from the current project and from previous projects, are what will help the team develop **estimates,** and in particular workload estimates (see Chapter 12 on Planning). These estimates are a shared responsibility between the project manager and the rest of the team. The project manager cannot unilaterally impose them on a team.

Activities of a Project Manager

So what is it exactly that a project manager is expected to do, according to the RUP?

In the RUP you will find that the activities are grouped by theme:

- Activities to launch a new project
- Activities to define and evolve all elements of the Software Development Plan

- Activities to start, run, and close a project, a phase, or an iteration
- Activities to monitor a project

Launching a New Project

Based on an initial Vision Document, a project manager develops an initial Business Case that contrasts the scope of the project (and its expected duration and cost) with the potential return. The Vision contains the gist of the requirements: what it is that you want to achieve. The Business Case articulates the rationale for doing this software project. The Vision and the Business Case should be revisited many times until a project can be initiated and approved. It is never too early to start identifying risks, that is, any event that may adversely affect the project or make it fail. These risks will be the first thing the project should focus on in the next iteration.

Developing the Software Development Plan

Depending on the scope and size of the project, a project manager will develop some or all of an SDP. The organization may have developed ready-made templates that are more specific than the ones you will find in the RUP, with large segments already prefilled.

There are two important parts of an SDP:

- Planning time and resources, in a project plan and a staffing plan (which we described more fully in Chapter 12).
- Specifying the process this project will use: artifacts to be developed and level of ceremony and formality resulting in a development case (as we described in Chapter 10). This includes specific guides, style guides, and conventions to be used in the project.

Other plans dealing with Configuration Management, documentation, testing, tools, and so on may have to be developed.

Starting and Closing Phases and Iteration

The project manager will plan in more detail the contents and objectives of phases and of iterations by specifying the success criteria that

will be used to evaluate the work at the concluding milestones. These activities will require extensive interactions with all the team members and cannot be done in an ivory tower. Each phase and iteration will need to be properly staffed and activities allocated to team members.

As an iteration (or a phase with its major milestone) concludes, the project manager will assess the results of the iteration or phase, and compare them with the expected results specified in the SDP. Discrepancies will trigger revision of the plans or rescoping the project differently. The process itself may be improved.

For example, looking at the risks previously identified ("Integration of technology X with middleware Y"), you assess that you have indeed successfully integrated them in a prototype and tested, therefore eliminating this as a risk.

Monitoring the Project

As an ongoing activity, the project manager will use some indicators to monitor progress and compare it to the plans. This can take various levels of formality and use a combination of metrics (such as defects discovery and resolution rates) and reviews (informal and formal) to assess conformance to plans and quality of the product.

For example, if the defects discovery rate drops dramatically, this is a signal (a) that the testing effort is stalling, (b) that the new builds are not bringing any new substantial functionality, or (c) simply that the product is becoming stable.

There is at least one assessment per iteration, and somewhat more formality at the closing of a phase, as these major milestones may involve some strategic decision about the pursuit of the project. They place you at a point where you can consider cancellation or a significant rescoping of the project.

Finding Your Way in the RUP

To get started with the RUP, it is vital that a project manager thoroughly understands the concept of **iterative development** and the

RUP lifecycle (phases and iterations). Then there are some key concepts: risk management, quality, metrics, and how the process is described (Roles, Activities, and Artifacts). As necessary, check the RUP Glossary for definitions. If you are familiar with project management, but not specifically with iterative software projects, it is in the area of **planning** that you may have the most to learn, and especially planning an iterative project (as described in Chapter 12).

You can enter the RUP via the Role: Project Manager and reach the various activities that define this role. Alternatively, you may start from the Artifact: Software Development Plan (its template and some examples). From there navigate to the various activities that contribute to its development, or more precisely, to the development of the various plans it contains. This will lead you to the more specialized roles of Configuration Manager, Test Manager, and so on.

On small projects, or in a small software development organization, it is highly likely that the same person who plays the role of project manager will also be the process engineer, defining the project's development case, facilitating the enactment of the process, and getting involved in process improvement activities as a result of iteration (or project) assessment. Then see the Role: Process Engineer.

Do not forget that a project manager will interact with many other roles and participate in their activities, in some form or another. In particular, the project manager will have to interact and coordinate almost daily with the Architect(s) and get involved in various reviews.

Conclusion

Following a defined process, such as an instance of the RUP, is not an easy way for a project manager to abdicate responsibilities and forgo common sense. The job does not consist in blindly developing any and all artifacts described in the RUP, hoping that the right thing will happen. The tasks do not consist of allocating all activities of the RUP to the team members and then saying, "Oh, I simply followed the RUP! I do not understand why we failed." Recall that you should

select out of the RUP the right set of artifacts, the right methods and techniques, and adapt them to your context. You must understand the project and the product deeply, and work with the architect, the analysts, the designers, and the testers.

You will be judged on concrete results, not on the means you have put in place.

You will be judged on concrete results, not on the means you have put in place. Your role is to steer and continuously adapt the process as the project unfolds, deciding which artifacts and which activities are bringing concrete results. To do this, you must get deeply involved in the project life, from a technical standpoint, to understand rapidly the key decisions to be made, to seize opportunities to get certain results faster, to manage the scope of the project, to "size" the process. This is done efficiently only in a collaborative manner, not by imposing a rigid bureaucracy, setting up a distance between project management and the rest of the team.

Remember also that all the management activities *not* described in the RUP are also very important. You are not managing machines; you are not managing behaviors; you are managing *people*. Just running around and telling them what to do and pointing at the RUP won't do. You are setting goals and establishing a software development culture, a culture of collaboration and trust. And this is done through a high and constant level of communication.

So, to summarize:

- The project manager is not an innocent bystander but is part of a team and works collaboratively with this team.
- The project manager is responsible for the development and modification of the Software Development Plan.
- The plan is based on a configured process, adapted to fit the context of the project.
- The project manager is responsible for making the appropriate tradeoffs to manage the scope of the project and of each iteration.
- The project manager is constantly focused on risks—any risks— and how to mitigate them, should they prove to be in the way of success.
- The project manager keeps the focus on real results, not on intermediate and sometimes abstract artifacts.

Resources for the Project Manager

Further Reading

Murray Cantor. *Software Leadership: A Guide to Successful Software Development*. Boston: Addison-Wesley, 2002.

Tom Gilb. *Principles of Software Engineering Management*. Reading, MA: Addison-Wesley, 1988.

James A. Highsmith. *Adaptive Software Development: A Collaborative Approach to Managing Complex Systems*. New York: Dorset House Publishing, 2000.

IEEE Standard 1490-1998. "Adoption of the PMI Guide to the Project Management Body of Knowledge." New York: IEEE, 1998.

IEEE Standard 1058-1998. "Standard for Software Project Management Plans." New York: IEEE, 1998.

Steve McConnell. *Software Project Survival Guide*. Redmond, WA: Microsoft Press, 1997.

Fergus O'Connell. *How to Run Successful Projects*. Upper Saddle River, NJ: Prentice-Hall, 1994.

PMI. *Guide to the Project Management Body of Knowledge (PMBOK Guide)*. William R. Duncan (editor). Newton Square, PA: Project Management Institute (PMI), 2000.

On the Web

Look in *The Rational Edge* (www.therationaledge.com) for management articles, in particular the various lively pieces by Joe Marasco, on his experience managing software projects. Check the "Franklin's Kite" section.

And see Philippe Kruchten, "From Waterfall to Iterative Development—A Tough Transition for Project Managers," in *The Rational Edge*, December 2000. http://www.therationaledge.com/content/dec_00/m_iterative.html.

Training Resources

The following training course has been developed to support RUP users; it is delivered by IBM Software and its partners (see www.rational.com for more information):

- Mastering the Management of Iterative Development (three days).

CHAPTER 15

An Analyst's Guide to the RUP

You are a business analyst, system analyst, product manager, or other person involved with business modeling, requirements management, or user-interface (UI) prototyping. This chapter provides an overview of the responsibilities of an analyst in a RUP project. We also provide resources such as training courses and recommend reading that will help make you more proficient as an analyst.

Your Mission as an Analyst

As an analyst you wear many hats, and you need a wide variety of skills. Your overall objective is to define and communicate to all stakeholders what the system should do. This can be broken down into the following high-level tasks:

- Understand the needs of the users
- Understand the needs of other stakeholders
- Document, prioritize, and communicate the requirements
- Negotiate requirements and facilitate customer acceptance of the application

Carrying out these tasks typically requires the following:

- Proficiency in managing relationships with a variety of stakeholders

The overall objective of the analyst is to define and communicate to all stakeholders what the system should do.

287

- A good understanding of the problem domain, or the ability to acquire this knowledge rapidly
- Thorough, clear, and concise written and oral communication
- The ability to write clear and concise requirements
- An overall understanding of the software development lifecycle and how the analyst's work fits into it

An analyst is primarily involved in the Business Modeling, Requirements, and Analysis & Design disciplines.

An analyst is primarily involved in the Business Modeling, Requirements, and Analysis & Design disciplines of the RUP. Figure 15.1 shows how the emphasis of these disciplines varies over the four phases.

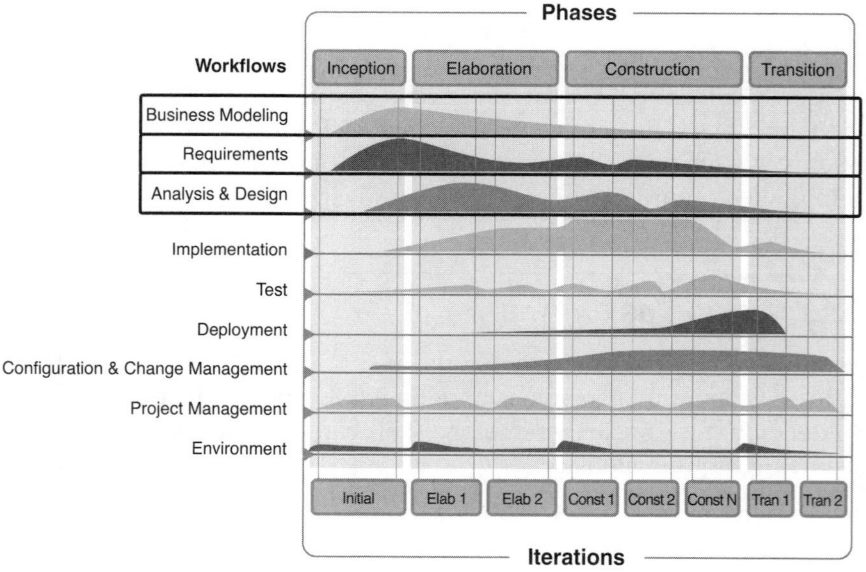

FIGURE 15.1 An Analyst's Involvement in the RUP Lifecycle. *An analyst is primarily involved in the RUP disciplines of Business Modeling, Requirements, and Analysis & Design—this means that they do most of their work in the Inception and Elaboration phases. Analysts also play an important role during Construction and Transition.*

- The analyst contributes most during the **Inception** and **Elaboration** phases, when requirements are identified and stabilized. The analyst's responsibility here is to ensure that the right application is built.
- During the **Construction** and **Transition** phases, the analyst is less involved, but there will still be some work with detailing requirements and analyzing the impact of any changing requirements or business models.

Where Do You Start?

The amount of effort required to define the right system varies tremendously. Depending on what impact new software systems have on your business, the analysis of the business operation may be anything from a large-scale business re-engineering effort to a minimal research effort. Let's look at a couple of different situations:

- **Business NOT well understood.** You first need to understand the business before you build the supporting software. This is when you need to do business engineering. Business engineering is a big field—we will summarize only a small area of it called **business modeling**.[1] The next section, Understand How Your Business Should Operate, briefly describes business modeling and how to translate business models into software requirements.
- **Business well understood.** Most applications are developed to support an existing, and well-understood, business. In this case, an analyst would commence working as described in the following sections, Understand Stakeholder Needs and Develop a Vision.

You first need to understand the business before you build the supporting software.

Understand How Your Business Should Operate

The RUP approach proposes a notation and process to be used for business engineering that are very similar to those used for software

---

1. For a more complete description of the RUP's approach to business engineering, see Jacobson 1994.

development. This approach facilitates communication between teams analyzing the business and teams developing software. Business engineering is primarily done by larger projects or organizations. Note that some of these techniques also may be used by smaller teams, but focus on only the parts of the business that are the most unclear or crucial for the set of software systems you plan to develop. The information is possibly captured less formally, but the thought process you go through is the same.

What business processes are required to support your business stakeholders?

You need to understand what business processes are required to support your business stakeholders. These processes are represented by business use cases, which describe the services your business will provide to your customers. The definition and the way business use cases are described are very similar to how software use cases are described, except the "system" being described is the entire business operation (a business system), not only the parts being automated. As an example, if your business is a store, your business use cases may be the following:

- **Provide information about available products.** Later, this can be implemented by salespersons in a store or by a Web site.
- **Accept and process order.** There may be many different software use cases to support this business use case, ranging from e-shopping to information systems supporting in-store salespersons.

The RUP product provides a simple path for deriving software system requirements from the business use-case and business object model.

The workflow of a business use case can be described textually in use-case descriptions as well as visually using UML diagrams (see Figure 15.2). You also describe the realization of those workflows in terms of how roles in the organization collaborate to execute the business process. Roles and deliverables of the process are represented by classes and objects in a business object model (see Figure 15.3).

You also need to identify the applications needed to support the business processes. The RUP product provides a simple path for deriving software system requirements from the business use-case and business object model.[2] Coupling the development of software features with the business processes they support helps you understand the

---

2. See Guidelines: Going from Business Models to Systems under Business Modeling, in the RUP product.

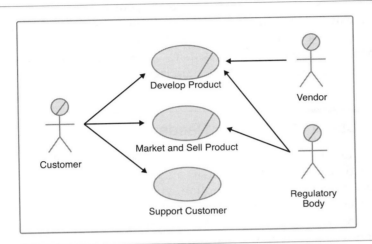

FIGURE 15.2 Business Use-Case Model for Product Company. *A business use-case model shows which business process (business use cases) is provided for which customers/business partners (business actors).*

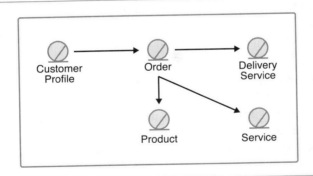

FIGURE 15.3 Business Object Model for Order. *A business object model captures the responsibilities, organizational units, and important concepts and items within your business, and how they relate to each other. This figure shows how the concept Order relates to other concepts, such as Customer Profile and Product. A model of concepts only is sometimes called a domain model, since it provides a good understanding of the problem domain.*

value various software features have for your business. Understanding the value of software features assists you in prioritizing work and investing project resources wisely to maximize business benefits when building the software systems. This is an area where many business-engineering approaches are lacking.

Understand Stakeholder Needs

A stakeholder is an individual or entity that is materially affected by the outcome of the system, such as a user, business sponsor, buyer, or product manager.

A stakeholder is an individual or entity that is materially affected by the outcome of the system, such as a user, business sponsor, buyer, or product manager. During Inception, you need to elicit requests from the project stakeholders to understand what their most important needs are. The collected stakeholder requests can be regarded as a "wish list" that will be used as primary input to define the high-level features of the system, as described in the Vision, which drives the specification of the more detailed software requirements.

You should identify a small stakeholder team (say, two to five people) that represents the various groups that have a stake in the project. If this team is too large, you can spend more time managing the group than understanding stakeholder needs. At the same time, you need balance—if the team is too small, you may not include everyone impacted by the results of the project.

The stakeholder wish list can be gathered through interviews or by arranging and facilitating a two- to four-hour workshop with the stakeholder team. During the session, discuss what the system should do, and document requests made by participants. You often need to get the discussion moving by asking leading questions such as, "What are the current problems you face with the existing system?", "What tasks do you spend the most time on today?", and "Which of your current tasks can be automated?"

As you document the requests, prioritize them, and note who made the request. You should also consider reviewing the results of the workshop with a representative subset of customers or users in a follow-up session. In this session, identify any issues that need to be clarified and, in turn, any tasks that need to be completed, and assign people to those tasks.

Stakeholder requests can be documented formally or informally, depending on the size and complexity of the project. For smaller projects, you might just create an informal wish list that is used as input for initial requirements work and then is thrown away. For larger projects—especially if contractual agreements are involved—you may choose to maintain a separate Stakeholder Request document.

Stakeholder requests can be documented formally or informally, depending on the size and complexity of the project.

As mentioned earlier, eliciting stakeholder requests is primarily done in Inception, with many updates in Elaboration. However, throughout the project, you will get useful requests from stakeholders. These are documented in Change Requests, and they should be continually reviewed to determine their suitability for inclusion in the project.

Also, if you are refining an existing system, reviewing change requests usually provides excellent information about stakeholder needs. Walk through all change requests, and identify which may qualify for inclusion in the next version of the system.

Develop a Vision

A **Vision** defines the stakeholders' view of the product to be developed, specified in terms of the stakeholders' key needs and features, and provides the contractual basis for the more detailed technical requirements. The most essential things captured in a Vision include the following:

- **Stakeholders list:** Customers, users, investors, product managers, designers, testers, and so on.
- **Constraints:** Budgetary constraints, a list of technology selections, operating systems, and required coexistence or compatibility with existing systems.
- **Problem statement:** A distinct description of the problem you are attempting to solve (described in more detail later).
- **Feature list:** A list of services provided by the system for the users of that system (described in more detail later).

As we discussed in Chapter 6, for very small projects this could be an informal document, maybe even an e-mail message capturing what was

on a whiteboard. For average-sized projects, you might write a **Vision Document** of a few pages; large projects may require quite an extensive Vision Document. Let's take a closer look at some of these sections.

Problem Statement

The **problem statement** forces the team to specify concretely the problem they are attempting to solve. The following format can be used:

> **The problem of** <describe the problem>
> **affects** <the stakeholders affected by the problem>.
> **The impact of which is** <what the impact of the problem is>.
> **A successful solution would** <list some key benefits of a successful solution>.

A problem statement could look like the following:

> **The problem of** untimely and improper resolution of customer service issues
> **affects** our customers, customer support reps, and service technicians.
> **The impact of which is** customer dissatisfaction, perceived lack of quality, unhappy employees, and loss of revenue.
> **A successful solution would** provide real-time access to a troubleshooting database by support representatives and facilitate dispatch of service technicians, in a timely manner, to only those locations in genuine need of assistance.

Feature List

A **feature** is a service provided by the system that can be observed by a user of the system, and that directly fulfills a stakeholder need. To identify the right set of features, you need to analyze the stakeholder requests and understand how they help provide the benefits described in the problem statement.

Each feature should have the following:

- A short description

- A **value attribute** indicating the business value the feature provides (for example, low, medium, or high)
- A **cost attribute** indicating how complex/costly the feature is to implement

By looking at the value and cost, you can now prioritize the features. You may, for example, choose to use priority levels of 1 through 5. A common problem in projects is assigning almost all features to Priority 1—this makes prioritization meaningless.[3] To avoid this, you can force separation of requirements so they are not all of the same priority level. There are many ways to achieve this—here is a typical approach to prioritization:

- Assume that you have only 50 percent or less of available resources. Assign the highest priority features you expect to be able to develop with those resources (yes, it will be a big guess, but when in doubt, be pessimistic) as Priority 1.
- Assume that you have only 80 percent of available resources. Assign the next set of high-priority features you expect to be able to develop with those resources as Priority 2.
- Assume that you have 100 percent of available resources. Assign the next set of high-priority features you expect to be able to develop with those resources as Priority 3.
- Assign the remaining features as Priorities 4 and 5 (that is, as candidates for future projects).

Prioritization forces you to make some preliminary, but tough, decisions on how to use your resources. If progress is slower than expected and, for example, you have to cut 20 percent of the features, you would in the example cut all Priority 3 features and postpone them to later projects. You will revisit and fine-tune the priority list many times during Inception and Elaboration. And you will use the list frequently in Construction and Transition to make sure that you make the right decisions if you need to descope the project to handle unexpected delays.

A common problem in projects is assigning almost all features to Priority 1— this makes prioritization meaningless.

Prioritization forces you to make some preliminary, but tough, decisions on how to use your resources.

---

3. It should be noted that in some rare cases, especially for embedded systems, all features really should be of Priority 1 because the system cannot be delivered without all of the specified features.

The analyst typically proposes the initial prioritization of features, reviews them with the project manager, architect, and the stakeholder team, and then modifies the list based on feedback.

Develop a Use-Case Model and Glossary

A use-case model describes a system's functional requirements in terms of actors and use cases. An **actor** represents a **type of user** of the system, or **another system** that will interact with the system. A **use case** describes how each actor will interact with the system.

Here are 10 steps that are quite useful—a "to-do" list to get the use-case model right:

Step 1:   Identify actors.

Step 2:   Identify use cases.

Step 3:   Do 1 and 2 again, and see if you need more actors for newly identified use cases, and vice versa.

Step 4:   Write a paragraph describing each actor and a couple of paragraphs about each use case.

Step 5:   Identify key "items" the system handles, and put them in a glossary or domain model. A **domain model** is a partial business model, showing only important concepts and how they relate to each other (see Figure 15.3).

Step 6:   Verify that you have steps in one or more use cases that create, maintain, and delete each of the "items" your system handles.

Step 7:   Identify the most essential or critical (architecturally significant) use cases (usually about 20 to 30 percent).

Step 8:   Describe the most essential or critical use cases in more detail.

Step 9:   Update the glossary or domain object model, and do lifecycle analysis of important concepts.

Step 10: Structure your use-case model.

The next section, Describe Requirements "Mile-Wide, Inch-Deep," details steps 1–7; the section Detail Actors and Use Cases details step 8; and the section Fine-Tune Your Model details steps 9 and 10.

Describe Requirements "Mile-Wide, Inch-Deep"

During Inception you need to provide a good understanding of the scope of the system, without going into too much detail. This is what we call a "mile-wide, inch-deep" understanding of the system (something we also talked about in Chapter 6). This is done in parallel with, or slightly after, eliciting stakeholder requests and documenting a Vision.

During Inception you need to provide a good understanding of the scope of the system, without going into too much detail.

So how do you produce this mile-wide, inch-deep description? For small projects, you get your team, your customer, and maybe other stakeholders together for a brainstorming meeting of a few hours. For larger projects, you may instead do a two-day workshop that includes all key stakeholders: project manager, architect, lead developer, customer, and a couple of analysts. During this session go through steps 1–7 as follows:

Step 1: **Analyze stakeholder requests and features to identify as many actors** (remember, actors represent both users and external systems with which the system interacts) as you can. Make sure that the actors represent roles, not titles or individual people. Any single person can typically play several roles, and many individuals may have the same role. Write a one-sentence description of actors as you find them. Do not spend too much time on this step; you will revisit this step many times.

Step 2: **For each actor, capture interactions with and usage of the system** in the form of use cases. A use case is a service, or a sequence of actions, that has a measurable value to the actor. It should be meaningful by itself. Write a one-sentence description of use cases as you find them.

Step 3: **For each of the use cases, determine whether it requires interaction with other users or systems.** This can be done by verbally walking through what happens when you execute the use case. In this way, you can find additional actors. Continue to go back and forth between finding actors and use cases until you feel the model has stabilized. You will most likely identify 80 percent of the actors and use cases in the first 20 percent of the time you spend. Therefore, you may want to cut the discovery period short when the rate of discovery slows down. You will revisit this model later.

Your results will probably look similar to Figure 15.4.

Step 4: **Write a paragraph describing each actor and a couple of paragraphs about each use case.** This can be done as a break-out session, where each person in the workshop is given two hours to describe, let's say, one actor and two to three use cases. Reassemble the group and review all descriptions. At this point you typically observe an interesting phenomenon: Although everyone agrees on the use-case names, they have their own interpretation of what the use case entails; now that there are actual detailed descriptions, the different interpretations are clear. As a result, you can usually come up with a few more use cases to cover all the functionality needed.

Step 5: **Create a Glossary** containing the key "items" the application deals with. For example, for an insurance application define

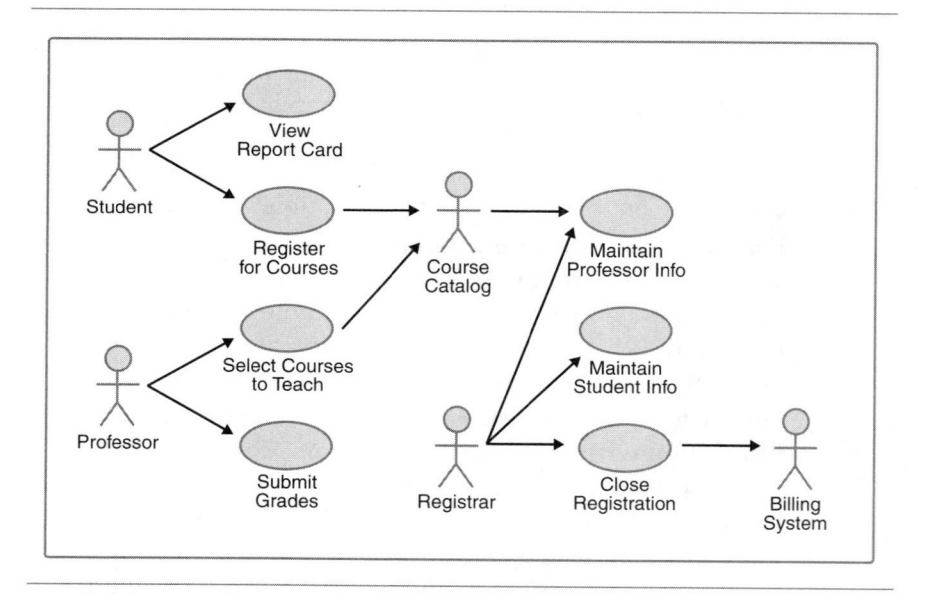

FIGURE 15.4 System Overview: Actors and Use Cases. *During a brainstorming meeting or use-case workshop, capture (on a whiteboard) the user groups and systems (actors) that will interact with your system, and the services (use cases) your system will provide to those actors.*

things such as claims, different types of policies, and so on. Also add common terminology that is used in the domain and with which the team or stakeholders may not be familiar. This glossary should help the participants to agree on a common terminology, as this is often a cause of miscommunication and misunderstanding. For many systems, it can be quite useful to graphically depict how one concept relates to other concepts. This can be done by modeling important concepts in a **domain model** (see Figure 15.3). A domain model allows you to capture a richer set of information about a concept such as how it relates to other concepts, allowing you to answer questions such as, "What type of policies exist, and how are they related to each other?", "Can a policy owner have any number of policies?", and "Must a claim be associated with a policy?" You can also use a domain model to give everybody an understanding of what key information is typically captured for a policy. Especially for complex systems, some formalism around essential concepts greatly hastens definition of requirements. Note that it is sometimes useful to do this step *before* step 1.

Step 6: **Review the glossary** or domain model and make sure there are use cases describing how each of the key "items" is created, maintained, and deleted. Do you have a use case that describes how to set up a policy? How to make changes to a policy? How to cancel a policy? You get the point. This is a great way of discovering holes in your use-case model.

Step 7: At this stage, you need to **identify the most essential or critical use cases** (up to 20 percent of the total). For some systems, you may have one or two use cases that capture the essence of the system, and most of the remaining use cases are there just to support them. If this is the case, you would identify a smaller percentage of use cases to be essential or critical. This activity is typically led by the architect, but analysts also need to participate (see the section Objective 2: Identify Key System Functionality, in Chapter 6, for more details on this).

Detail Actors and Use Cases

Step 8: Perform this step during Inception for the most essential and critical use cases. Most of this activity is, however, performed

During Elaboration, you finalize the use cases described in Inception, as well as detail almost all other use cases.

during Elaboration, where you finalize the use cases described in Inception, as well as detail almost all other use cases. You may also detail and finalize a smaller set of use cases first in Construction (see the section Describe the Remaining Use Cases and Other Requirements, in Chapter 8, for more information).

It is essential to understand that a use case contains many scenarios. As an example, the use case Transfer Balance may allow you to transfer a balance from a Checking, Savings, or Broker Account to a Checking, Savings, or Broker Account. So there are nine different transfer combinations. Each one of these nine transfers can have any number of outcomes, including Successful or Insufficient Funds. Also, there may be a series of error conditions, such as Connection to Server Not Available, and alternative flows of events, such as Receiving Account in Other Bank (potentially allowing the user to launch a Wire Transfer use case).

It usually takes just a few hours to produce a good draft of the most essential and typical use-case scenarios. For most systems, such a draft is one to two pages long. It generally takes considerably longer to complete the use case by detailing all scenarios within the use case. Detailed use cases are typically two to six pages long, but they can be much longer for systems with complex sequencing, such as telecom systems, or they can be shorter when there is limited sequencing and few business rules to be applied, such as viewing, but not updating, a limited set of information. For smaller projects, where you have the same person doing analysis and design of the use case, or projects building applications where maintenance is not considered a major issue, you may consider not documenting all possible scenarios to save time.

Guidelines for Detailing Use Cases

Here are some guidelines that you may find useful when detailing a use case:

- Identify the steps in the flow of events (see Figure 15.5) for the most common scenario of the use case, referred to as the basic flow of events or the "Happy Day" scenario—this is a scenario where everything goes as expected. In the earlier example, that could be Transfer Balance from a Checking to a Savings Account when there are sufficient funds.

- Describe each of the steps for that scenario.
- For each of these steps, identify all the things that could go wrong, or all exceptions from the Happy Day scenario. Document these alternative flows of events as If XX, then YY…, structured as sub-bullets under their respective steps.
- Continue to describe each alternative flow of events in detail. If the alternative flow of events becomes longer than a paragraph, place it in a separate section toward the end of the use-case description, and reference it from the step where it previously was described. This restructuring makes it easier to distinguish the Happy Day scenario, since the use-case description would otherwise be chopped into too many long parallel flows.
- If you have a lot of business rules, define these business rules outside the use case, as you do for the glossary. If you are using Rational tools, you can, for example, create a requirements type called Business Rule. Within your use-case description, reference in each section the business rules that should be applied. This way of handling business rules is especially good if the same business rules are referenced from many different use cases.
- Add pre- and postconditions; that is, clarify how the use case starts and ends. A precondition is the state of the system that is required before the use case can be started. A postcondition is the state the system can be in after the use case has ended.[4]

It should be noted that for many systems, use-case descriptions should be complemented with a user-interface prototype (see the section Develop User-Interface Prototypes, below).

For many systems, use-case descriptions should be complemented with a user-interface prototype.

Another important warning is now due: Always keep "the Spirit of the RUP" in mind, especially "Stay focused on executable software" (see Chapter 2). It is easy to become too focused on perfecting the requirements, and we have seen many projects go under because the focus has turned to academic discussions on how to document requirements, rather than on documenting the requirements *well enough* to enable successful implementation and testing of the system. As an analyst, you

---

4. See Bittner 2003 and Cockburn 2001.

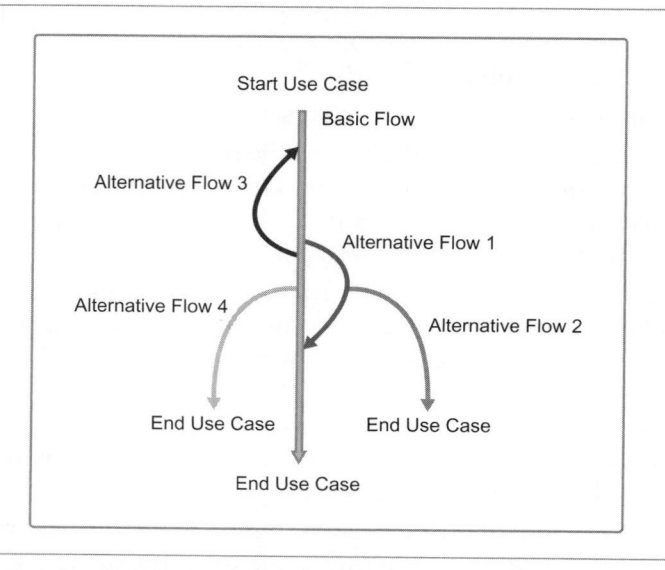

FIGURE 15.5 Structuring of Flows of Events. *The typical structure of a flow of events: The straight arrow represents the basic flow of events, and the curves represent alternative paths relative to "normal." Some alternative paths return to the basic flow of events, while others end the use case. A scenario is a combination of main and alternate flows from start to finish through a use case.*

should also work closely with the developer designing and implemeting the use case (it may even be the same person taking on both roles). Work hand-in-hand with this person to understand whether the requirements can be optimized. We discuss this in the section Describe the Remaining Use Cases and Other Requirements, in Chapter 8.

Example: Use-Case Specification for Register for Courses

A use-case specification details the sequence of events within a use case, without describing implementation details such as the layout and exact presentation of information, or how the functionality should be implemented. It should be easy to read for users and should provide sufficient detail to add value to developers implementing the use case.

Course Registration System: Use-Case Specification for Register for Courses

1. Brief Description

This use case allows a Student to register for course offerings in the current semester. The Student can also modify or delete course selections if changes are made within the add/drop period at the beginning of the semester. The Course Catalog System provides a list of all the course offerings for the current semester.

The main actor of this use case is the Student. The Course Catalog System is an actor within the use case.

2. Flow of Events

The use case begins when the Student selects to Register for Courses.

2.1 Basic Flow: Register for Courses

1. The Student selects to Register for Courses.

2. The system displays a blank schedule.

3. The system retrieves a list of available course offerings from the Course Catalog System.

4. The Student selects one or more primary and alternate course offerings from the list of available offerings. The user can at any time add or remove courses from the list of selected courses. Once the selections are complete the Student submits the schedule.

5. For each selected course offering, the system verifies that the Student has the necessary prerequisites and that the course offering is open.

    a. If the Student has the necessary prerequisites, and the course offering is not full, the system adds the Student to the selected course offering. The course offering is marked as "enrolled in" in the schedule.

    b. If the Student does not have the necessary prerequisites, or if the selected course offering is full, an error message is displayed. The Student can either select a different course offering or cancel the operation, at which point the use case is restarted.

6. The system saves the schedule.

2.2 Alternative Flows

2.2.1 Modify Course Registration

1. The Student selects to modify the current course registration schedule.

2. The system retrieves and displays the Student's current schedule (the schedule for the current semester).

3. The system retrieves a list of all the course offerings available for the current semester from the Course Catalog System. The system displays the list to the Student.

4. The Student can then modify the course selections by deleting and adding new courses. The Student selects the courses to add from the list of available courses. The Student also selects any course offerings to delete from the existing schedule. Once the edits are complete the Student submits the schedule to indicate completion with the selection of courses.

5. Subflow 2.1.5 is performed for each selected course offering.

6. The system saves the schedule.

2.2.2 Delete Course Registration

1. The Student selects to delete a schedule.

2. The system retrieves and displays the Student's current schedule.

3. The Student selects to delete the schedule.

4. The system prompts the Student to verify the deletion.

5. The Student verifies the deletion.

6. The system deletes the schedule.

2.2.3 Save a Schedule

At any point, the Student may choose to save a schedule without submitting it. The current schedule is saved, but the student is not added to any of the selected course offerings. The course offerings are marked as "selected" in the schedule.

Fine-Tune Your Models

Toward the end of Inception, as well as occasionally during later phases, it's wise to spend some time updating your use-case model and glossary.

Step 9:   In parallel with writing the detailed use-case descriptions, **update the glossary or domain model.** A good glossary will save you a lot of grief later in the project and will accelerate the writing of use cases. While writing use-case descriptions, did you run across any important concepts that need to be added to your glossary? Are your use cases referencing the correct glossary items/domain objects, or are concepts already defined reinvented?

Another thing to consider when you are working with the glossary/domain model is to revisit step 6. Go through the lifecycle of any new concepts defined, and make sure that you have use cases that describe how to create, maintain, and delete that concept.

Step 10: You can structure your use-case model **by creating relationships between actors and use cases,** such as inheritance between actors, or includes, extends, or generalizations between use cases. The first thing we recommend is to **use these constructs only** if you are an expert use-case modeler. We see these constructs misused more often than not, and you can build perfectly fine systems without using them.

If you are interested in using these, we recommend you to wait until Elaboration, or at least until very late in Inception. We also recommend you not use a relationship except when you can make a convincing case for it. When in doubt, go for simplicity.

As you restructure your use-case model, you will need to revisit the use-case description for each use case involved.

Develop User-Interface Prototypes

Analysts either develop user-interface prototypes or work closely with the people who develop them. The development of UI prototypes can be divided into two main groups: conceptual prototypes and use-case storyboards or prototypes.

- **Conceptual Prototype.** During Inception, in parallel with developing the vision, describing the most essential use cases, and producing a business case for the system, you need to develop a conceptual prototype to visualize and demonstrate key concepts and capabilities to enable stakeholders to understand better the system being built. Often, a conceptual prototype contains not only UI prototypes, but also some underlying functionality.

  The prototype should answer questions such as, "Are you proposing a new user paradigm?", "What capabilities will the application offer?", "To what user types will the application appeal?", and "What is the potential functionality offered by the most critical use cases?"

  Answers, or potential answers, to all of these questions facilitate the big decision you make at the end of Inception: Should you develop the envisioned product?

- **Use-Case Storyboard or Use-Case Prototype.** In late Inception, throughout Elaboration, and into early Construction, you want to develop UI prototypes in parallel with use-case descriptions to enhance your understanding of the use cases. How much time you spend on this differs greatly depending on the application.

Develop Use-Case Storyboard or Prototype

For more **technical applications** with a strong focus on sequencing and interaction with other systems, you would create a use-case storyboard only for some key use cases to showcase a few different screens.

For **database-focused applications** of the Create, Read, Update, Delete (CRUD) nature, you should try to do a UI prototype for each use case, not so much to mitigate risks associated with the UI, but to increase the speed and accuracy in developing use-case descriptions (see step 8). The following procedure has been used successfully to accelerate the development of use cases, while increasing the value of the use-case description feedback provided by users and customers:

1. Have one person (the UI designer) responsible for UI prototypes to ensure consistency across use cases. For large projects with more than five to eight analysts, you may need more than one UI designer.

2. When an analyst has produced a first draft of the use-case description, review it with the UI designer. Together sketch out what information needs to be displayed and what screens will be needed. Later, the UI designer may merge or split screens based on available space, so do not focus too much on details at this point. Doing this walkthrough allows the analyst to get valuable and early feedback on the use case. You will likely discover inconsistencies in information managed by the use cases, as well as in the flow of events.

3. The UI designer creates a mock-up of the screens. This can be done rapidly using the GUI Builder of the IDE you are using, providing developers with a great starting point when designing, implementing, and testing the use case. Do not add any logic behind the screens; just print the screens for later review. In parallel, the analyst details the use-case description.

4. The UI designer and analyst review the screen shots and use them to walk through the use case. Corrections are made to screen shots and to use-case descriptions as holes or discrepancies are identified.

5. The analyst meets with the users and/or customers to walk through the use case. The review is done as a storyboard, where the screen shots are used to clarify the flow of events. It is often beneficial to leave the material on-site for a day or two after the meeting so it can be reviewed in detail.

6. Update use cases and screen shots based on feedback.

This approach normally provides many of the following benefits:

- Increased consistency in the UI
- Accelerated completion of use-case descriptions
- Improved feedback from users

- Accelerated design, implementation, and testing of use cases
- Enhanced communication between analysts and developers

It should be noted that there is also a clear risk that users, UI designers, and analysts seek to perfect the UI prototypes, which could lead to analysis-paralysis. Your goal is **not to finalize the UI;** your goal is to get a reasonably good UI to facilitate effective communication with the users on what the system should do, allowing you to finalize the use cases more rapidly.

Note that projects with a very strong focus on user experience may choose to formally model the user interface using UML models. This is done by representing screens with stereotyped analysis classes, allowing you to show the interaction between the users (actors) and the screens through UML diagrams such as sequence diagrams. This is described in more detail in *The User-Experience Modeling Plug-In for the RUP*, available through the Rational Developer Network, as well as in Conallen 2000.

Capture Nonfunctional Requirements

Nonfunctional requirements typically have a significant impact on the architecture and on user satisfaction. These requirements may, however, not always be as clearly articulated by users and stakeholders as are the functional requirements. This means that the analyst needs to identify, document, and confirm the nonfunctional requirements, such as:

- **Quality attributes,** including usability, reliability, performance, and supportability requirements.
- **Legal and regulatory requirements,** and application standards.
- **Other requirements,** such as operating systems and environments, compatibility requirements, and design constraints.

A major objective in the Elaboration phase is to verify that you can sufficiently support many of the nonfunctional requirements: performance, usability, and so on.

Nonfunctional requirements are captured primarily during Inception and early Elaboration, but they may be revised throughout the project. They are documented in the RUP artifact called the Supplementary Specification. It should be noted that a major objective in the Elaboration phase is to verify that you can sufficiently support

many of the nonfunctional requirements such as usability, reliability, performance, operating systems, environments, and compatibility with other systems.

Update and Refine Requirements

In iterative development, requirements evolve incrementally. As described earlier, a majority of the work in defining the requirements is done in Inception and Elaboration. As discussed in the section Describe the Remaining Use Cases and Other Requirements, in Chapter 8, some less-critical use cases are described first in Construction. It should be noted, however, that as you design, implement, and test the various use cases, as you expose the system to users, and as you learn more about the problem domain and the implemented solution, you will need to continually refine the requirements.

Today's systems are too complex to allow you to define the right system from the beginning. This is why you need to be very open to reasonable modifications to the requirements during Inception and Elaboration. Major modifications ("Are you changing the scope or the vision of the system?", "Should you?") need to be carefully considered and discussed.

As your investment in the design, implementation, and testing of the system increases and as the delivery date creeps closer, you need to be more careful about allowing changes to requirements. You need to consider carefully the impact of each change on risk, cost, schedule, and resources, compared to the value the change will bring. In many cases, you need to state, "This is a great suggestion for improvement, and we should absolutely consider implementing this change in a *later* version of the system." But if the customer insists, you should make it clear what the cost will be and let the customer decide whether to cut scope or extend the project. In many projects, however, it is the Change Control Board or the project manager making decisions as to whether to allow late changes to requirements. Analysts also need to understand the overall approach to changes in requirements so they can support and guide people in making the right decision.

Ensure That the Requirements Are Delivered and Tested

During Transition, the last of the four lifecycle phases of the RUP, you transition the product to the user in the target environment. One of the steps involved in the deployment is acceptance testing, to verify that the software is ready and can be used by the users to perform those functions and tasks the software was built for. Product acceptance testing often involves more than execution of the software for readiness; it also involves all product artifacts delivered to the customer(s), such as training, documentation, and packaging.

Acceptance testing is the responsibility of the tester, but the analyst needs to be actively involved in the process to ensure that the user requirements are satisfied and properly tested.

The Analyst's Role in the Rational Unified Process

The RUP product provides a more fine-grained representation of the analyst's role by describing its more specialized roles:

- System analyst
- Business designer
- Business-model reviewer
- Business-process analyst
- Requirements reviewer
- Requirements specifier
- Test analyst
- User-interface designer

In this chapter, we captured all of these specialized roles—with the exception of test analyst—within the super-role of analyst. It should also be noted that many organizations may consider the tasks of a user-interface designer to be developer tasks, rather than analyst tasks.

Resources for Analysts

Below are some resources for analysts seeking a better understanding of how to work within a RUP project.

Further Reading

Kurt Bittner and Ian Spence. *Use Case Modeling*. Boston: Addison-Wesley, 2003.

Alistair Cockburn. *Writing Effective Use Cases*. Boston: Addison-Wesley, 2001.

Ivar Jacobson, Maria Ericsson, and Agneta Jacobson. *The Object Advantage: Business Process Reengineering with Object Technology*. Reading, MA: Addison-Wesley, 1994.

Philippe Kruchten. *The Rational Unified Process: An Introduction, Second Edition*. Boston: Addison-Wesley, 2000.

Dean Leffingwell and Don Widrig. *Managing Software Requirements: A Unified Approach*. Boston: Addison-Wesley, 2000.

Training Resources

The following training courses have been develop to support RUP users; they are delivered by IBM Software and its partners (see www.rational.com for more information).

- Principles of the Rational Unified Process: Web-based training.
- Essentials of the Rational Unified Process (two days).
- Principles of Use-Case Modeling with UML: Web-based training.
- Mastering Requirements Management with Use Cases (three days).

CHAPTER 16

An Architect's Guide to the RUP

You are a software architect, and you are about to use the RUP product. This chapter is a guide to help you understand your role in a software development project using the RUP approach. You will find a definition of the **role** of an architect and its interactions with other roles. We will define **architecture** and describe the various **artifacts** that an architect may develop. Finally, we will review some of the key RUP **activities** in which architects are involved.

The Mission of an Architect

A software architect leads and coordinates **technical** activities and artifacts throughout the project. A software architect coordinates some of the key design decisions in terms of technologies, structure, and organization of the software system. In contrast to the other roles defined in the RUP approach, the software architect's view is one of breadth, as opposed to one of depth.

A software architect leads and coordinates technical activities and artifacts throughout the project.

A Jack-of-All-Trades

How do we characterize the ideal architect? Around 25 B.C., the Roman architect Vitruvius wrote, "The ideal architect should be a person of letters, a mathematician, familiar with historical studies, a diligent

student of philosophy, acquainted with music, not ignorant of medicine, learned in the responses of jurisconsults, familiar with astronomy and astronomical calculations." This is quite a challenge!

A software architect must grasp issues quickly and make educated, critical judgments in the absence of complete information.

In a similar fashion, a software architect must be well rounded and possess maturity, vision, and a depth of experience that allows for grasping issues quickly and making educated, critical judgments in the absence of complete information. More specifically, the software architect, or the members of the architecture team, must combine these attributes:

- **Experience** in both the problem domain (through a thorough understanding of the requirements) and the software engineering domain. If there is a team, these qualities can be spread across the team members, but at least one software architect must provide the global vision for the project. The software architect must understand the key technologies available or be able to quickly bring in the appropriate competencies.

- **Leadership** in order to drive the technical effort across the various teams and to make critical decisions under pressure and make those decisions stick. To be effective, the software architect and the project manager must work closely together, with the software architect leading the technical issues and the project manager leading the business and administrative issues.

- **Communication** to earn trust, to persuade, to motivate, and to mentor. The software architect cannot lead by decree, only by the consent of the rest of the project team. In order to be effective, the software architect must earn the respect of the project team, the project manager, the customer, and the user community, as well as the management team.

- **Goal-oriented and proactive** with a relentless focus on results. The software architect is the technical driving force behind the project, not a visionary or dreamer. The life of a successful software architect is a long series of suboptimal decisions often made in the dark and under pressure. A perfectionist who spends a lot of time on issues would not be appropriate for the job.

A Person or a Team?

If the project is large enough, then several people, grouped in a software architecture team, will play this role. A project with more than 30 people all together may want to create an architecture team. If this is your case, the goal in assembling such a team is to have a good mix of talents, covering a wide spectrum of experience and sharing a common understanding of the software engineering process. The architecture team should not be a mere committee of representatives from various teams, domains, or contractors. Software architecture is a full-time function, with staff permanently dedicated to it. We often write "the software architect does...." Understand that we mean collectively the persons playing that role at a given point in time.

A Vertex of Communication

The architect is not a lone designer, operating from a technological ivory tower, but rather plays a major communication role in the development organization.

Communication Between Project Management and Development

In the movie industry, the director is responsible for the artistic content of the movie—the direction of actors. It is very rare that the director will also play the role of the executive producer, the latter being more focused on planning, finance, budget, crews, supplies, set construction, and so on. But at the same time, these two roles need to be very closely coordinated. They need to speak to each other constantly, especially in a moving and ever-changing environment. Similarly, in a software project, the architect and the project manager will need to be in constant communication (although careful not to do each other's job). We will see later that the architect will play a major role in planning the contents of an iteration, in identifying and addressing technical risks, and in helping the project manager with strategic and tactical changes.

Communication Between Internal
Parties and External Stakeholders

The architect will also interface the outside world with the rest of the team—architecture team and project team—on the technical matters. The Vision Document and the requirements developed by the analysts provide the major input to the architect's work, from which the architect will extract the architecturally significant requirements that will contribute to shape the system. When multiple external parties—customers, contractors, and so on—are involved, this aspect of the job may become quite time-consuming.

Communication Between Various Development Teams

Especially in a large organization, the architects will also play a role of communication and coordination, on the technical front, between various development teams. They will make sure that interfaces are defined and respected; they will scout for the potential for reuse; and they will participate in reviews, striving to ensure a consistent style for the development of the system, to preserve what Frederick Brooks called its "architectural integrity." Also, this role is often continuous and informal; when things get tough, the architect plays an arbiter role between teams and takes part in the decision of a Change Control Board[1] if a CCB is instituted.

Architecture

Let us slow down and back up for a while to define a bit more what we mean by "software architecture" and to define a few other key concepts. Architecture (with a capital "A") is a discipline, an art, but architecture (with a small "a") also designates a "thing," a property of all systems, and the focus of the work of the architect.

---

1. A Change Control Board is a small group of people who review and approve proposed changes to baselined artifacts.

Architecture Defined

Software **architecture** encompasses the set of significant decisions about the organization of a software system:

- Selection of the structural elements and their interfaces, by which a system is composed
- Behavior as specified in collaborations among those elements
- Composition of these structural and behavioral elements into larger subsystems
- Architectural style that guides this organization

Software architecture is also concerned with

- Usage
- Functionality
- Performance
- Resilience
- Reuse
- Comprehensibility
- Economic and technology constraints and tradeoffs
- Aesthetic concerns

This is more than a one-line definition; it is a whole menu! Yes, architecture, both as an artifact and as a discipline, is quite challenging, and if you are new to the role of architect, be ready for a wild ride. Architecture is quite a complex thing. Note, however, that the architect focuses only on the architecturally significant requirements and the corresponding architecturally significant design decisions (see Figure 16.1). By "architecturally significant," we mean the ones that will have a long and lasting effect on the system performance, quality, and scalability, as opposed to the myriad other design decisions that will be made during the construction of the system. The architect does not bear the responsibility of making *all* design decisions.

The architect focuses on the architecturally significant requirements and the corresponding architecturally significant design decisions.

Models and Views

As the architecture of a system may be quite challenging to describe, and as it is the focus of attention of multiple parties, or stakeholders,

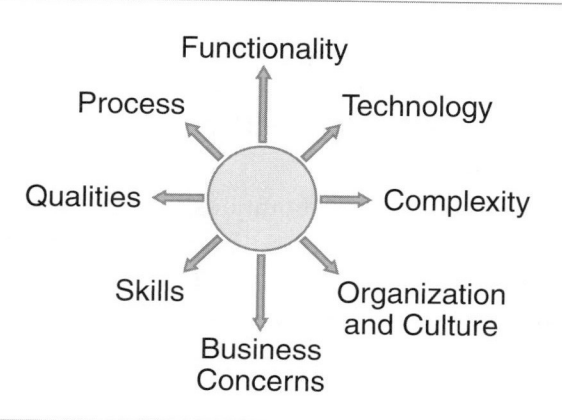

FIGURE 16.1 Architecting: The Art of Compromise. *Architects need to consider and balance the impact along a number of different dimensions when making architectural decisions. This forces the architects to constantly make difficult tradeoffs.*

one approach to organizing its description is to use multiple viewpoints. The description of architecture is organized in **views,** each focusing on one aspect of architecture, leaving the other perspectives aside. In turn, each view may be described by a UML model or simply descriptive text.

Depending on the specific nature of your project, your architecture will have one of the following views:

- A **logical view** (existing for any system), showing the various elements of the software and their structure: classes, packages, and so on.

- A **process view,** in the case of a distributed and concurrent system, showing the parallelism between various entities, and how communication and synchronization are achieved.

- An **implementation view,** showing how the implementation elements (source code files, executable, and so on) are organized in the development environment.

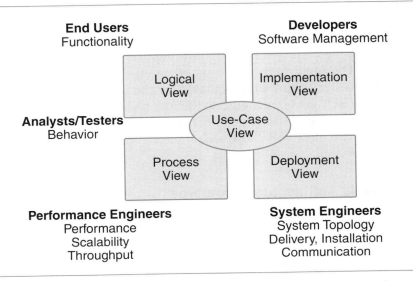

FIGURE 16.2 The 4+1 Views of Architecture. *The use-case view contains the architecturally significant use cases and represents the problem space. It ties together the other four views in the solution space. (From Kruchten 1995).*

- A **deployment view,** showing how physically at runtime the various runtime components are replicated and deployed, and how they communicate.
- A **use-case view,** capturing the most significant requirements: use cases or parts of use cases that have some great impact on the architecture, as well as significant nonfunctional requirements (see Figure 16.2). This may include use-case realizations to illustrate how the system works.

The four first views are in the solution space, and the last one ties them with the problem space.

Software Architecture Document

The main responsibility of the architect is to describe the architecture of the system in a major artifact of the RUP product, called the **Software Architecture Document (SAD).** For many projects, this may be the only

part of the design that is described in an actual document, as most design aspects can be documented in UML models and in the code itself. The more stakeholders that are interested in understanding or influencing the architecture, the more important this document will be. The SAD is organized along a set of views, chosen among the ones we listed earlier, or any other suitable for the project. The SAD template in the RUP is very general, so the first task of an architect will be to tailor it to suit the specific context and needs of the project. In particular, the architect will chose which views are relevant and how to document them.

Executable Architectural Prototype

The architectural decisions are validated using an architectural prototype.

The SAD is only an intent, a document. The architectural decisions are validated using an architectural prototype, and the architect is responsible for driving the implementation of this prototype that will subsequently evolve to become the complete system. The prototype is used to validate the architecture, to demonstrate that all major technical risks have been retired, to serve as a baseline for the rest of the development. Its development is also a good way to bring the development organization up to speed with tools, languages, technologies, processes, and performance calibration.

Architectural Mechanisms

Architectural mechanisms represent common, concrete solutions to frequently encountered problems. They may be patterns of structure, patterns of behavior, or both. They provide standard solutions to problems such as garbage collection, persistent storage, list management, "shopping cart" implementation, communication with external systems through a certain protocol, and so on. They play an important role in the description of an architecture.

Additional Architecture?

Architects may develop other RUP artifacts, for example, to analyze tradeoffs between possible solutions or **guidelines** to convey principles and guidelines to the rest of the development organization.

Architects will contribute to RUP artifacts such as risk lists, project plan and iteration plans, vision, requirements, use cases, and so on.

Outside the bounds of an individual project, architects may want to establish an enterprise architecture, including technology choices and development paradigms. Are you organizing around reuse? How should you achieve it? Should you develop all applications on the J2EE platform, where communication between building blocks is done through message queues? What are these major reusable building blocks, and how will they roughly evolve over a series of projects? Do you instead embrace the emerging Web services capability to allow different applications to reuse components across platforms?

An Evolving Role

Describing the RUP approach for an architect is a bit of a challenge, as this role evolves throughout the lifecycle—Inception, Elaboration, Construction, and Transition—and also during evolution or maintenance cycles.

During **Inception,** working with the emerging vision, an architect will evaluate possible implementation strategies and feedback feasibility to the requirements work, as well as costs to the management. As the system takes shape, a possible architecture is defined and sometimes even prototyped to assess its effectiveness: a proof-of-concept prototype for the candidate Architecture. Certain delicate parts of the system may also be prototyped to prove a concept feasible, or to help drive a decision to develop the system—or not develop it, in some cases! For example, if there is a strong doubt, build a crude prototype to show that your distributed system will support the number of transactions you expect.

It is during the **Elaboration** phase that the Architect has the most crucial role, and often several persons will be involved. An objective of Elaboration is to flesh out the Software Architecture Document and to validate the choices made by developing an executable architectural prototype. The milestone that concludes this phase is called the Lifecycle Architecture (LCA) Milestone, and this is where hopefully the architects can baseline an architecture. Faced now with some more tangible

It is during the Elaboration phase that the Architect has the most crucial role.

elements other than requirements simply drawn on paper or sketchy design ideas, this architectural effort may result in a revision of the requirements and the vision. For example, your new prototype may show that you have some performance issues to be addressed. But the role of the architect does not abruptly stop at the LCA Milestone.

In Construction, software architects are responsible for overseeing the implementation of the rest of the system.

In **Construction,** as in building architecture, software architects are responsible for overseeing the implementation of the rest of the system, making sure that the original architectural intent is not compromised. Often architectural adjustments and additions are necessary. The architect will play go-between and arbiter between teams, deciding where an aspect must be developed, making sure that guidelines are followed, or capturing new information in the guidelines. Involved in design reviews, architects are well placed to attract the attention of project management on some staffing issues: imbalance between teams, lack of resources, lack of training, and so on. They can also identify further opportunities for reuse or acquisition of ready-made software.

One may think that the role of architects is almost nil in the **Transition** phase, that they may now retire in peace or move to greener pastures. Not quite! As things get tough toward the delivery date, the architect is involved in critical decisions about major defects: what to fix and how, especially vigilant so that hasty or uninformed decisions that could fix one subsystem but break another one are not made. Lots of nasty mistakes can be made in that last stretch to the finish line, wiping out the benefits of architectural work.

What Do Architects Do?

David Dikel and his colleagues, authors of *Software Architecture: Organizational Principles and Patterns,* have captured the essence of the activities of the architect in a model they call VRAPS, which stands for Vision, Rhythm, Anticipation, Partnering, and Simplification.

Vision

"Vision is the mapping of future values to architectural constraints, as measured by how well the architecture's structures and goals are clear, compelling, congruent, and flexible."[2] Developing an architectural vision permits a better definition of the scope of the architectural endeavor and sets the right level of expectations among the stakeholders (internal and external). It also allows early detection of when the expectations fail to align, and it makes tacit knowledge about architecture visible to its users.

The architectural vision is clearly articulated in the **Software Architecture Document,** which must tie to the overall project **Vision Document.** Many of the activities related to architecture in the RUP Elaboration phase contribute to this architectural vision.

Rhythm

"Rhythm is the recurring, predictable exchange of workproducts within an architecture group and across their customers and suppliers."[3] It is about the lifecycle, the cycles and iterations, their visibility and predictability, how the organization will evolve an architecture over time, and how the various components will unfold and integrate. It is both about timing and about the content of a release and the quality of that content. It deals with synchronization between stakeholders, about re-evaluation. The RUP has a three-tier "tempo": cycle, iteration, and build. The initial development cycle brings a clear focus on architecture through its Elaboration phase. Subsequent evolution cycles will also have an Elaboration phase to evolve, refine, and simplify the architecture. Each cycle and phase is decomposed in iterations, which provide organizationwide synchronization points, focusing on a release of products, initially leading to an architectural baseline, and then evolving to a gradually more complete product of increasing quality. Then, in each iteration, the regular builds force a focus on value and force closure on concrete issues.

---

2. See Dikel 2001.
3. Ibid.

Anticipation

"Anticipation is the extent to which those who build and implement the architecture predict, validate, and adapt the architecture to changing technology, competition, and customer needs."[4] The hardest objective of an architect is balancing long-term vision with immediate needs in the context of high technology churn. How do you avoid getting on the nasty tracks of too much bleeding edge and tunnel vision? Here you see how the various principles start playing each other: A healthy rhythm will force regular reviews and re-evaluation of the architectural vision.

Partnering

"Partnering is the extent to which architecture stakeholders maintain clear, cooperative roles and maximize the value they deliver and receive."[5] Do not do it all. Build cooperative organizations, internally and externally. Maximize the ultimate value for critical stakeholders, not the amount of local invention and development. Make sure that there is a clear and compelling agreement between the various stakeholders, in the sense of the "win-win" approach preached by Barry Boehm and others. The architect is a negotiator, a mediator, a go-between, an ombudsman. The architect is keen on reuse.

Simplification

"Simplification is the intelligent clarification and minimization of both the architecture and the organizational environment in which it functions."[6] The architecture continues to be used, but at the same time the cost of using it, and therefore its complexity, must be reduced: no fluff, no overgeneralization of the problems leading to overgeneral solutions. The architect understands the essential minimal requirements and builds them into the core elements of the architecture. The overall business case for evolving the architecture remains clear. Some architectural refactoring does take place.

---

4. Ibid.
5. Ibid.
6. Ibid.

The Architect's Activities in the RUP

It is hard to reduce the activities of the architect to a small set of recipes. Too much will depend on the context, the nature of the system, its size, or whether it is "green-field" development, an extension of an existing system, or the re-engineering of a legacy application.

Besides the Software Architecture Document and the architectural views it describes, the RUP describes several activities for the architect (see Figure 16.3). We will group them into three "buckets":

- Working with the requirements and the project management
- Refining the architecture
- Maintaining the architectural integrity

Working with the Requirements and Project Management

These activities are usually at the early stages of a project, where the architect's role is straddling across project management, requirements management, and analysis and design.

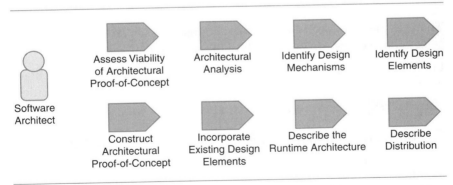

FIGURE 16.3 Overview of the Architect's Activities. *An architect is responsible for a wide set of activities, including activities related to requirements and project management, refining the architecture, and maintaining architectural integrity.*

Prioritize Use Cases

This activity encompasses the role of the architect in the planning of iterations, working jointly with the project manager. Based on the risks that must be mitigated in a given iteration, and based on which part of the system must be completed (when we are in the later part of the development cycle), the architect will select which parts of which use cases should be implemented in the upcoming iteration. We have seen this described in Chapter 6 on Inception.

Architectural Analysis

Based on the vision and the key use cases, an architect will develop the architectural vision we described earlier by developing an overview of the architecture, identifying which existing assets can be used or reused to minimize work, and giving a structure to the logical view of the architecture.

This structure is populated with **key abstractions,** usually deriving from the domain. They often are classes such as Customer, Order, Inventory, and so on, and key parts or attributes of these key classes. The architect also identifies fundamental analysis mechanisms and patterns to connect and give behavior to these classes. These analysis mechanisms are implementation-independent. They cover issues like persistency, communication, synchronization, and security. They will later be bound to concrete implementations.

Then, using these candidate abstractions (classes and patterns), the selected use cases can be described in use-case realizations.

Finally, all these individual decisions must be put together in a single coherent architecture, eliminating redundancy, looking at similarities, and exploiting them.

Construct an Architectural Proof-of-Concept Prototype

We saw in Chapter 6 on Inception that in bold, new projects, where a lot of unchartered territory has to be covered before making wise development choices, it may be necessary to build prototypes just to help scope the system, assess feasibility, or view the reality of a risk or the efficiency of a solution.

Refining the Architecture

This is where technological choices are made, validated, and documented. These activities mostly contribute to the development of the executable architectural baseline of the system, and their outcome is documented mainly in the SAD. These activities are illustrated in Chapter 7 on Elaboration.

Identify Design Mechanisms

The architect must now choose appropriate designs to realize the analysis mechanisms identified earlier. For example, shall persistency be on disk or in memory, using a database or a simple file? Often the choice of an infrastructure (a middleware) will bring a choice of possible designs. Then these designs must be mapped onto concrete implementation mechanisms.

Identify Design Elements

Similarly, the architect must know how the various key elements will be defined in the software. This is a core activity, where all the design skills of the architect can be used, as well as all the wealth of guidance on design that is contained in the RUP product. The only danger is in the architect going overboard and getting lost in this activity: too far, too deep, and too detailed.

Incorporate Existing Design Elements

Very often all this work must not be done in a vacuum. There are large opportunities for **reuse,** from platforms, from other similar projects, from legacy systems. Sometimes this takes the form of reverse-engineering existing elements to integrate them in the new system.

Structure Implementation Model

Having made some of the major choices, the implementation structure must be defined: Where will the implementation artifacts be stored? What about source code, executable, documentation, models? What will be under configuration and version control? Where will the reusable parts be? This structure must also allow developers to work in an efficient manner without stepping on each other's feet. Issues such as individual or team workspaces, integration spaces, and Configuration Management must also be considered when building this aspect of the architecture.

Describe Distribution and Describe the Runtime Architecture

Similarly, if the system is distributed and concurrent, processes, tasks, and various other issues of parallelism must be resolved and organized in separate views: the process view and the deployment view.

The architect describes the runtime architecture by

- Analyzing concurrency requirements.
- Identifying processes and threads.
- Identifying inter-process communication mechanisms.
- Allocating inter-process coordination resources.
- Identifying process lifecycles.
- Mapping processes onto the implementation environment.
- Distributing model elements among processes.

For distributed systems, the architect describes the distribution by outlining the physical nodes. This includes defining the network configuration and allocating processes to nodes.

A few years ago, our colleague Grady Booch was involved in a project that illustrated the importance of concurrency and load balancing. For a new generation of armored rocket launchers, he was designing advanced software to help maneuver the vehicle and analyze incoming fire. The design review showed some major flaws: When under fire, an operator could barely maneuver the vehicle, let alone scoot quickly away and hide. The solution was another allocation of modeling elements to processes and of processes to physical nodes, as well as different priorities for the runtime processes, so that neither the same processes nor the same processors would simultaneously handle the maneuvering of the vehicle and the analysis of incoming fire.

Maintaining Architectural Integrity

There are a certain number of auxiliary but important activities that are also the architect's responsibility. They either pertain to the assessment of the architecture, or they contribute to maintaining architectural integrity throughout the development cycle.

Develop Design Guidelines

The architects not only need to design or select an architecture, but they must also communicate on how to use it and how to exploit the elements of the architecture in a consistent manner; they even set up the rules on how to extend and change it. There may be many hidden assumptions in the architecture that must be spelled out clearly to all of the other designers, testers, and integrators in order not to break the architecture.

Develop Programming Guidelines

This is similar to the design guidelines, but it exploits the feature of a chosen programming language to achieve certain architectural intent.

Review the Architecture

The purpose of architectural reviews is

- To uncover any unknown or perceived risks in the schedule or budget.
- To detect any architectural design flaws. Architectural flaws are known to be the hardest to fix and the most damaging in the long run.
- To detect a potential mismatch between the requirements and the architecture: overdesign, unrealistic requirements, or missing requirements. In particular the assessment may examine some aspects often neglected in the areas of operation, administration,

and maintenance. How is the system installed or updated? How do we transition the current databases?

- To evaluate one or more specific architectural qualities: performance, reliability, modifiability, security, and safety.
- To identify reuse opportunities.

This review is conducted as apart of the LCA Milestone at the end of Elaboration. Without enumerating them here, it is highly likely that an architect will be involved in other reviews, defined in the Project Management discipline of the RUP, as well as be a key player in the Change Control Board to decide how and when critical issues must be resolved.

The Architect's Roles in the RUP

If you're a software architect, you are likely to play several of the roles defined in the RUP. First and foremost, the architect will fulfill the role described in the RUP as Software Architect. But the architect will also often be a Designer and an Architecture Reviewer.

Often the architect will be an Implementer, especially when contributing to the development of the architectural prototype early in the Elaboration phase, or a proof-of-concept prototype during Inception.

It is preferable that the role of the Analyst should be played by a different person to keep a healthy separation of concerns and to avoid polluting the requirements with the design, or vice versa. Ideally, the analyst should remain an advocate for the customer (although an enlightened advocate who understands the technical issues and the emerging design). It is true, however, that on many small projects the line is blurred between the analysts and the architects.

It is rarely a good idea to have an architect play the role of Project Manager, except on very small projects.

It is not too uncommon to see the architect play the role of Process Engineer, because often he or she has the right level of experience with the software development process to potentially fulfill this role.

Finding Your Way in the RUP Product

As an architect, to get started with the RUP, first understand some of the fundamental concepts: iterative development, the RUP lifecycle (phases and iterations), risk management, and then understand some of the concepts directly related to architecture: components and the various Architectural Views. As necessary, check the Glossary for definitions.

Then you can enter the RUP via the Role: Software Architect and reach the various activities that define this role. Alternatively, you may start from the Artifact: Software Architecture Document (its template and an example). From there navigate to the various activities that contribute to its development. A third track into the RUP is to start from the Roadmap: Developing Component Solutions.

As required in your specific case, you can then dive into more specialized issues, the Concepts: Concurrency and the use of Capsule, Data Modeling, Business Architecture, and so on.

Do not forget that the architect will interact with many other roles and participate in their activities, in some form or another. Use the search engine with the word Architecture or Architect.

Resources for the Architect

Further Reading

Len Bass, Paul Clements, and Rick Kazman. *Software Architecture in Practice.* Reading, MA: Addison-Wesley, 1998.

Jan Bosch. *Design and Use of Software Architecture: Designing and Evolving a Product-Line Approach.* Boston: Addison-Wesley, 2000.

Frank Buschmann, Regine Meunier, Hans Rohnert, Peter Sommerlad, and Michael Stal. *Pattern-Oriented Software Architecture: A System of Patterns.* New York: John Wiley & Sons, 1996.

Paul Clements, Felix Bachmann, Len Bass, David Garlan, James Ivers, Reed Little, Robert Nord, and Judith Stafford. *Documenting Software Architectures: Views and Beyond*. Boston: Addison-Wesley, 2002.

Paul Clements, Rick Kazman, and Mark Klein. *Evaluating Software Architecture*. Boston: Addison-Wesley, 2002.

Paul Clements and Linda Northrop. *Software Product Lines: Practice and Patterns*. Boston: Addison-Wesley, 2002.

David M. Dikel, David Kane, and James R. Wilson. *Software Architecture: Organizational Principles and Patterns*, Upper Saddle River, NJ: Prentice-Hall, 2001.

Christine Hofmeister, Robert Nord, and Dilip Soni. *Applied Software Architecture*. Boston: Addison-Wesley, 2000.

IEEE 1471:2000. "Recommended Practice for Architectural Representation." Los Alamitos, CA: Software Engineering Standards Committee of the IEEE Computer Society, 2000.

ISO/IEC 10746:1995. *Reference Model of Open Distributed Processing (RM-ODP)* (ITU Rec. X901). Geneva, Switzerland: ISO, 1995.

Ivar Jacobson, Martin Griss, and Patrik Jonsson. *Software Reuse: Architecture, Process and Organization for Business Success*. Reading, MA: Addison-Wesley, 1997.

Philippe Kruchten. "Common Misconceptions About Software Architecture," in *The Rational Edge*, April 2001.

Philippe Kruchten. "The Tao of the Software Architect," in *The Rational Edge*, March 2001.

Philippe Kruchten. "The 4+1 View of Architecture," in *IEEE Software* 6 (12), 1995.

Eberhardt Rechtin and Mark Maier. *The Art of System Architecting*. Boca Raton, FL: CRC Books, 1997.

Bran Selic, Garth Gullekson, and Paul Ward. *Real-Time Object-Oriented Modeling*. New York: John Wiley & Sons, 1994.

Mary Shaw and David Garlan. *Software Architecture: Perspectives on an Emerging Discipline*. Upper Saddle River, NJ: Prentice-Hall, 1996.

Marcus Vitruvius Pollio, De Architecura, circa 25 B.C. at http://www.ukans.edu/history/index/europe/ancient_rome/L/Roman/Texts/Vitruvius/1*.html.

Bernard I. Witt, F. Terry Baker, and Everett W. Merritt. *Software Architecture and Design: Principles, Models, and Methods.* New York: Van Nostrand Reinhold, 1995.

Useful Web Sites

Here are some useful starting points for a Web search of software architecture information:

- Software Engineering Institute: http://www.sei.cmu.edu/architecture/sw_architecture.html.
- WorldWide Institute of Software Architects: http://www.wwisa.org.
- Dana Bredemeyer's Resources for Software Architects: http://www.bredemeyer.com.

CHAPTER 17

A Developer's Guide to the RUP

You are a developer involved with analysis, design, implementation, integration, or developer testing. This chapter will guide you in using the RUP approach. You will find an overview of the developer responsibilities in a RUP project and resources, such as recommended training courses and reading, that will make you a more proficient developer.

Your Mission as a Developer

When we talk about the Developer, we talk about a role. A RUP project may have many people taking on a role, or one person taking on many roles or many partial roles. So you may, for example, take on a subset of the role of a developer, as well as a subset of the responsibilities of an analyst. Also note that in this chapter we briefly cover integration and database design. In many projects, especially larger projects, integration may be done by somebody with the title Configuration Manager, who may not do the tasks of analysis, design, implementation, or developer testing. Similarly, database design may be done by somebody with the title of Database Administrator (DBA), rather than a person with the title Developer.

As a developer, your overall objective is to translate requirements into executable code of sufficient quality.

As a developer, your overall objective is to translate requirements into executable code of sufficient quality. This needs to be done in close collaboration with the architect (see Chapter 16) to ensure that the design complies with the overall architecture. The developer's work can be broken down into the following high-level tasks:

- Understand the requirements and design constraints
- Design, implement, and test software that addresses the requirements
- Design, implement, and test any necessary databases
- Frequently integrate your application with the work of other developers

To carry out these tasks effectively, you need the following skills:

- You need to understand how requirements are documented.
- You need to have a solid understanding of the implementation technology and tools to be used, such as J2EE, .NET, the IDE you are using, visual modeling tools, and the deployment platform.
- You need to be creative, yet structured, keeping a good balance between finding clever solutions to tricky problems and developing in a disciplined fashion.
- You need to be quality conscious and make sure that checked-in code is tested.

As a developer, your contributions are critical (see Figure 17.1), especially during Construction, when the majority of code is designed, implemented, and tested. You also participate in Elaboration, when you design, implement, and test architecturally significant scenarios to help verify that the architecture is good enough. During Elaboration, you also implement architectural mechanisms, that is, reusable solutions to common problems such as how to deal with persistency or inter-process communication. You continue to refine the application through defect-fixing in Transition, and you may also spend some time in Inception building conceptual prototypes.

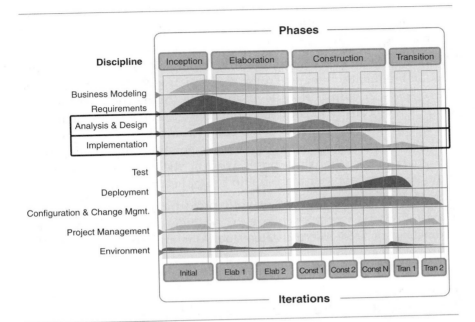

FIGURE 17.1 A Developer's Role in the RUP. *A developer is primarily involved in the RUP disciplines of Analysis & Design and Implementation—this means that they do most of their work in the Elaboration and Construction phases. Developers also play an important role during Transition and a minor role in Inception.*

Overview of the Developer's Tasks

A developer's tasks can be divided into the following categories (each of which is described in a later section):

- Understand the requirements and design constraints
- Design, implement, and test use cases and components
- Design, implement, and test any necessary databases
- Frequently integrate your application with the work of other developers

After the tasks have been explored, the section Developer Best Practices, later in this chapter, provides a toolbox of techniques to choose from as required by your project.

All of the developer's tasks are done iteratively, as indicated in the section Frequently Integrate Your Application with the Work of Other Developers. It is important to keep this in mind when reading this chapter. Typically, you complete some design, some implementation, some testing, come up with some good ideas which you implement, and then reverse-engineer your implementation into an improved design. For instructional purposes, we describe the thought process in a more sequential order than should be applied in practice.

Note that based on the size of your project and how formally you choose to work, you may choose to document some of the described artifacts (especially intermediate artifacts) in an informal manner (for example, on a whiteboard).

Understand the Requirements and Design Constraints

As a developer, it is essential that you understand the requirements. The first step is to read through the Vision, which gives a high-level understanding of what the system should do, providing you with the bigger context of how your piece of the project fits in the overall solution.

Functional requirements are primarily documented in use cases.

Functional requirements are primarily documented in use cases. You may be responsible for implementing the capabilities of anything from a partial use case to several use cases. To get acquainted with a use case, read through the use-case description. You find an example of the use-case description in the section Detail Actors and Use Cases, in Chapter 15. It is also essential that you review or take part in the development of the user-interface prototype. It will provide you with a better understanding of what capabilities the users expect from the use case. You can find more information about the user-interface prototype in the section Develop User-Interface Prototypes, in Chapter 15. Especially for smaller projects, you may have the same person doing analysis and design of a use case. This automatically provides the developer with an in-depth understanding of the use case, since he or she participated in describing it.

Nonfunctional requirements are documented in the Supplementary Specification, in the RUP, which contains requirements on performance, usability, platform support, and technical and other constraints. For example, you may not use any open-source software in your application. It is important that you read through this document, so you can choose the right technical solution within the constraints in which your implementation must reside. Note that for smaller projects with less ceremony, these nonfunctional requirements may not all be documented. If this is the case, you need to communicate with analysts and other stakeholders to ensure you have a good understanding of the nonfunctional requirements.

Nonfunctional requirements are documented in the Supplementary Specification.

As a developer, you are responsible for architectural control of the part of the system that you design. This means that you need to work hand-in-hand with the architect to ensure that your design fits within the overall architecture. Information about which architectural mechanisms (common solutions to common problems) are supposed to be used is found in the Software Architecture Document. Here you may find ready-made solutions for how to handle communication with external systems, deal with persistency, handle garbage collection, and so on. The SAD also contains information about the major building blocks and their interfaces—information that will help you understand the architecture within which your code will coexist. For smaller projects with less ceremony, architectural decisions and architectural mechanisms may not all be documented in the SAD. In this case, you need to work closely with the architect, making sure that you fully understand the architecture.

As you design, implement, and test your solution, it is essential that you communicate and demonstrate progress to the extended team, including representatives of the user. By demonstrating partial solutions, you can get early feedback, allowing you to make necessary improvements to your implementations when it is easiest to do so.

As you design, implement, and test your solution, it is essential that you communicate and demonstrate progress to the extended team.

As you design, implement, and test the application, you are likely to notice inconsistencies or "holes" in the requirements. It is important that you provide the analyst with this information, so the analyst can correct or refine the use cases.

Design, Implement, and Test Use Cases and Components

You want to make sure that you design, implement, and test the user capabilities you have agreed to deliver. These capabilities are primarily captured in use-case descriptions and associated user-interface prototypes. As discussed earlier in the section Understand the Requirements and Design Constraints, you find constraints on how to implement the use cases in both the Supplementary Specification and the Software Architecture Document.

You want to design, implement, and test the most essential use cases in Elaboration, which we describe in more detail in the section Use Architecturally Significant Use Cases to Drive the Architecture, in Chapter 7. Note that in Elaboration, you typically implement only the most important scenarios for those use cases, not the complete use case. During each iteration in Construction, you will implement more and more use cases and complete the use cases that were previously only partially implemented. By the end of Construction, all use cases should be fully implemented, but they may still require some minor modifications in Transition, based on user feedback and found defects.

Design Use-Case Realizations and Components

The design representation of a use case is called use-case realization.

The design representation of a use case is called use-case realization. It describes how a particular use case is realized within the design model in terms of collaborating components. Different developers prefer different approaches when producing a use-case realization. In this section we will describe an approach that has proven valuable by facilitating communication between analysts and developers, by providing a step-by-step guide to identifying good components, and by forcing the design to address the requirements—but no more. Let's take a look at this five-step approach to producing a use-case realization, dividing the work into an analysis section and a design section:

Step 1: Produce a first-draft outline for what analysis objects are needed to provide the collaboration.

Step 2: Distribute behavior to analysis classes.

Step 3: Detail analysis classes and unify the analysis model.

Step 4: Do use-case design.

Step 5: Detail each design class and unify the design model.

It should be noted that for very simple and data-centric use cases, especially when implementing them in a powerful programming language such as a fourth-generation language (4GL, for example, Visual Basic and PowerBuilder), you typically do not need to go through all these steps (more about this later).

Note that you need to choose the right level of formality for your project. Some developers prefer to capture the output from steps 1 through 3 on whiteboards or even in their heads; others prefer to capture it directly in a visual modeling tool. Some developers may even be inclined to jump directly to step 4. This forces you to move directly from high-level requirements to detailed design decisions. It also makes it harder for you to communicate with the analyst to make sure that you understand the requirements (part of step 1), and it makes it more difficult to come up with a design that complies with the architecture and is unified since you did not do step 3. This means that if you skip steps 1 through 3, you need to mitigate these risks, for example by having experienced developers, by developing less-complex systems, by having developers who understand the requirements well, and by having strong architects on your team.

Finally, the suggested approach works no matter if you are using object-oriented programming languages or other programming languages, as long as your language supports implementation of components through encapsulation.

Let's take a closer look at these steps.

Step 1: Produce a first-draft outline for what analysis objects are needed to provide the collaboration.

Many people new to object-oriented development find it difficult to identify good objects. The RUP provides concrete guidelines that

greatly facilitate this task by dividing classes into three categories, or so-called "stereotypes":

Boundary classes. Provide an interface toward actors or protocols for interaction with external systems.

Examples: User screens or http:// protocols.

Control classes. Encapsulate the sequencing or behavior of the use case.

Examples: Scheduler or RegistrationController.

Entity classes. Store (normally persistent) information about some phenomenon, such as an event, a person, or a real-life object, and contain the business rules associated with that information.

Examples: Student, Schedule, or Course Offering.

Use-case realizations follow a typical analysis pattern. There is usually

- **One boundary class** for each actor involved in the use case to encapsulate the interface toward that actor.
- **One control class** for each use case to encapsulate the sequencing within that use case.
- **As many entity classes as needed** to store information about various phenomena that need to be represented.

Many of the entity classes needed may already be created (at least toward the second half of Construction), but you may have to add a few additional entity objects during this step. Place objects from the classes you need in a diagram, often called a "View of Participating Classes (VOPC)," and create relationships to show how their instances are communicating. Figure 17.2 is an example of such a diagram. Collaborate closely with the analyst responsible for the use case. Creating a VOPC often highlights holes in the use-case description. You should also consider collaborating closely with the architect, since the architect may be able to help you to rapidly produce a good

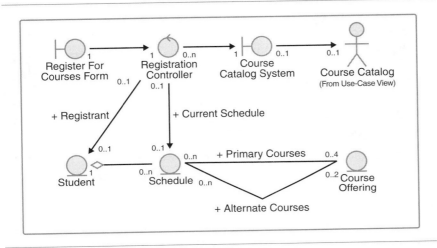

FIGURE 17.2 Example of the View of Participating Classes. *The View of Participating Classes shows the analysis classes whose instances participate in a given use case. It provides a high-level understanding of what classes are involved, without focusing on details such as what operations are involved at what time to provide the functionality of the use case.*

first-draft model that is consistent with the rest of the system. Involving the architect can radically reduce the amount of time you need to spend on step 3. Our experience also shows that people new to object-oriented techniques need help the first few times doing this step.

Step 2: *Distribute behavior to analysis classes.*

To verify that you have all the classes you need and to understand the responsibilities of each class, you need to describe how the identified objects are collaborating with each other. For those new to component-based development, we have found that a very useful learning tool is to do this as a fun group exercise, similar to the CRC card technique introduced by Kent Beck and Ward Cunningham.[1] Get your

---

1. See Beck 1998.

team together and have each person play the role of either one of the objects or one of the actors. To represent operations invoked[2] upon various objects, someone (actor/object) passes an item (such as a ball) to the person (actor/object) he or she wants to request a service from. A scribe documents the interaction and the identified responsibility of the actor/object. Then the person with the ball takes a turn at making a request, and so on. Let's look at an example of how this role-play would work for the use case Register for Course for a course registration system (shown in Figure 17.3).

1. The person representing the actor Student passes the ball to the person representing an instance of the boundary class *RegisterForCoursesForm* stating that the actor wants to create a schedule.

2. The person representing an instance of the boundary class *RegisterForCoursesForm* sends a request "get course offerings" to the person representing the instance of the class *RegistrationController*.

3. The person representing an instance of the boundary class *RegistrationController*...

4.   ...And so on.

During this role-play, you come to understand the responsibilities of each class. Any missing classes will be apparent when you have the ball and there is no instance of a class from which to request a needed service.

This description represents an extremely simplified view of this activity; you can find more guidance in the RUP in the activity Use-Case Analysis. Typically, the operations identified at this stage are at a high level, and many of them will later be broken down into several smaller operations involving more objects.

---

2. Invoking an operation means that one object sends a message to another object instructing it what to do.

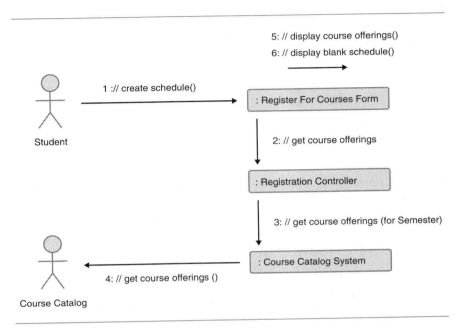

5: // display course offerings()

6: // display blank schedule()

1 :// create schedule()

: Register For Courses Form

Student

2: // get course offerings

: Registration Controller

3: // get course offerings (for Semester)

: Course Catalog System

4: // get course offerings ()

Course Catalog

FIGURE 17.3 Example of a Collaboration Diagram. *A collaboration diagram shows the dynamic behavior of a use case. It specifies the order in which operations are invoked to provide the functionality of the use case (or part of the use case). In this example, to Register for Courses, (1) the Student invokes the operation Create Schedule on an instance of the class RegisterForCoursesForm, (2) RegisterForCoursesForm invokes the operation "get course offerings" on RegistrationController, and so on.*

Step 3: Detail analysis classes and unify the analysis model.

During the role-play you need to document the responsibilities (operations) of each class by describing the operations and the data (attributes) the class needs to handle.

The next step is to review the responsibilities and associations of the identified classes. To do this, you need to work with other developers and architects to understand the bigger picture. What you are trying to address in this step is to ensure that different developers have not

identified different analysis classes that do almost the same thing (in which case you will have to decide whether they should be merged) and refactor the analysis model to make sure that it supports, rather than breaks, the architecture of your system. You should answer questions such as the following:

- Are there classes that should be merged or split?
- What associations are needed between classes?
- Are there opportunities for reuse?
- Should some of the classes be generalized?

The steps that follow will continue to refine the analysis model, and in the future if you want to maintain the analysis model separately, you take a snapshot of the model at this stage for future reference.

Step 4: Do use-case design.

During use-case design, you continue to detail the collaboration diagram created in step 2. Do this in parallel with step 5, "Detail each design class and unify the design model." Specify in detail each operation and its parameters. In many cases, you'll notice that a previously identified high-level operation needs to be broken down into several smaller operations, potentially involving additional classes identified (one analysis class may often be implemented by two or more design classes; see below).

For use cases in which the order of invoked operations is significant, you typically want to document the use-case collaboration in a sequence diagram, rather than in a collaboration diagram (see Figure 17.4). When implementing simple use cases (such as online viewing of database records, or updates to those database records with few business rules involved) and using powerful 4GLs such as Visual Basic or PowerBuilder, it is normally less essential to document the exact sequence in which operations are invoked, since the language environment takes care of a lot of the involved logic for you (such as how to synchronize values of various fields on a screen with the corresponding database tables). In such cases, you may not bother to produce a more detailed documentation for the use-case collaboration other than the View of Participating Classes (see Figure 17.2).

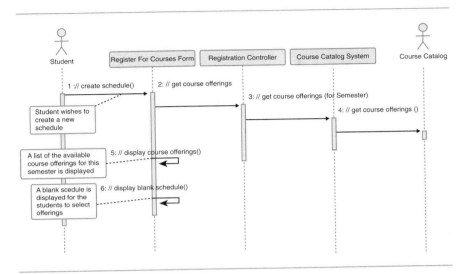

FIGURE 17.4 Example of a Sequence Diagram. *A sequence diagram shows the same information as a collaboration diagram, but presents it in a way that provides a clearer overview of the sequencing. Time flows from top to bottom. Each column represents an instance of a class, and the arrows represent that an operation is invoked.*

You will also take advantage of your identified architectural mechanisms, which provide solutions for dealing with persistent storage, inter-process communication, transaction management, security, message routing, error reporting, and so on. We describe architectural mechanisms in more detail in Chapters 7 and 16.

Step 5: *Detail each design class and unify the design model.*

In parallel with use-case design, detail the description of each design class. Specify each operation needed to support the key scenarios, as well as required attributes. Provide the level of detail necessary to implement the class. In many cases, an analysis class will be implemented by two or more design classes. For example, when implementing the analysis class *CourseCatalogSystem*, you may need a series

of design classes to implement a persistent storage of a set of database tables and related business rules for updating these tables.

Since a design class may participate in several different use cases, several developers may have a say in what the design class should look like. You need to decide whether to allow several people to change a design class (and then also have a collective ownership of the implementation and unit testing of that component). If you decide not to have collective ownership, there should still be a developer responsible for the design, implementation, and testing of each use case to make sure that you deliver the capabilities expected by the users. It should be noted that collective ownership typically works for smaller systems with more experienced developers. When developing larger systems, developers will not be familiar with large parts of the system, and the risk is too great that they will not understand the complexities of a component's necessary changes. This may also be the case for smaller systems where inexperienced developers may introduce too many defects when modifying a component's design or implementation.

When designing classes, keep in mind established design patterns, such as the so-called Gang of Four patterns.[3] You may find these and other patterns useful for solving common design problems.

Similar to step 3, you need to work with other developers and architects to unify the design model. You want to ensure that different developers have not identified different design classes doing very similar things (in this case you will have to decide whether they should they be merged) and to ensure that you are producing a design model that supports, rather than breaks, the system architecture. As an example, for layered architectures you need not only to decide in which layer various components reside, but also to make sure that the relationships between components don't break any rules you may have set up about visibility between layers.

---

3. See Gamma 1995.

Implement Use Cases and Components

Since implementing use cases is done component-by-component, some of the components you need may already be implemented or partially implemented. Based on whether you have collective owner- ship, you either develop or refine the components yourself, or you work with another developer to ensure they understand what needs to be done. A design model can greatly facilitate this communication.

Your project should have programming guidelines for the language(s) you are using, and as a developer, it is important that you follow these guidelines to ensure consistency within your project and optimal usage of the language. The RUP product provides you with programming guidelines for some languages (or you can use your own guidelines).

Some developers are good at abstract thinking and always prefer to cre- ate a design and then implement it. Other developers find it more pro- ductive to do a lot of the low-level design while coding. This is perfectly fine—do whatever is the most effective for you—but update your design to reflect your code to ensure that the code is maintainable and understandable by others. This is facilitated by using a visual modeling environment that can round-trip engineer your code. Through reverse engineering you can capture the static design model, but you need to recreate the dynamics, that is, show how the various components inter- act with each other to provide the required functionality.

It is also important to continually integrate your code, something we talk more about in the section Frequently Integrate Your Application.

In many cases, code reviews can radically improve the quality of your code. Some developers find great value in pair programming, mean- ing that two developers work side-by-side to write the code. These and other best practices are described in more detail in the section Developer Best Practices.

Developer Testing

As a developer, you need to continuously test your implementation to verify that it provides the required functionality and performance. As mentioned earlier, code reviews can reveal some defects by statically

parsing and analyzing the source files, but you also need to understand whether your application provides expected behavior. The only way of determining that is by monitoring the application during its execution at runtime. Runtime analysis ensures that your application uses memory efficiently and without errors, that your components are fast and scalable, and that you test everything before you check in the source files.

To test whether components provide required functionality, you may need to design and implement test drivers and test stubs to emulate other components that will interact with your component(s). Some visual modeling environments can automatically generate these test drivers and stubs for you. Once the stubs are ready, you can run a number of test scenarios. Typically these test scenarios are derived from the use-case scenarios in which the component(s) takes part, since the use-case scenarios identify typical ways in which the components will interact with each other when the users are using the application. You also look at the Supplementary Specification to understand other constraints that need to be tested.

Runtime analysis can radically reduce the amount of time that needs to be spent on integration and system testing of your code.

There are many other problems that can be hard to detect later in the project, such as memory leaks or performance problems. As a developer, you can radically reduce the amount of time that needs to be spent on integration and system testing by doing runtime analysis of your code. Runtime analysis is done with tools that examine an application's execution details for method, object, or source line of code. Inadequate memory usage can significantly reduce scalability and can be very difficult to optimize later in the development cycle. In some cases, memory leaks can cause an application to crash when it runs out of available memory. Another reason to perform runtime analysis is to find performance bottlenecks. Runtime analysis tools can identify the root cause of performance problems in code (see Figure 17.5). Using such tools in parallel with reviewing the use cases can help ensure that all common usage scenarios have good enough performance.

Automated test tools can also help you identify what code has been tested. This can help you to optimize unit and component tests to cover more use-case scenarios and thus make sure that your code is bug free. If you do not test the code, how can you know whether it will function or perform as expected?

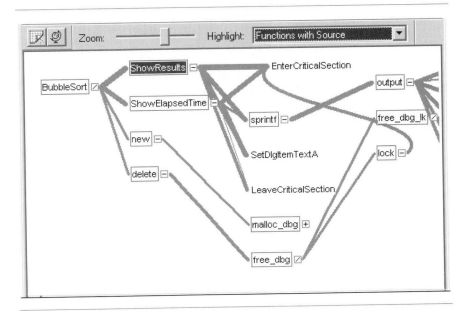

FIGURE 17.5 Runtime Analysis Can Detect Performance Bottlenecks. *Tools such as Rational PurifyPlus monitor the execution of an application, or components, to identify excessive or erroneous memory usage, performance bottlenecks, and untested code. In this screen shot, we see potential performance bottlenecks identified by thick lines, showing that the execution of these operations is much slower than the rest of the application. For each potential bottleneck, the developer can determine whether it represents a real issue by comparing the screen to common scenarios represented by the use case.*

Design, Implement, and Test Any Necessary Databases

Most systems have a database, and you need to understand how persistent data is to be stored in, and retrieved from, the database. A first assumption is to have a database table for each persistent design class, with a column for each attribute containing persistent data. This provides a very simplified, first-draft logical database.

If you are using relational databases and doing object-oriented development, you need to pay special attention to when and how persistent data shall be retrieved from the database and placed into instantiated objects, and how to design the physical database to achieve required performance. Using an object-oriented database makes the mapping easier by automating a lot of the logics involved.

During Elaboration, you want to decide how to handle persistency in your system, and then design, implement, and test one or several architectural mechanisms that can be reused for persistency issues. Also establish the major database structures (tables, indexes, and primary and foreign key columns) to support the architecturally significant scenarios. In addition, representative data volumes should be loaded into the databases to support architectural performance testing. Based on the results of performance testing, the data model may need to be optimized, including but not limited to denormalization, optimizing physical storage attributes or distribution, or indexing.

In Construction, additional columns may be added to tables, views may be created to support query and reporting requirements, and indexes may be created to optimize performance, but major restructuring of tables should not occur. This would be a sign that the architecture was not stable and that Construction was started prematurely, or that you have evolving requirements that add architectural risks to the project.

You can find comprehensive guidance within the Rational Unified Process in the area of database design (see the activity Database Design and the Guidelines: Data Model). You'll also find useful information in Ambler 2000.

Frequently Integrate Your Application with the Work of Other Developers

A build demonstrates a subset of the capabilities to be provided in the final product.

Frequent integration of your application is a core principle when doing iterative development. When you integrate an application you create a **build,** which is an operational version of the system or part of the system that demonstrates a subset of the capabilities to be provided in the final product.

A build is not, however, the same as a release, which is the end result of an iteration. If you have a month-long iteration, you may produce daily builds, where each build is a small step closer to the release planned for the end of the iteration. Frequent builds ensure engineering progress by allowing you to validate that the code implemented since the last build works properly with other code. A build may be somewhat unstable, providing limited or no additional user functionality. A release, on the other hand, should be stable and offer new user functionality and mitigation of technical risks, all according to the iteration plan.

You typically want to minimize the time between builds to enable rapid feedback, especially in late Construction and Transition, but there is a cost associated with each build. The larger the size of your system, and the larger and more distributed your team is, the more expensive it is to do frequent builds. A good Configuration Management system with support for automated build management can significantly reduce the cost of doing frequent builds. Also note that the longer the time between builds, the more expensive the build will be because there will be more integration issues to resolve.

A team of three co-located developers with very primitive Configuration Management tool support may find that they can do daily builds, while a 100-person team distributed over several locations may accomplish only weekly builds in Inception and Elaboration, biweekly builds in Construction, and daily builds in Transition. The same 100-person team distributed over several locations, but without an effective Configuration Management system, may be able to do only monthly builds, in practice making it very difficult to do iterative development. As an example of what can be achieved with good automation and a good Configuration and Change Management process, Rational products are typically built using daily builds for at least the last 100 days of each major product release. These builds integrate the work of several hundred developers (who are distributed over many sites on three continents) building the various editions of Rational Suite.

Configuration Management Workspaces

A workspace provides each project member with an environment that selects and presents the appropriate version of each file.

As projects grow in size, it is increasingly important to set up private workspaces. A workspace provides each project member with an environment that selects and presents the appropriate version of each file. The workspace provides control over both sharing and isolation so the developers can stay isolated from changes made by others, but at the same time, they are able to unit-test their changes with changes made by certain other developers. A workspace also works as a "time capsule," allowing a developer, analyst, tester, or other team members to see older versions of binaries, documents, tests, tools, and other objects. This is of great help when maintaining the system.

When a developer has implemented and tested a component or a set of components so they are stable, the developer moves them into a common workspace, often called an **integration workspace.** The person responsible for producing builds does so from the components in the integration workspace. This ensures that builds are created only from components that have been validated by the developer.

Note that Configuration Management tools are valuable to all team members, not only developers, ensuring that you keep track of all project artifacts.

Integration Planning

When doing iterative development, it becomes increasingly complex to plan builds and integration testing. For each iteration, you need to do an **Integration Build Plan,** specifying what capabilities should be testable in each build, and which components you need to integrate to produce the build with required capabilities, such as use cases, parts of use cases, or other functionality that can be tested.

Integration planning is essential since components are often dependent on each other in some way. To get a certain capability, you may find from the use-case realizations that you need Component A. But Component A may require the existence of Components B and C to be compilable. Component C may require the existence of Component D, and so on. In many cases, it is sufficient just to do a very shallow implementation of Components B, C, and D, allowing you to save a lot of time by focusing on the most essential functionality, while still being able to integrate your system. The Integration Build Plan specifies which components need to be developed, and allows you to improve your iteration plan and understand which stubs need to be developed.

You also need to decide which version of each component should be included in the build. It is not always the latest version, since a developer may be working on future capabilities of the component, temporarily putting it in an unstable state. As a developer, you need to review the Integration Build Plan to ensure you are developing the right components in the right order and moving them into the integration workspace.

Produce a Build

When producing a build, the developer is responsible for delivering and integrating the components in the integration workspace according to the Integration Build Plan. Depending on the complexity and number of components to be integrated, it is often more efficient to produce the target build in a number of steps, adding more components with each step and producing a series of intermediate "mini" builds. These are subjected to a minimal integration test (usually a subset of the tests described in the Integration Build Plan for the target build) to ensure that what is added is compatible with what already exists in the system integration workspace. It is easier to isolate and diagnose problems using this approach.

Once the build has been produced, all developers must rebase their workspace to update it with the developments of the others. The build is also made available for testing, so it can be tested while development continues working on the next build. With frequent builds, you need to automate regression testing to keep testing costs down. In this way, hundreds or thousands of regression tests can be run daily or weekly, ensuring that newly introduced defects are rapidly found.

With frequent builds, you need to automate regression testing to keep testing costs down.

Developer Best Practices

In this section, we describe some of the more popular best practices for designing, implementing, and unit-testing code; we also indicate when the practices are applicable. Many of these practices have been around for some time but have been further elaborated on and popularized by the Agile Movement, especially XP.[4] Some of these best practices were described earlier in this chapter:

- **Test frequently** (see the sections Developer Testing and Produce a Build).
- **Integrate continuously** (see the section Frequently Integrate Your Application with the Work of Other Developers).
- **Perform runtime analysis** (see the section Developer Testing).

Other best practices are

- Test first.
- Refactor your code.
- Use patterns, architectural mechanisms, and other reusable assets.
- Keep your design simple.
- Pair programming.

Test First

The idea behind test first is to write and implement the test cases first and then write the code.

The idea behind test first[5] is to write and implement the test cases first and then write the code. The code is written as simply as possible and then improved until the test case passes. The programmer selects a task, writes one or two very simple unit test cases that fail because the unit is not performing the task, and then modifies the program to make the tests pass. The programmer continually adds more test cases and makes them pass until the software does everything it is supposed to do. If you apply this best practice, you should consider combining it with refactoring, or you may end up with overly complex implementations. Test first works well with a use-case-driven

---

4. See Beck 2000.
5. See Beck 2000.

approach, since use cases provide you with a good base for early iden-tification of test cases. Kent Beck and others are also working on an approach called Test-First Design that describes how to integrate test first into your design process.

Refactor Your Code and Design

Refactoring[6] is building a component or set of components by making numerous small and well-defined changes to improve their structure without modifying their functionality. The aim is to simplify and improve upon the existing solution to get higher quality and more maintainable code. After each small improvement, you need to run through your tests to ensure that nothing broke. This means that you need to combine refactoring with the test-first best practice. The com-bination of test first and refactoring has been successfully used in many projects.

Note that refactoring should not be used as a substitute for good design and architecture. There are limits to what refactoring can accomplish. It is also important to remember that "Perfection is the enemy of suc-cess."[7] There is a time when a component is sufficiently structured and further improvements will have a very low return on investment.

Use Patterns, Architectural Mechanisms, and Other Reusable Assets

The "not invented here" mentality is a major hurdle to overcome in becoming a good developer. Rather than submitting to this way of think-ing, you should seek opportunities to reuse solutions that work. You need to be aware of the architectural mechanisms you are using within your projects, and which patterns are available from platform vendors and other sources.[8] Naturally, you can also use other sources such as project class libraries, as well as other available third-party components.

---

6. See Newkirk 2001 and Fowler 1999.
7. See Gilb 1988.
8. See Gamma 1995.

Note that to reduce potential liabilities, some companies have clear restrictions in terms of which shareware components can be used.

Working closely with the architecture team and reviewing the Software Architecture Document should help you in maximizing reuse. If your company is producing reusable assets, you should consider documenting and packaging these assets using a standard called Reuse Asset Specification (RAS). This specification provides guidelines for how to structure and document the assets so they are easy to understand and use. RAS assets can automatically be understood and unpackaged by other tools, such as Rational XDE.

Keep Your Design Simple

The fundamental idea behind keeping the design simple is to only design for what is needed right now. The underlying assumption is that when you design for future capabilities, you do not have enough information to create the right design, and you typically end up with a more complex design than is warranted by the problem you are trying to solve.

You need to balance the benefit of making a simple design with the advantage of thinking one step ahead.

On the other hand, if you create a design without considering future capabilities, you may end up with a nonoptimal design requiring major rework. You need to balance the benefit of making a simple design with the advantage of thinking one step ahead. The more experienced you are and the better you know what the future application looks like, the more you can think ahead. But be careful not to add unnecessary complexity, making your product overly intricate and difficult to maintain.

When designing, always make sure that you work with the architect to ensure that your design is consistent with the overall architecture. The architect may also be able to guide you in the appropriate level of simplicity for the design versus how much to design for future capabilities.

Pair Programming

Pair programming[9] is a practice of two developers working side-by-side to produce code while sharing one workstation. One developer

9. See Martin 2001.

drives the workstation while the other looks on, carefully watching the code being produced. The driver thinks tactically and is concerned with the code. The observer validates syntax and thinks strategically about the whole program. It is important that the roles are traded frequently.

Many projects, and some preliminary research, reveal that code is written with fewer defects when using pair programming than when a single developer writes the code.[10] However, a fair amount of people dislike this best practice; they find that it slows down skilled programmers. As with all best practices, you need to figure out what fits your project, your culture, and the personality of your developers.

The Developer Role in the Rational Unified Process

The RUP product provides a more fine-grained representation of the Developer role by describing more specialized roles. This chapter describes the responsibilities of the specialized roles listed here in italics. The roles of a Software Architect and Architecture Reviewer are described in Chapter 16, and the role of a Test Designer is described in Chapter 18. We do not describe the Capsule Designer in this book, since this role is applicable only for real-time systems.

- Capsule Designer
- *Code Reviewer*
- *Database Designer*
- *Implementer*
- *Integrator*
- Software Architect
- Architecture Reviewer
- *Design Reviewer*
- *Designer*
- Test Designer

---

10. See Williams 2000.

Available Resources for Developers

Below are some resources for developers seeking a better understanding of how to work within a RUP project.

Recommended Reading

Scott Ambler and Larry Constantine. *The Unified Process Construction Phase.* Lawrence, KS: CMP Books, 2000, pp. 163–170.

Kent Beck. *Extreme Programming Explained: Embrace Change.* Boston: Addison-Wesley, 2000.

Grady Booch. *Object-Oriented Analysis and Design with Applications, Second Edition.* Menlo Park, CA: Addison-Wesley, 1994.

Erich Gamma, Richard Helm, Ralph Johnson, and John Vlissides. *Design Patterns: Elements of Reusable Object-Oriented Software.* Reading, MA: Addison-Wesley, 1995.

Philippe Kruchten. *The Rational Unified Process: An Introduction, Second Edition.* Boston: Addison-Wesley, 2000.

James Newkirk and Robert Martin. *Extreme Programming in Practice.* Boston: Addison-Wesley, 2001.

Recommended Training

The following training courses have been developed to support RUP users. They are delivered by IBM Software and its partners (see www.rational.com for more information).

- Principles of the Rational Unified Process: Web-based training.
- Essentials of the Rational Unified Process: Instructor led (two days).
- Principles of Visual Modeling: Web-based training.
- Principles of Use-Case Modeling with UML: Web-based training.
- Principles of Analysis: Web-based training.
- Object-Oriented Analysis Using UML: Instructor led (three days).
- Object-Oriented Design Using UML: Instructor led (four days).

CHAPTER 18

A Tester's Guide to the RUP

And what is good, Phaedrus,
And what is not good—
Need we ask anyone to tell us these things?

(Plato, circa 370 B.C.)

You are a tester or you are responsible for some aspect of software quality assessment in your organization. This chapter is a guide to help you start with the RUP. You will find definitions of the major concepts we are using in the RUP relative to testing, our philosophy of testing, and a description of the key artifacts you may be responsible for, and we will introduce you to the major activities involving the tester.[1]

The Mission of the Tester

The focus of the tester is primarily about **Objective Assessment.** Testers offer their services to other parts of the development organization to help assess the software product based on appropriate criteria, such as perceived quality, conformance to standards, and defect discovery. The evaluations provided by this service help other team players (developers, managers, even customers) to make the right

---

1. This chapter was developed with Paul Szymkowiak.

decisions about their next actions, based on demonstrable and objective information. Anyone who is serious about producing an excellent product faces two problems in particular:

- How do you know when the product is "good enough"?
- If the product is not yet good enough, how do you assure that your teammates know it?

The answer to the first question determines when an organization releases a product. The answer to the second question prevents the organization from releasing a bad product.

The Concept of Product Quality in the RUP

You may be thinking, "I don't want to ship a merely satisfactory product; I want to ship a great product." Let's explore that. What happens when you tell your coworkers, your management, or your investors that your quality standards are high, and that you intend to ship a great product? If it's early in the project cycle, they probably nod and smile. Everyone likes quality. However, if it's late in the project cycle, you're probably under a lot of pressure to complete the project, and creating a great product may require that you engage in extensive testing, fix many problems (even small ones), add features, or even scrap and rewrite a large part of the code. You will also have to resolve disputes over different visions of "good" quality. Greatness is hard work. Perfection is even harder. Eventually, the people who control the project will come to you and say something like, "Perfection would be nice, but we have to be practical. We're running a business. Quality is good, but not quality at any cost. As you know, all software has bugs."

Greatness can be a motivating goal. It appeals to the pride you have in your work. But there are problems with using what amounts to "if quality is good, more quality must be better" to justify the pursuit of excellence. For one thing, to make such an argument can make you seem like a quality fanatic, rather than a balanced thinker. For another thing, it ignores the cost factor. In leaving cost out of the picture, the "more is better" argument also ignores diminishing returns. The better your product, the harder it is to justify further improvement. While you labor to gold plate one aspect of a product, you must ignore other aspects of the product, or the potential opportunities presented by other projects. Every day, the business has to make choices about the best use of resources, and it must consider factors other than quality.

The RUP product has incorporated and extended the concept of Good Enough Quality (GEQ) from the work of James Bach.[2] This GEQ concept provides, paradoxically, a more effective argument than "more is better," because it provides a target that is either achievable or not achievable, in which case it becomes a de facto argument for canceling or rechartering the project.

Paradigms of "Good Enough"

Most businesses practice some form of "good enough reasoning" about their products. The only ones that don't are those that believe they have achieved perfection, because they lack the imagination and skill to see how their products might be improved.

Here are some models of the "good enough" approach. Some of them are more effective than others, depending on the situation, but all have their weaknesses:

- **Not Too Bad ("We're not dead yet").** Our quality only has to be good enough so we can continue to stay in business. Make it good enough so that we aren't successfully sued.

- **Positive Infallibility ("Anything we do is good").** Our organization is the best in the world. Because we're so good, anything we do is automatically good. Think about success. Don't think about failure because "negative" thinking makes for poor quality.

- **Righteous Exhaustion ("Perfection or bust").** No product is good enough; it's effort that counts. And only our complete exhaustion will be a good enough level of effort. Business issues are not our concern. We will do everything we possibly can to make it perfect. Since we'll never be finished improving, someone will have to come in and pry it from our fingers if they want it. Then they will bear the blame for any quality problems, not us.

---

2. See Bach 1997.

- **Customer Is Always Right ("Customers seem to like it").** If customers like it, it must be good enough. Of course, you can't please everybody all the time. And if a current or potential customer doesn't like the product, it's up to them to let us know. We can't read their minds. Quality by market share?

- **Defined Process ("We follow a good process").** Quality is the result of the process we use to build the product. We have defined our process, and we think it's a good process. Therefore, as long as we follow the process, a good-enough product will inevitably result.

- **Static Requirements ("We satisfy the requirements").** We have defined quality in terms of objective, quantifiable, noncontroversial goals. If we meet those goals, then we have a good-enough product, no matter what other subjective, nonquantifiable, controversial goals might be suggested.

- **Accountability ("We fulfill our promises").** Quality is defined by contract. We promise to do certain things and achieve certain goals. If we fulfill our contract, that is good enough.

- **Advocacy ("We make every reasonable effort").** We advocate for excellence. Throughout the project, we look for ways to prevent problems, and to find and fix the ones we can't prevent. If we work faithfully toward excellence, that will be good enough.

- **Dynamic Tradeoff ("We weigh many factors").** With respect to our mission and the situation at hand, a product is good enough when it has sufficient benefits and no critical problems, its benefits sufficiently outweigh its noncritical problems, and it would cause more harm than good to continue improving it.

However, for certain types of applications—safety-critical systems, which may endanger human life—failure (or more precisely, certain types of failure) is simply not an option.

The Cost of Quality

Is a high-quality product necessarily more expensive? Depending on a lot of factors, such as process, skill, technology, tools, environment, and culture, you may be able to produce a much higher-quality product for the same cost than would otherwise be possible. A more testable and maintainable product will cost less to improve over the long run. Conversely, there are costs associated with poor quality, such as support costs and costs to the customer.

The cost of quality is a complex issue, and it is difficult to make broad generalizations. However, we can say with certainty that we can always spend more time on much better tests, much more error handling, and fixing or rewriting every part of the product. No matter how good you are, quality does cost something. And if you can't think of more improvements to make, it's more likely that you've reached the upper limit of your imagination, not of quality. There must be a point of "diminishing returns," a point where your "test ROI" becomes negative.

The cost of quality is a complex issue, and it is difficult to make broad generalizations.

In the software industry, GEQ is viewed more as a response to one particular cost over any other—the cost of not releasing the product soon enough. The specter of a market window, or an external deadline, imposes tangible penalties upon us if we can't meet the challenge to deliver on time. That's why the project endings are so often characterized by frenzied triage. If you want to know what an organization really believes is good enough and how well prepared they are for it, witness the last three days of any six-month software project; see what happens when a new problem is reported on the last day.

Wouldn't Quantification Help?

It can be tempting to reduce quality to a number and then set a numerical threshold that represents good-enough quality. The problem with that is you can measure only factors that relate to quality. But you can't measure quality itself. This is partly because the word "quality" is just a label for a relationship between a person and a thing. The statement "this product is high in quality" is just another way of saying, "Somebody values this product." It's a statement not only about the product, but also about people and the surrounding context. Even if the product stays the same, people and situations change, so there can be no single, static, true measure of quality. Read (or reread) Robert Pirsig's *Zen and the Art of Motorcycle Maintenance*, which states, "At the leading edge there are no subjects, no objects, only the track of Quality ahead, and if you have no formal

You can measure only factors that relate to quality. But you can't measure quality itself.

way of evaluating, no way of acknowledging this Quality, then the train has no way of knowing where to go."[3]

There are many measures you might use to get a sense of quality, even if you can't measure it completely and objectively. Even so, the question of what quality is good enough requires sophisticated judgment. You can't escape from the fact that, in the end, people have to think it through and make a judgment. For a simple product, that judgment might be easy. For a complex, high-stakes product, it's very hard. Making this call is not the responsibility of the tester, but the tester does provide the information for this decision. Finally, the definition of quality also depends on the problem space; quality for NASA or for surgical automation has a very different meaning from quality for a customer service rep's workstation and a different meaning from quality for a stock exchange.

Conformance to Standards

Assessment implies the comparison of the product to some standard. One standard of reference that often comes to mind is the requirements—the "specs" for the system. There may be other standards referred to, either formal standards, such as a Usability or Accessibility standard, or implicit standards, such as those related to look and feel (for example, we want it to match Windows 2000 conventions). There are also standards that are industry-specific: standards for the biomedical industry, the pharmaceutical industry, the aeronautical industry, and so on.

In practice, assessment is not just about comparing the software product against the requirements and other specification artifacts. We use—implicitly or explicitly—other standards for determining whether quality is acceptable. There are two important concerns that often require a broader consideration than the documented specifications:

- Are the specifications themselves complete? By their nature, specifications are somewhat abstract and evolve over the life of the project as a greater understanding of the problem and appropriate

---

3. See Pirsig, 1977, p. 277.

solutions are gained. Are there additional things you should assess that may be somewhat ambiguous or missing from the specifications?

- What exceptional events or conditions might cause the software to break? Specifications often overlook a number of exceptional concerns that are arguably more apparent to a tester. Sometimes that is because the requirements specifier—the analyst—is not familiar with certain aspects of the problem or solution domain, or because the exceptional requirements are regarded as implicit.

A diligent tester will consider tests that help to expose issues that arise from implied and omitted requirements.

The Quality Assurance Plan, which is part of the Software Development Plan and under responsibility of the Project Manager, defines the overarching approach to GEQ on the project and the techniques that will be used to assess whether an acceptable level of quality is being achieved (see also Chapter 12).

What Is Testing?

The Test discipline of the RUP product acts in many respects as a service provider to the other disciplines. **Testing** focuses primarily on the evaluation or assessment of quality and is realized through a number of core practices:

- Finding and documenting gaps in GEQ
- Generally advising team members about perceived software quality
- Validating through concrete demonstration the assumptions made in design and requirement specifications
- Validating that the software product functions as it was designed to function
- Validating that the requirements have been implemented appropriately

An interesting, but somewhat subtle difference between the Test Discipline and the other disciplines in RUP is that testing is essentially tasked with finding and exposing weaknesses in the software product.

The challenge is to avoid an approach that does not suitably and effectively challenge the software and expose its inherent problems and weaknesses, and an approach that is so negative that it is unlikely to ever find the quality of the software product acceptable.

For this effort to be successful, it necessitates a somewhat negative and destructive, rather than constructive, approach: "How could this software fail?" The challenge is to avoid both the approach that does not suitably and effectively challenge the software and expose its inherent problems and weaknesses, and the approach that is so negative that it is unlikely to ever find the quality of the software product acceptable.

Based on information presented in various surveys and essays, software testing is said to account for 30 to 50 percent of total software development costs. It is, therefore, perhaps surprising to note that most people believe computer software is not well tested before it is delivered. This contradiction is rooted in a few key issues:

- Testing is usually done late in the lifecycle, keeping project risks and the number of unknown factors very high for far too long, rather than testing with every iteration, as the RUP advocates.

- Testability is not considered in the product design (again, contrary to the RUP) and thereby increases the complexity of testing many times over, making test automation difficult, and in some cases making certain types of tests impossible.

- Test planning is done in isolation from the system under test (SUT), before any actual testing, when the least is known about the system under test. In contrast, the RUP advocates detailed test planning by iteration, using the experience of the previous iteration.

Beyond these issues, we also have to acknowledge that testing software is enormously challenging. The different ways a given program can behave are unquantifiable, and the number of potential tests for that program is arguably limited only by the imagination of the tester.

Testing is typically done without a guiding methodology, resulting in a wide variance of success from project to project.

Often, testing is typically done without a guiding methodology, resulting in a wide variance of success from project to project and organization to organization; success is primarily a factor of the quality, skills, and experience of the individual tester. Testing also suffers when insufficient use is made of productivity tools, to make the laborious aspects of testing manageable. A lot of testing is conducted without tools that allow the effective management of test assets such as extensive Test Data, without tools to evaluate detailed Test Results, and without appropriate support for automated test execution. While the flexibility of use and complexity of software makes "complete" testing an impossible goal in all but the most trivial systems, an appropriately chosen methodology and the use of proper supporting tools can improve the productivity and effectiveness of the software testing effort.

For "safety-critical" systems where a failure can harm people (such as air-traffic control, missile guidance, or medical delivery systems), high-quality software is essential for the success of the system. For a typical MIS system, the criticality of the system may not be as immediately obvious as in a safety-critical system, but it's likely that a serious defect could cost the business using the software considerable expense in lost revenue or possible legal costs. In this "information age" of increasing demand on the provision of electronically delivered services over media such as the Internet, many MIS systems are now considered "mission-critical"—that is, when software failures occur in these systems, companies cannot fulfill their functions and experience massive losses.

Many projects do not pay much attention to performance testing until very late in the development cycle. For systems that will be in continuous use (24/7), for distributed systems, and for systems that must scale up to large numbers of simultaneous users, it is important to assess early and continuously to verify that the expected performance will be met. This can start in the Elaboration phase when enough of the architecture is in place to start exercising the system under various load conditions.

A continuous approach to quality, initiated early in the software lifecycle, can significantly lower the cost of completing and maintaining the software. This greatly reduces the risk associated with deploying poor-quality software.

It is important to assess early and continuously to verify that the expected performance will be met.

A continuous approach to quality, initiated early in the software lifecycle, can significantly lower the cost of completing and maintaining the software.

The RUP Testing Philosophy

In a traditional, waterfall approach, up to 80 percent of the test project time can be spent planning the test effort and defining test cases (but not actually conducting any testing at all). Then toward the end of the lifecycle, 20 percent of the effort is typically spent running

and debugging tests. Often an additional 20 percent (yes, we are now over budget!) is then required to fix anything in the product that did not pass the tests.

The test philosophy in the RUP takes a different approach and can be summarized as a small set of principles:

- **Iterative development.** Testing does not start with just test plans. The tests themselves are developed early and conducted early, and a useful subset of them is accumulated in regression suites, iteration after iteration. This enables early feedback of important information to the rest of the development team, permits the tests themselves to mature as the problem and solution spaces are better understood, and enables the inclusion in the evolving software design of required testability mechanisms. To account for the changing tactical objectives of the tester throughout the iterative lifecycle, we will introduce the concept of **mission.**

- **Low up-front documentation.** Detailed Test planning is defined iteration by iteration, based on a governing master Test plan, to meet the needs of the team and match the objectives of the iteration. For example, during the Elaboration phase, we focus on architecture and so the test effort should focus on testing the key architectural elements as they evolve in each iteration. The performance of key end-to-end scenarios should be assessed—typically under load—even though the user interface may be rudimentary. But beyond this semiformal artifact that defines the test plan for each iteration, there is not a lot of up-front specification paperwork developed.

- **Holistic approach.** The approach to identifying appropriate tests is not strictly and solely based on deriving tests from requirements. After all, the requirements rarely specify what the system should *not* do; they do not enumerate all the possible crashes and sources of errors. These have to come from elsewhere. Tests in the RUP are derived from the requirements *and* from other sources. We will see this later, embodied in the concept of **test-idea list.**

- **Automation.** Testing starts early in the RUP lifecycle, is repeated again and again, and could be very time-consuming, so many aspects must be supported by tools: tools to design tests, to run tests, and to analyze results.

Mission

The concept of an evaluation **mission,** as used in the RUP approach, has been derived from the work of James Bach in identifying different missions commonly adopted by software test teams. Bach advocates using a simple heuristic model for test planning. This model recognizes that different missions govern the activities and deliverables of the testing effort, and that selecting an appropriate mission is a key aspect of test planning.[4]

The evaluation mission identifies a simple statement the test team can remember in order to stay focused on their overall goal and appropriate deliverables for a given iteration. This is especially important in situations where the team is faced with a number of possibly conflicting missions. A test team without an evaluation mission often describes their goal with statements such as "We test everything" or "We just do testing." They're concerned with simply performing the test activities and overlook how those activities should be adjusted to suit the current project context or iteration context to achieve an appropriate goal.

The evaluation mission identifies a simple statement the test team can focus on for a given iteration.

Mission statements shouldn't be too complex or incorporate too many conflicting goals. The best mission statements are simple, short, succinct—and achievable. Here are some ideas for mission statements you might adopt for a given iteration:

- Find as many defects as possible.
- Find important problems fast.
- Assess perceived quality risks.
- Advise about perceived project risks.
- Advise about perceived quality.
- Certify to a given standard.
- Assess conformance to a specification (requirements, design, or product claims).

---

4. See Kaner 2002.

Test Cycles

A **test cycle** is a period of independent test activity that includes, among other things, the execution and evaluation of tests. Each iteration can contain multiple test cycles—the majority of iterations contain at least one. Each test cycle starts with the assessment of a software build's stability before it's accepted by the test team for more thorough and detailed testing.

The RUP recommends that each build be regarded as potentially requiring a cycle of testing (that is, a test cycle), but there is no strong coupling between build and test cycle. If each build may be "smoke-tested" to verify the build process, a test cycle may be longer than the build. Typically, Inception iterations of new projects don't produce builds, but iterations in all other phases do. Although each build is a potential candidate for a cycle of testing, there are various reasons why you might not decide to test every software build. Sometimes it will be appropriate to distribute the work effort to test a single software build across multiple test cycles.

The Test Discipline in the RUP Product

We will now turn to the RUP and examine how testing is described. It is mostly confined within the Testing Discipline. We will review the various roles involved, the artifacts produced, and the activities and their workflow.

Various Roles Related to Test in the RUP

There are four roles provided in the RUP focusing on test-related activities:

- Test Manager
- Test Analyst
- Test Designer
- Tester

These roles represent a natural and complete grouping of skills and responsibilities. As a tester in a small organization, you may be called to play all four roles. In larger organizations, some specialization may take place to allocate the roles to different individuals.

It's important to recognize that the roles in the RUP represent a related group of responsibilities—represented by RUP activities—that are partitioned around a set of skills required to fulfill those responsibilities. This partitioning allows for many different choices about how a project team might assign the roles to individuals. These roles are based around four sets of fundamental skills: management, analysis, development, and test.

Key Test Artifacts

- **Test evaluation summary.** Since the purpose of testing is to provide an objective assessment of a build, the most important artifact is the **test evaluation summary**—more important than the test plan. One such evaluation summary is ideally created for each test cycle, or for each build to be tested, but at least one per iteration. This artifact presents an objective assessment of the build, from the perspective of the agreed mission. It refers indirectly to defects and other anomalies (often stored in a change request database), emphasizing the critical ones. It also assesses the results of activities targeted at addressing risks that were driving the iteration, and it presents an assessment of the test effort itself in terms of the extent of testing (often described as "coverage") against plan and the relative effectiveness of the test effort. This is your most important artifact in communicating with the rest of the team.

- **Test Plan.** Matching the two-level Project Plan and Iteration Plan described in Chapter 12, in larger projects we find a Master Test Plan governing the whole project and then a **Test Plan** specifying the mission and the specific test objectives for each iteration.

  The Master Test Plan may be constrained by a Quality Assurance Plan (if there is one) found in the project's Software Development Plan. And similarly, the individual Test Plans for each iteration are constrained by the Master Test Plan.

- **Test-idea list.** A **test-idea list** is an informal listing resulting from considering various things that might necessitate a test being undertaken (and, again, not necessarily related to the requirements). This list is often created by brainstorming with other team members, such as a tester collaborating with a developer or analyst. This list is subsequently used to direct the testing effort by sorting it based on a number of factors: time and effort it would

take, importance to customer, likelihood of finding problems, and so on. An organization may keep one or more catalogs of abstract test ideas to enable reuse from iteration to iteration, project to project. The RUP product contains some examples of test-idea catalogs and guidance on creating and maintaining them.

- **Test suite.** A **test suite** is a group of related tests, which when executed together give a good assessment of a general area of concern. A test suite is the realization of one or more test ideas or test cases and consists of test scripts and test data.

- **Test scripts.** These are the procedural aspects of the test, the step-by-step instructions to execute to test. **Test scripts** may be manually or—to varying degrees—automatically executed.

  Test scripts and test suites are the area where automation will kick-in, allowing the testers to manage and run again and again large numbers of tests, and automate the production of a large part of the test evaluation summary.

- **Test cases.** Test cases tie testing activity to the software under test so that you can look at progress over time. Each answer to the question, "What are you going to test?" is a **test motivator,** and each answer to "And how are you going to test it?" is a **test case.**

  Test cases are more abstract than the scripts. In addition, they define preconditions, processing conditions, and postconditions: They represent a high-level specification for one or more tests. They are likely derived from test motivators such as the requirements, and in the RUP, many are derived from use cases.[5] Use cases are one of the primary sources of test cases, but not the sole source, and they must be complemented by other test ideas.

  In many projects there is a clear danger of spending an inordinate amount of time formalizing test-case specifications, using up valuable time that could otherwise be spent on real, concrete testing. However, test-case specifications add value and are necessary in certain types of development, specifically for mission- or safety-critical systems, for particularly complex tests, and for tests that require careful consideration of multiple resources (both in terms of hardware and in terms of people), such as system performance testing. Note that not every test script needs to be related to a test case.

---

5. See Heumann 2001.

- **Defect.** Unfortunately—depending on your point of view—testing uncovers defects. A **defect** is a kind of change request, and may lead to a fix in some subsequent build or iteration. Defects are a useful source of metrics that the project manager will be able to use to understand not only the quality of the product over time, but also the quality of the process, and the quality and efficiency of the test process itself. You should be careful, though, to clearly differentiate a defect in the application from a defect in the test itself.

- **Workload model.** To support performance testing, a **workload model** may be developed, describing typical and exceptional load conditions that the system must support.

You will find in the RUP some other artifacts related to testing. A **test interface specification** contains additional requirements to be placed on the software to enable it to be tested efficiently; this concern is often called **testability.** The **test automation architecture** shows the design of the test harness and the various testing tools and mechanisms that will be used to automate the testing of the software product being developed. This test automation architecture may need to handle various architectural mechanisms such as **concurrency** (running two or more automated tests concurrently), **distribution** (distributing automated tests to run on remote nodes), **maintainability** (ease of maintenance of the automated tests as they evolve), and so on.

Activities of the Tester

Now that we understand the major artifacts involved in testing, let us review the principal activities that create, update, or use these artifacts. There are six main groups of testing activities in the RUP (see Figure 18.1):

- Define test mission
- Verify test approach
- Validate build stability (smoke test)
- Test and evaluate
- Achieve acceptable mission
- Improve test assets

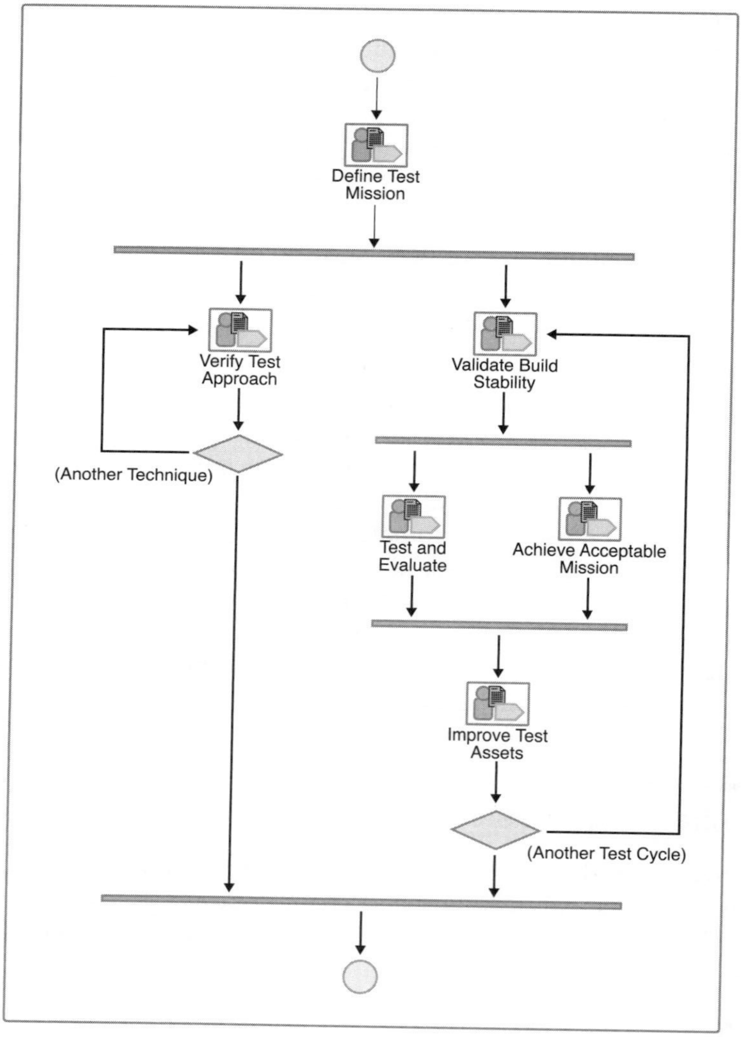

FIGURE 18.1 The Overall Test Workflow. *The high-level test activities captured in this figure are done at least once for each iteration. Also within the iteration, testing is done in an iterative fashion (as indicated by the recursive arrows).*

These activities are done at least once per iteration. Their focus, however, will vary across the lifecycle.

- In **Inception,** the execution of this workflow may be very sketchy. The mission for a new project that produces no build could be simply to "warm up," try some test ideas, put together the tools and test harnesses, and define with other developers some testability requirements. Some testing may be done just by a walkthrough of the design.

- In **Elaboration,** you will primarily focus on testing the architecture and key architecturally significant requirements, many of them nonfunctional (performance, scalability, integration with other products), assessing whether the major architectural risks have been mitigated. You will also test the testing strategy and the test architecture (the tools you have put in place to support testing).

- In **Construction,** the focus on the test mission will shift toward more functional testing, validating all functionality described in the use cases, leading to a meaningful first beta system. Nonfunctional testing, and in particular performance testing, will continue to monitor progress in performance tuning, or detect rapidly that an evolution of the system results in a loss of performance.

- In **Transition,** your final rush to product release, the focus will be on overall quality, robustness, and usability and on achieving the expected level of quality to allow the release of the product.

In other words, the testing mission is perfectly aligned with the objectives of the phases and does not consist, as in traditional processes, of a long period of leisurely test planning and test development, followed by a frenetic and hurried test period.

We will now review the activities in more detail.

Define Test Mission

You will identify the appropriate focus of the test effort for the upcoming iteration and will gain agreement with stakeholders on the goals that will direct the test effort.

For each iteration, this work is focused mainly on

- Identifying the objectives for the testing effort and deliverable artifacts.
- Identifying a good resource utilization strategy.
- Defining the appropriate scope and boundaries for the test effort.
- Outlining the approach that will be used, including the tool automation.
- Defining how progress will be monitored and assessed.

And we have seen how the mission may evolve throughout the lifecycle.

Verify Test Approach

You will demonstrate that the various test techniques and test tools outlined in the Test Approach will facilitate the required testing. You verify by demonstration that the approach will work, produces accurate results, and is appropriate for the available resources. The objective is to gain an understanding of the constraints and limitations of each tool and technique in the context of your specific project, and either to find an appropriate implementation solution for each technique or to find alternative techniques that can be implemented. This helps to mitigate the risk of discovering too late in the project lifecycle that the test approach is unworkable.

For each iteration, this work is focused mainly on

- Verifying early that the intended Test Approach will work and that it produces results of value.
- Establishing the basic infrastructure to enable and support the Test Approach.
- Obtaining commitment from the development team to provide and support the required testability to achieve the Test Approach.
- Identifying the scope, boundaries, limitations, and constraints of each tool and technique.

Validate Build Stability (Smoke Test)

You will first validate that the build is stable enough for detailed test and evaluation efforts to begin. This work is also referred to as a "smoke test," build verification test, build regression test, sanity check, or acceptance into testing. This work helps prevent the test resources from being wasted on a futile and fruitless testing effort.

For each build to be tested, this work is focused on

- Making an assessment of the stability and testability of the build: Can you install it, load it, and start it?
- Gaining an initial understanding—or confirming the expectation—of the development work delivered in the build: What was effectively integrated into this build?
- Making a decision to accept the build as suitable for use—guided by the evaluation mission—in further testing, or to conduct further testing against a previous build. Again, not all builds are suitable for a test cycle, and there is no point wasting too much testing time and effort on an unsatisfactory build.

Test and Evaluate

This is testing per se. You must achieve appropriate breadth and depth of the test effort to enable a sufficient test evaluation, relative of course to the iteration's Evaluation Mission. Typically performed once per test cycle, after accepting a build, this work involves performing the core tactical work of the test and evaluation effort—namely the implementation, execution, and evaluation of specific tests and the corresponding reporting of incidents that are encountered. Testing tools will help select the appropriate tests and execute them—when they can be run automatically.

For each test cycle, this work focuses mainly on

- Providing ongoing evaluation and assessment of the Target Test Items.
- Recording the appropriate information necessary to diagnose and resolve any identified issues.
- Achieving suitable breadth and depth in the test and evaluation work.
- Providing feedback on the most likely areas of potential quality risk.

Achieve an Acceptable Mission

At the same time, you must deliver a useful evaluation result from the test effort to your stakeholders—where useful evaluation results are assessed in terms of the Mission. In most cases that will mean focusing your efforts on helping the project team achieve the Iteration Plan objectives that apply to the current test cycle.

For each test cycle, this work focuses mainly on

- Actively prioritizing the minimal set of necessary tests that must be conducted to achieve the Evaluation Mission.
- Advocating the resolution of important issues that have a significant negative impact on the Evaluation Mission.
- Advocating appropriate product quality.
- Identifying regressions in quality introduced between test cycles.
- Where appropriate, revising the Evaluation Mission in light of the evaluation findings so as to provide useful evaluation information to the project team.

Improve Test Assets

As always with any good process, at the end of a test cycle or at least at the end of the iteration, you must close the loop, provide some feedback on the process itself, and take advantage of the iterative nature of the lifecycle to maintain and improve your test assets. This is important especially if the intention is to reuse the assets developed in the current test cycle in subsequent test cycles or even in another project.

For each test cycle, this work focuses mainly on

- Adding the minimal set of additional tests to validate the stability of subsequent builds.
- Assembling Test Scripts into additional appropriate Test Suites.
- Removing test assets that no longer serve a useful purpose or have become uneconomic to maintain.
- Maintaining Test Environment Configurations and Test Data sets.
- Exploring opportunities for reuse and productivity improvements.

- Conducting general maintenance of and making improvements to the maintainability of test automation assets.
- Documenting lessons learned—both good and bad practices discovered during the test cycle. This should be done at least at the end of the iteration.

Other Related Activities

Do not restrict your RUP investigation to the discipline, though. Testers and quality engineers are likely to be involved in many other activities in the RUP. For example:

- Defining the Quality Assurance Plan (part of the SDP).
- Participating in various reviews of the requirements and of the design, from which they will glean test ideas.
- Participating in the activities of the Change Control Board to review defects and decide their fate.

Conclusion

Testing in the RUP is about continuously providing the management and the development teams with an objective assessment of the quality of the product. It is not about ticking all the checkmarks for all the requirements (even if this plays a role) in one massive shot done toward the end of the project lifecycle.

The expected level of quality and the requirements both evolve during the lifecycle, and testing should evolve with them. Testing can start early, since iterative development produces testable code early, and can therefore provide crucial feedback, both on the product and on the process so that they can evolve as required—feedback that is sorely missing in more traditional approaches.

The role of the tester or the quality engineer in the RUP is not primarily to find defects, but to provide other team members—developers and managers—with an objective assessment of the quality of the product. Testing is not a complete, separate workflow, parallel to or appended to software development, but fully integrated in the iterative cycle of the

RUP. Taking advantage of iterations, testing becomes an almost-continuous process that continually feeds back into the requirements, the design, and the management of the project. It is then a collaborative activity, no longer an adversarial or rubber-stamping activity. It is also more effectively automated by tools. Testing in the RUP embraces a practical and flexible notion of Good Enough Quality that takes into account the balance between the cost of testing and the desired level of quality based on the context.

Resources for Testers

Further Reading

James Bach. "Good Enough Quality: Beyond the Buzzword," in *IEEE Computer*, 30 (8), August 1997, 96–98.

Boris Beizer. *Black Box Testing*. New York: John Wiley & Sons, Inc., 1995.

Rex Black. *Managing the Testing Process*. Redmond, WA: Microsoft Press, 1999.

Jim Heumann. "Generating Test Cases from Use Cases," in *The Rational Edge*, June 2001. http://www.therationaledge.com/content/jun_01/m_cases_jh.html.

Cem Kaner, James Bach, and Bret Pettichord. *Lessons Learned in Software Testing*. New York: John Wiley & Sons, Inc., 2002.

Cem Kaner, Jack Falk, and Hung Quoc Nguyen. *Testing Computer Software, Second Edition*. New York: John Wiley & Sons, Inc., 1999.

Brian Marick. "Faults of Omission," in *Software Testing and Quality Engineering Magazine*, January 2000.

Glenford J. Myers. *The Art of Software Testing*. New York: John Wiley & Sons, 1979.

Robert Pirsig, *Zen and the Art of Motorcycle Maintenance*. New York: Bantam Books, 1977.

Connie U. Smith and Lloyd Williams. *Performance Solutions: A Practical Guide to Creating Responsive, Scalable Software*. Boston: Addison-Wesley, 2002.

Training Resources

The following training courses have been developed to support RUP users; they are delivered by Rational Software and its partners (see www.rational.com for more information).

Principles of Software Testing for Testers (two days).

Essentials of Functional Testing (two days).

Essentials of XDE Tester, Java, and Web Edition: The Basics of Performance Testing (four hours).

GLOSSARY

In this glossary, only the terms that are specific to the RUP or that have a slightly different meaning in the RUP are defined. Terms in italics are defined elsewhere in the glossary.

Activity   A unit of work in the RUP that a *role* may be asked to perform. An activity may be decomposed in steps. Activities produce or modify *artifacts*.

Actor   Someone or something, outside the system (or business), that interacts with the system (or business).

Artifact   A piece of information that is produced, modified, or used by a process, defines an area of responsibility, and is subject to version control. An artifact can be a model, a model element, or a document.

Base   See *RUP Base.*

Baseline   A reviewed and approved release of artifacts that constitutes an agreed-on basis for evolution or development and that can be changed only through a formal procedure, such as a change and configuration control procedure.

Build   An operational version of a system or part of a system that demonstrates a subset of the capabilities to be provided in the final product.

Builder   See *RUP Builder.*

Component   A nontrivial, nearly independent, and replaceable part of a system that fulfills a clear function in the context of a well-defined architecture. A component conforms to and provides the

physical realization of a set of interfaces. See also *Process Component*.

Construction   The third *phase* of the RUP development cycle, where most of the software is developed.

Cycle   A complete pass through all four *phases* of the RUP (*Inception, Elaboration, Construction,* and *Transition*), resulting in an external product release.

Deployment   A *discipline* in the RUP whose purpose is to ensure a successful transition of the developed system to its users.

Development Case   The actual process used by the performing organization. It is developed as a configuration, or customization, of the RUP product and is adapted to the project's needs.

Discipline   A logical grouping of *role, activities, artifacts,* and other process guidance in the description of a process.

Elaboration   The second *phase* of the RUP development *cycle,* where the product's *vision,* its requirements, and its architecture are fully defined.

Extended Help   A RUP feature allowing associated software development tools to provide a context to the RUP, which will make the RUP display appropriate topics based on the given context.

Inception   The first *phase* of the RUP development *cycle,* where the scope of the project and its motivations are defined.

Iteration   A distinct sequence of *activities* with a plan and evaluation criteria resulting in a *release* (internal or external).

Milestone   The point in time at which an *iteration* or a *phase* formally ends, corresponding to a *release* point.

Modeler   See *RUP Modeler.*

MyRUP   The RUP browser allowing you to view the process, search, use the index, navigate graphically, and create your own personalized *process views* of your RUP *Process Configuration.*

Organizer   See *RUP Organizer.*

Phase The time between two major project *milestones*, during which a well-defined set of objectives is met, *artifacts* are completed, and decisions are made to move or not to move into the next phase.

Plug-In A RUP Plug-In is a deployable unit for one or several RUP *Process Components* that can be readily "dropped" onto a *RUP Base* to extend it. A RUP Plug-In can be compiled into a physical file, allowing it to be moved around and added to a *RUP Library* with a compatible *RUP Base*.

Process Component A RUP Process Component is a coherent, quasi-independent "chunk" or module of process knowledge that can be named, packaged, exchanged, and assembled with other process components.

Process Configuration A RUP Process Configuration is a browsable set of RUP *Process Components* that constitutes a complete process ("complete" from the perspective of a particular use). It is a Web site that sits on the user's machine or a server. RUP Process Configurations are compiled with *RUP Builder*.

Process View A feature of *MyRUP* allowing you to customize what parts of the RUP *Process Configuration* you want to see in your *MyRUP* tree browser as well as external links. Process views can be role-based (for example, analyst, developer, tester) or personalized for the needs of a specific user.

Prototype A *release* that is not necessarily subject to change management and configuration control. A prototype may be thrown away or may evolve into becoming the final system.

Rational Process Workbench (RPW) A process authoring toolkit. It is a combination of tools, processes, and other assets that allow a process engineer to develop RUP *Plug-Ins*. The RPW includes RUP *Modeler*, RUP *Organizer*, a *RUP Library*, and process guidance for process authoring.

Release A subset of the end product that is the object of evaluation at a *milestone*. A release is a stable, executable version of the product, together with any *artifacts* necessary to use this release, such as release notes or installation instructions. A release can be internal or external. An internal release is used only by the development organization as part of a *milestone*, or for a demonstration to users or customers. An external release (or delivery) is delivered to end-users.

Risk   An ongoing or upcoming concern that has a significant probability of adversely affecting the success of major *milestones*.

Role   A definition of the behavior and responsibilities of an individual, or a set of individuals, working together as a team.

RPW   See *Rational Process Workbench*.

RUP Base   A collection of RUP *Process Components* meant to be extended by applying plug-ins to generate RUP *Process Configurations*. It resides in a *RUP Library*.

RUP Builder   A tool within the RUP product used to create RUP *Process Configurations* out of a *RUP Base* and any number of RUP *Plug-Ins*.

RUP Exchange   A place on the Rational Developer Network where RUP *Plug-Ins* together with other process-related material are made available to the user community.

RUP Library   A collection of *Process Components* out of which a set of RUP *Process Configurations* may be compiled with *RUP Builder*. New process components can be added to a *RUP Library* through the means of RUP *Plug-Ins*.

RUP Modeler   A component of *Rational Process Workbench*. It allows a process engineer to visually model process elements such as *activities, artifacts, roles, disciplines,* and *tool mentors* and their relationships; assemble them into RUP *Process Components*; and compile them into RUP *Plug-Ins*. RUP Modeler is an add-in to Rational XDE and works in conjunction with *RUP Organizer*.

RUP Organizer   A component of *Rational Process Workbench*. It allows you to associate content files with process elements such *activities, artifacts, roles, disciplines,* and *tool mentors* and to compile these RUP *Process Components* to create a RUP *Plug-In* with the new or modified files. The files can be examples, guidelines, or reusable assets. RUP Organizer also allows you to modify *Extended Help*.

Scenario A described use-case instance or a subset of a *use case*.

Step A subset of an *activity*. Not all steps needs to be performed each time an *activity* is invoked.

Tool Mentor A description that provides practical guidance on how to perform specific process *activities* or *steps* using a specific software tool.

Transition The fourth and last *phase* of the RUP development *cycle*, which results in a final product *release*.

Use Case A sequence of actions a system performs that yields an observable result of value to a particular *actor*. A use-case class contains all main, alternate, and exception flows of events that are related to producing the "observable result of value."

Vision The user's or customer's view of the product to be developed, specified summarily at the level of key stakeholders' needs and major features of the system.

Workflow The sequence of activities performed in a business that produces a result of observable value to an individual actor of the business. Workflows in the software engineering process can be expressed in terms of sequences of *activities*.

IBLIOGRAPHY

The Rational Edge can be found at http://www.therationaledge.com.

Albrecht 1979   Allan J. Albrecht. "Measuring Applications Development Productivity," in *Proceedings of IBM Applications Development Joint SHARE/GUIDE Symposium*, Monterey, CA: 1979, 83–92.

Ambler 1998   Scott Ambler. *Process Patterns: Building Large-Scale Systems Using Object Technology.* New York: SIGS Books/Cambridge University Press, 1998.

Ambler 1999   Scott Ambler. *More Process Patterns: Delivering Large-Scale Systems Using Object Technology.* New York: SIGS Books/ Cambridge University Press, 1999.

Ambler 2000   Scott Ambler and Larry Constantine. *The Unified Process Construction Phase.* Lawrence, KS: CMP Books, 2000, 163–170.

Bach 1997   James Bach. "Good Enough Quality: Beyond the Buzzword," in *IEEE Computer*, 30 (8), August 1997, 96–98.

Bach 2001   James Bach. "What Is Exploratory Testing? (And How It Differs from Scripted Testing)," in *Software Testing and Quality Engineering Magazine*, January 29, 2001.

Bass 1998   Len Bass, Paul Clements, and Rick Kazman. *Software Architecture in Practice.* Reading, MA: Addison-Wesley, 1998.

Beck 1998   Kent Beck. *CRC: The Essence of Objects.* Upper Saddle River, NJ: Prentice-Hall, 1998.

Beck 2000   Kent Beck. *Extreme Programming Explained: Embrace Change.* Boston: Addison-Wesley, 2000.

Beck 2001   Kent Beck and Martin Fowler. *Planning Extreme Programming.* Boston: Addison-Wesley, 2001.

Beizer 1995   Boris Beizer. *Black Box Testing*. New York: John Wiley & Sons, Inc., 1995.

Binder 2000   Robert V. Binder. *Testing Object-Oriented Systems: Models, Patterns, and Tools*. Boston: Addison-Wesley, 2000.

Bittner 2003   Kurt Bittner and Ian Spence. *Use Case Modeling*. Boston: Addison-Wesley, 2003.

Black 1999   Rex Black. *Managing the Testing Process*. Redmond, WA: Microsoft Press, 1999.

Boehm 1981   Barry W. Boehm. *Software Engineering Economics*. Upper Saddle River, NJ: Prentice-Hall, 1981.

Boehm 1986   Barry W. Boehm. "A Spiral Model of Software Development and Enhancement," in *ACM SIGSOFT Software Engineering Notes*, 11, August 1986, 22–42.

Boehm 1991   Barry W. Boehm. "Software Risk Management: Principles and Practices," in *IEEE Software*, 8 (1), January 1991, 32–41.

Boehm 1996   Barry W. Boehm. "Anchoring the Software Process," in *IEEE Software*, 13 (4), July 1996, 73–82.

Boehm 2001   Barry W. Boehm, et al. *Software Cost Estimation with COCOMO II*. Upper Saddle River, NJ: Prentice-Hall, 2001.

Boehm 2002   Barry W. Boehm, "Get Ready for Agile Methods, with Care," in *IEEE Computer*, 35 (1), January 2002, 64–69.

Booch 1994   Grady Booch. *Object-Oriented Analysis and Design with Applications, Second Edition*. Menlo Park, CA: Addison-Wesley, 1994.

Booch 1996   Grady Booch. *Object Solutions: Managing the Object-Oriented Project*. Menlo Park, CA: Addison-Wesley, 1996.

Booch 1999   Grady Booch, James Rumbaugh, and Ivar Jacobson. *The Unified Modeling Language User Guide*. Reading, MA: Addison-Wesley, 1999.

Booch 2001   Grady Booch. "The Illusion of Simplicity," in *Software Development Magazine*, February 2001, 57–59.

Bosch 2000   Jan Bosch. *Design and Use of Software Architecture: Adopting and Evolving a Product-Line Approach*. Boston: Addison-Wesley, 2000.

Brooks 1995   Frederick P. Brooks, Jr. *The Mythical Man-Month (Anniversary Edition)*. Reading, MA: Addison-Wesley, 1995.

Buschmann 1996   Frank Buschmann, Regine Meunier, Hans Rohnert, Peter Sommerlad, and Michael Stal. *Pattern-Oriented Software Architecture: A System of Patterns*. New York: John Wiley & Sons, Inc., 1996.

Cantor 2002   Murray Cantor. *Software Leadership: A Guide to Successful Software Development*. Boston: Addison-Wesley, 2002.

Charette 1989   Robert Charette. *Software Engineering Risk Analysis and Management*. New York: McGraw-Hill, 1989.

Clements 2002a   Paul Clements, Felix Bachmann, Len Bass, David Garlan, James Ivers, Reed Little, Robert Nord, and Judith Stafford. *Documenting Software Architectures: Views and Beyond*. Boston: Addison-Wesley, 2002.

Clements 2002b   Paul Clements, Rick Kazman, and Mark Klein. *Evaluating Software Architecture*. Boston: Addison-Wesley, 2002.

Clements 2002c   Paul Clements and Linda Northrop. *Software Product Lines: Practice and Patterns*. Boston: Addison-Wesley, 2002.

Cockburn 2001   Alistair Cockburn. *Writing Effective Use Cases*. Boston: Addison-Wesley, 2001.

Cockburn 2002   Alistair Cockburn. *Agile Software Development*. Boston: Addison-Wesley, 2002.

Conallen 2000   Jim Conallen. *Building Web Applications with UML*. Boston: Addison-Wesley, 2000.

Constantine 1999   Larry Constantine and Lucy Lockwood. *Software for Use*. Reading, MA: Addison-Wesley, 1999.

Cooper 1999   Alan Cooper. *The Inmates Are Running the Asylum*. Indianapolis, IN: Sams, 1999.

Derniame 1999   Jean-Claude Derniame, Badara Ali Kaba, and David Graham Wastell. *Software Process: Principles, Methodology, and Technology*. LNCS #1500. Berlin, Germany: Springer-Verlag, 1999.

Dikel 2001   David M. Dikel, David Kane, and James R. Wilson. *Software Architecture: Organizational Principles and Patterns*. Upper Saddle River, NJ: Prentice-Hall, 2001.

Eeles 2003 Peter Eeles, Kelli Houston, and Wojtek Kozaczynski. *Building J2EE Applications with the Rational Unified Process.* Boston: Addison-Wesley, 2003.

Eriksson 2000 Hans-Erik Eriksson and Magnus Penker. *Business Modeling with UML: Business Patterns at Work.* New York: John Wiley & Sons, Inc., 2000.

Fowler 1997 Martin Fowler and Kendall Scott. *UML Distilled: A Brief Guide to Applying the Standard Object Modeling Language.* Reading, MA: Addison-Wesley, 1997.

Fowler 1999 Martin Fowler, Kent Beck, John Brant, William Opdyke, and Don Roberts. *Refactoring: Improving the Design of Existing Code.* Reading, MA: Addison-Wesley, 1999.

Freedman 1990 Daniel P. Freedman and Gerald M. Weinberg. *Handbook of Walkthroughs, Inspections, and Technical Reviews: Evaluating Programs, Projects, and Products, Third Edition.* New York: Dorset House, 1990.

Gamma 1995 Erich Gamma, Richard Helm, Ralph Johnson, and John Vlissides. *Design Patterns: Elements of Reusable Object-Oriented Software.* Reading, MA: Addison-Wesley, 1995.

Gilb 1988 Tom Gilb. *Principles of Software Engineering Management.* Reading, MA: Addison-Wesley, 1988.

Graham 1997 Ian Graham, Brian Henderson-Sellers, and Houman Younessi. *The Open Process Specification.* Reading, MA: Addison-Wesley, 1997.

Heumann 2001 Jim Heumann. "Generating Test Cases from Use Cases," in *The Rational Edge*, June 2001.

Highsmith 2000 James A. Highsmith. *Adaptive Software Development: A Collaborative Approach to Managing Complex Systems.* New York: Dorset House, 2000.

Hofmeister 2000 Christine Hofmeister, Robert Nord, and Dilip Soni. *Applied Software Architecture.* Boston: Addison-Wesley, 2000.

Humphrey 1989 Watts Humphrey. *Managing the Software Process.* Reading, MA: Addison-Wesley, 1989.

Humphrey 1995 Watts Humphrey. *A Discipline for Software Engineering.* Reading, MA: Addison-Wesley, 1995.

Humphrey 1997   Watts Humphrey. *Introduction to the Personal Software Process*. Reading, MA: Addison-Wesley, 1997.

IEEE 1991   IEEE Standard 829-1991. "Standard for Software Test Documentation." New York: IEEE, 1991.

IEEE 1998a   IEEE Standard 1490-1998. "Adoption of the PMI Guide to PMBOK." New York: IEEE, 1998.

IEEE 1998b   IEEE Standard 1058-1998. "Standard for Software Project Management Plans." New York: IEEE, 1998.

IEEE 2000   IEEE Standard 1471-2000. "Recommended Practice for Architectural Description of Software-Intensive Systems." Los Alamitos, CA: IEEE Computer Society, 2000.

ISO/IEC 1995   ISO/IEC 10746:1995. *Reference Model of Open Distributed Processing (RM-ODP)* (ITU Rec. X901). Geneva, Switzerland: ISO, 1995.

ISO/IEC 1998   ISO/IEC 15504:1998. *Information Technologies— Software Process Assessment*. Geneva, Switzerland: ISO, 1998.

Jacobson 1992   Ivar Jacobson, Magnus Christerson, Patrik Jonsson, and Gunnar Övergaard. *Object-Oriented Software Engineering: A Use Case Driven Approach*. Reading, MA: Addison-Wesley, 1992.

Jacobson 1994   Ivar Jacobson, Maria Ericsson, and Agneta Jacobson. *The Object Advantage: Business Process Reengineering with Object Technology*. Reading, MA: Addison-Wesley, 1994.

Jacobson 1997   Ivar Jacobson, Martin Griss, and Patrik Jonsson. *Software Reuse: Architecture, Process and Organization for Business Success*. Reading, MA: Addison-Wesley, 1997.

Jacobson 1999   Ivar Jacobson, Grady Booch, and James Rumbaugh. *The Unified Software Development Process*. Reading, MA: Addison-Wesley, 1999.

Jeffries 2001   Ron Jeffries, Ann Anderson, and Chet Hendrickson. *Extreme Programming Installed*. Boston, MA: Addison-Wesley, 2001.

Kaner 1999   Cem Kaner, Jack Falk, and Hung Quoc Nguyen. *Testing Computer Software, Second Edition*. New York: John Wiley & Sons, Inc., 1999.

Kaner 2002   Cem Kaner, James Bach, and Bret Pettichord. *Lessons Learned in Software Testing.* New York: John Wiley & Sons, Inc., 2002.

Kroll 2001   Per Kroll. "The RUP: An Industry-Wide Platform for Best Practices," in *The Rational Edge*, December 2001.

Kruchten 1995   Philippe Kruchten. "The 4+1 View Model of Architecture," in *IEEE Software,* 6 (12), 1995, 45–50.

Kruchten 1996   Philippe Kruchten. "A Rational Development Process," in *CrossTalk*, 9 (7), July 1996, 11–16.

Kruchten 1999   Philippe Kruchten. "The Software Architect, and the Software Architecture Team," in *Software Architecture*, P. Donohue (ed.). Boston: Kluwer Academic Publishers, 1999, 565–583.

Kruchten 2000a   Philippe Kruchten. *The Rational Unified Process: An Introduction, Second Edition.* Boston: Addison-Wesley, 2000.

Kruchten 2000b   Philippe Kruchten. "From Waterfall to Iterative Development: A Tough Transition for Project Managers," in *The Rational Edge*, December 2000.

Kruchten 2001a   Philippe Kruchten. "What Is the Rational Unified Process?" in *The Rational Edge*, January 2001.

Kruchten 2001b   Philippe Kruchten. "The Tao of the Software Architect," in *The Rational Edge*, March 2001.

Kruchten 2001c   Philippe Kruchten. "Common Misconceptions About Software Architecture," in *The Rational Edge*, April 2001.

Kruchten 2002   Philippe Kruchten. "A Software Development Process for a Team of One," in *The Rational Edge*, February 2002.

Leffingwell 2000   Dean Leffingwell and Don Widrig. *Managing Software Requirements: A Unified Approach.* Boston: Addison-Wesley, 2000.

Marick 2000   Brian Marick. "Faults of Omission," in *Software Testing and Quality Engineering Magazine,* January 2000.

Martin 2001   Robert C. Martin and Robert S. Koss. *An Extreme Programming Episode.* Vernon Hills, IL: Object Mentor, 2001.

McCarthy 1995   Jim McCarthy. *Dynamics of Software Development.* Redmond, WA: Microsoft Press, 1995.

McConnell 1993   Steve McConnell. *Code Complete: A Practical Handbook of Software Construction.* Redmond, WA: Microsoft Press, 1993.

McConnell 1997   Steve McConnell. *Software Project Survival Guide.* Redmond, WA: Microsoft Press, 1997.

McCormack 2001   Alan McCormack. "Product-Development Practices That Work: How Internet Companies Build Software," in *MIT Sloan Management Review*, 42 (2), Winter 2001, 75–84.

Myers 1979   Glenford J. Myers. *The Art of Software Testing.* New York: John Wiley & Sons, Inc., 1979.

Newkirk 2001   James Newkirk and Robert Martin. *Extreme Programming in Practice.* Boston: Addison-Wesley, 2001.

O'Connell 1994   Fergus O'Connell. *How to Run Successful Projects.* Upper Saddle River, NJ: Prentice-Hall, 1994.

OMG 2001   Object Management Group. *Software Process Engineering Metamodel (SPEM).* OMG, doc ad/01-03-08, April 2, 2001. http://cgi.omg.org/cgi-bin/doc?ad/01-03-08.

Osterweil 1987   Leon J. Osterweil. "Software Processes Are Software Too," in *Proceedings 9th ICSE*, 1987, 2–13.

Pirsig 1977   Robert Pirsig. *Zen and the Art of Motorcycle Maintenance.* New York: Bantam Books, 1977.

PMI 2000   Project Management Institute. *Guide to the Project Management Body of Knowledge (PMBOK Guide).* W. Duncan (editor). Newton Square, PA: PMI, 2000.

Pressman 2001   Roger S. Pressman. *Software Engineering: A Practitioner's Approach, Fifth Edition.* Boston: McGraw-Hill Higher Education, 2001.

Probasco 2000   Leslee Probasco. "Ten Essentials of RUP," in *The Rational Edge*, December 2000.

Quatrani 1998   Terry Quatrani. *Visual Modeling with Rational Rose and UML.* Reading, MA: Addison-Wesley, 1998.

Rechtin 1997   Eberhardt Rechtin and Mark Maier. *The Art of Systems Architecting.* Boca Raton, FL: CRC Books, 1997.

Robillard 2003   Pierre Robillard and Philippe Kruchten. *Software Engineering Process with the UPEDU.* Boston: Addison-Wesley, 2003.

Royce 1998   Walker Royce. *Software Project Management: A Unified Framework.* Reading, MA: Addison-Wesley, 1998.

Royce 2002   Walker Royce. "CMM vs. CMMI: From Conventional to Modern Software Development," in *The Rational Edge*, February 2002.

Rumbaugh 1991   James Rumbaugh, Michael Blaha, William Lorensen, Frederick Eddy, and William Premerlani. *Object-Oriented Modeling and Design.* Upper Saddle River, NJ: Prentice-Hall, 1991.

Rumbaugh 1998   James Rumbaugh, Ivar Jacobson, and Grady Booch. *UML Reference Manual.* Reading, MA: Addison-Wesley, 1998.

Schwaber 2002   Ken Schwaber and Mike Beedle. *Agile Software Development with SCRUM.* Upper Saddle River, NJ: Prentice-Hall, 2002.

Selic 1994   Bran Selic, Garth Gullekson, and Paul Ward. *Real-Time Object-Oriented Modeling*, New York: John Wiley & Sons, Inc., 1994.

Shaw 1996   Mary Shaw and David Garlan. *Software Architecture: Perspectives on an Emerging Discipline.* Upper Saddle River, NJ: Prentice-Hall, 1996.

Smith 2002   Connie U. Smith and Lloyd Williams. *Performance Solutions: A Practical Guide to Creating Responsive, Scalable Software.* Boston: Addison-Wesley, 2002.

Stapleton 1998   Jennifer Stapleton. *DSDM, Dynamic Systems Development Method: The Method in Practice.* Reading, MA: Addison-Wesley, 1998.

Thai 2001   Thuan Thai and Hoang Q. Lam. *.NET Framework Essentials.* Sebastopol, CA: O'Reilly, 2001.

Thayer 1997   Richard H. Thayer (ed.). *Software Engineering Project Management, Second Edition.* Los Alamitos, CA: IEEE Computer Society Press, 1997.

Wiegers 2000   Karl Wiegers. "Stop Promising Miracles," in *Software Development*, February 2000.

Williams 2000   Laurie Williams, Robert R. Kessler, Ward Cunningham, and Ron Jeffries. "Strengthening the Case for Pair Programming," in *IEEE Software*, 17 (4), 2000, 19–25.

Witt 1994   Bernard I. Witt, F. Terry Baker, and Everett W. Merritt. *Software Architecture and Design: Principles, Models, and Methods.* New York: Van Nostrand Reinhold, 1994.

Yourdon 1997   Edward Yourdon. *Death March: Managing "Mission Impossible" Projects.* Upper Saddle River, NJ: Prentice-Hall, 1997.

INDEX

Rational Minds and Addison-Wesley Authors—
What a Combination!

Developing Enterprise Java Applications with J2EE and UML
Khawar Zaman Ahmed, Cary E. Umrysh
Foreword by Grady Booch

0-201-73829-5

Use Case Modeling
Kurt Bittner, Ian Spence

0-201-70913-9

Object-Oriented Analysis and Design with Applications
Grady Booch
SECOND EDITION

0-8053-5340-2

Object Solutions
Managing the Object-Oriented Project
Grady Booch

0-8053-0594-7

The Unified Modeling Language User Guide
Grady Booch, James Rumbaugh, Ivar Jacobson
The ultimate tutorial to the UML, from the original designers

0-201-57168-4

Software Leadership
A Guide to Successful Software Development
Murray Cantor

0-201-70044-1

Building Web Applications with UML
SECOND EDITION
Jim Conallen
Foreword by Grady Booch

0-201-73038-3

Building J2EE Applications with the Rational Unified Process
Peter Eeles, Kelli Houston, Wojtek Kozaczynski

0-201-79166-8

The Object Advantage
Business Process Reengineering with Object Technology
Ivar Jacobson

0-201-42289-1

Object-Oriented Software Engineering
A Use Case Driven Approach
Ivar Jacobson
COMPUTER LANGUAGE Productivity Award Winner 1992

0-201-54435-0

Software Reuse
Architecture, Process and Organization for Business Success
Ivar Jacobson · Martin Griss · Patrik Jonsson

0-201-92476-5

The Unified Software Development Process
Ivar Jacobson, Grady Booch, James Rumbaugh
The complete guide to the Unified Process from the original designers

0-201-57169-2

The Rational Unified Process An Introduction
SECOND EDITION
Philippe Kruchten

0-201-70710-1

Managing Software Requirements
SECOND EDITION
A Use Case Approach
Dean Leffingwell, Don Widrig

0-321-12247-X

UML for Database Design
Eric J. Naiburg, Robert A. Maksimchuk
Foreword by Grady Booch

0-201-72163-5

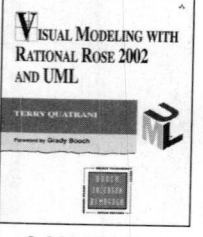

Visual Modeling with Rational Rose 2002 and UML
Terry Quatrani
Foreword by Grady Booch

0-201-72932-6

Software Project Management
A Unified Framework
Walker Royce
Foreword by Barry Boehm

0-201-30958-0

The Unified Modeling Language Reference Manual
James Rumbaugh, Ivar Jacobson, Grady Booch
The definitive reference to the UML from the original designers

0-201-30998-X

Software Configuration Management Strategies and Rational ClearCase®
A Practical Introduction
Brian A. White
Foreword by Geoffrey M. Clemm

0-201-60478-7

The Rational Unified Process Made Easy
A Practitioner's Guide to the RUP
Per Kroll, Philippe Kruchten
Foreword by Grady Booch

0-321-16609-4

For more information on these books by Rational Software Corporation employees, please go to **www.awprofessional.com**